Landscape Modernism Renounced

Christopher Tunnard is one of the most influential figures in landscape architecture. He was the first author on Modernism in landscape in the English language. Yet during the latter half of his career, he was at the forefront of the movement to save the city, becoming an acclaimed author sympathetic to preservation.

David Jacques and Jan Woudstra provide the first comprehensive study of the life and work of Christopher Tunnard. They explore his key role in the evolution of landscape architecture during the twentieth century, tracking his changing ideology through his writings, original drawings and records, and the experience of his family, friends and colleagues.

Reflective and deeply insightful into a career that still resonates in the discipline today, this is prime reading for students, academics and professionals of landscape architecture, history and theory.

David Jacques is a landscape historian, conservationist and town planner.

Jan Woudstra is Reader in Landscape History and Theory at the University of Sheffield and a leading expert in Modernism in landscape.

D1237167

Figure 1 Christopher Tunnard, landscape architect, town planner and preservationist during his days as a professor at Yale University.
(Source: National Parks Service, Jefferson National Expansion Memorial, 1948)

Landscape Modernism Renounced

The Career of Christopher Tunnard (1910–1979)

David Jacques and Jan Woudstra

With contributions by Elen Deming, David Jacques, Lance Neckar, Ann Satterthwaite and Jan Woudstra
With foreword by Christopher (Rusty) Tunnard

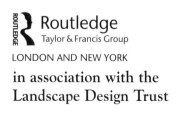

Routledge
Taylor & Francis Group

LONDON AND NEW YORK

in association with the
Landscape Design Trust

First published 2009
by Routledge
2 Park Square, Milton Park, Abingdon, Oxon OX14 4RN

Simultaneously published in the USA and Canada
by Routledge
270 Madison Avenue, New York, NY 10016, USA

Routledge is an imprint of the Taylor & Francis Group, an informa business

© 2009 David Jacques and Jan Woudstra

Typeset in Goudy by
Pindar NZ, Auckland, New Zealand
Printed and bound in Great Britain by
TJ International Ltd, Padstow, Cornwall

British Library Cataloguing in Publication Data
A catalogue record for this book is available from the British Library

Library of Congress Cataloging in Publication Data
Jacques, David.
Landscape modernism renounced: the career of Christopher Tunnard
(1910–1979) / David Jacques and Jan Woudstra.
    p. cm.
  Includes bibliographical references and index.
  1. Tunnard, Christopher. 2. Landscape architects—British Colombia—
Biography. 3. Modern movement (Architecture) 4. Landscape
design—England—History—20th century. 5. Landscape design—United
States—History—20th century. I. Woudstra, Jan. II. Title.
  SB469.386.C2J33 2009
  712.092—dc22   [B] 2008054732

ISBN10: 0-415-49720-5 (hbk)
ISBN10: 0-415-49722-1 (pbk)

ISBN13: 978-0-415-49720-6 (hbk)
ISBN13: 978-0-415-49722-0 (pbk)

To Karen and Laurence, without whose patience this book would have been finished long ago

Contents

Illustrations

All illustrations are reproduced with permission of the copyright holders and their successors, insofar as it has been possible to trace them.

Abbreviations

AJ:	*Architects' Journal*
AR:	*Architectural Review*
ASLA:	American Society of Landscape Architects
Clark Papers:	Royal Commission on the Ancient and Historical Monuments of Scotland (RCAHMS), MS/758: H F Clark Collection
ILA:	Institute of Landscape Architects (In 1978 changed name to Landscape Institute)
L&G:	*Landscape and Garden*
LI:	Landscape Institute
Lindley Library:	Royal Horticultural Society, Lindley Library
RIBA:	Royal Institute of British Architects
Tunnard Papers:	Yale University, Sterling Memorial Library, Manuscripts and Archives, Group 1070: Christopher Tunnard Papers

Acknowledgements

We gratefully acknowledge the contributions of the following:

Elen Deming

Dr M. Elen Deming became Head of Landscape Architecture at the University of Illinois in 2008, having previously been Associate Professor of Landscape Architecture at the State University of New York (SUNY) College of Environmental Science and Forestry. Prior to her academic career, Deming was an Associate and project designer at Sasaki Associates (Boston). Her doctorate from the Graduate School of Design, Harvard University, was in Landscape History and Theory. She is currently Editor of *Landscape Journal*, the official journal of the Council of Educators in Landscape Architecture.

Dr Deming has previously written on 'the empathic approach', and contributed to that section in this book.

Lance Neckar

Lance Neckar is Professor and Head of Department of Landscape Architecture at the University of Minnesota in Minneapolis. His article 'Strident Modernism/ Ambivalent Reconsiderations: Christopher Tunnard's Gardens in the Modern Landscape' in the *Journal of Garden History* in 1990 was the first academic study of Tunnard's thinking on landscape. He afterwards contributed to *Modern Landscape Architecture: A Critical Review* (1993), edited by Marc Treib, with an article on 'Christopher Tunnard: The Garden in the Modern Landscape'.

Professor Neckar contributed most of the biographical detail of Tunnard's time at Harvard, and very many facts and observations relating to Tunnard's pre-war artistic interests, his work with students at both Harvard and Yale, his emergence as a planner, and his life's work in retrospect, particularly in the last chapter.

Ann Satterthwaite

Ann Satterthwaite, A.I.C.P., is a city planner in Washington, DC, who received a Master's degree in City Planning in 1960 from Yale University, and has been involved in amenity planning, including landscapes, natural resources, and townscapes. She was chairman of the National Association for Olmsted Parks, wrote the preservation chapter in *Man-Made America*, and a book on the history of shopping, *Going Shopping: Consumer Choices and Community Consequences* (2001). She considers herself fortunate to have had Christopher Tunnard as a teacher, mentor, and friend, so has been able to draw own her own memories and experiences. However, she was helped by discussions with some of his friends and associates like George and Polly Hamilton of Williamstown, MA; Rudi Favretti of Mansfield, CT; Henry Hope Reed; Christopher Russell Tunnard, and Harry J. Wexler of New Haven, CT.

Ann Satterthwaite contributed to the biographical material for Tunnard's time at Yale, provided much of the bibliography, and provided material on the role of aesthetics, the old and new, and the relationship of man-made and natural environments within the chapter on 'Civic Art and Design'.

Rusty Tunnard

Christopher Russell (Rusty) Tunnard is the son of Christopher Tunnard and Lydia Evans Tunnard of Boston, MA. He teaches international business at The Fletcher School of Law and Diplomacy of Tufts University and in Europe. He was for many years a management consultant with the firm Arthur D. Little in Europe and the U.S. and maintains a private consulting practice. He accompanied his father on trips abroad and provided photographs of Italy and elsewhere for *World with a View* (1979) which was dedicated to him. He donated his father's papers to Yale in 1983. He is married, with two grown children, and he lives in the Boston area.

Other acknowledgements

As far as possible contributions of other individuals are to be found in the endnotes, but the following deserve particular mention:

Edward Baker (Executive Director of The New London County Historical Society), Pierre Bazin (of the Institut pour le Développement Forestier in Rennes), Chloe Bennet (née Clark), MacKenzie Bennett (of the Museum of Modern Art archives), Alan and Sylvia Blanc, Mr Chapman (of L.G. Mouchel & Partners), Serge Chermayeff, Jennifer R. Clark (Archivist, National Park Service, Jefferson National Expansion Memorial), Paul Davis (of Davis & Bayne, Architects), Mary Daniels (Frances Loeb Library, Graduate School of Design, Harvard University), Annabel Downs (and the Landscape Institute library for extreme helpfulness), Brent Elliott of the Lindley Library, Laurie Fricker, Dr John Glenn (of Anderson and Glenn Conservation Architects), E.J.P. Hardman (bursar of Marlborough College in 1989), Ian Kitson, Paul Miller (Preservation Society of Newport County, RI), David Mulford (editor of the *Wisley Garden Club Journal* at 1989), Alan Powers, Tricia Royston (Librarians, New London County Historical Society), Vincent Scully (for permission to quote privately printed text), Laurence Pattacini for providing a sketch of the Bentley Wood model, The

Province of British Columbia Archives and Records Service, English Heritage, The Royal Commission on the Ancient and Historical Monuments of Scotland, The University of Liverpool Archives, The University of Reading Archives and Manuscripts, The University of Victoria (BC) Archives, Harvard Design School Loeb Library Special Collections, and Yale University Library Manuscripts and Archives.

Grateful (and all posthumous, alas) thanks are due to the following who allowed David Jacques to take notes during conversations or interviews in or around 1989: Marjorie Clark, Sylvia Crowe, Gordon Cullen, Brian Hackett, Geoffrey Jellicoe, J.M. Richards, Willi Soukop, Dorothy Stroud, Peter Tunnard, William Stearn and Peter Youngman. Thanks are also due to Lance Neckar's interviewees: Rusty Tunnard and the late Edward Larrabee Barnes, Serge Chermayeff, Garrett Eckbo and Dan Kiley.

Preface

This book on Christopher Tunnard had its origins in 1987 when I joined English Heritage as its first Inspector of Historic Parks and Gardens. I was conscious that the new 'Register of Parks and Gardens of Special Historic Interest' omitted post-1939 landscapes, and I approached the Landscape Institute for advice. Matters did not run smoothly, as the effects of the October 1987 Great Storm occupied all my time. However, I planned to see a number of eminent members of the profession for inspiration, and in 1989 I did get around to seeing these sages. I also found a fellow enthusiast for Tunnard in Alan Blanc who organised visits to St Ann's Hill and to Gordon Cullen's tumbledown studio, 'The Conkers', not far away in Wraysbury. I found time to spend a few days in 1989 amongst the Tunnard Papers at Yale, and provided some of my researches there to Ian Kitson who was reworking his Architectural Association thesis as an article on Gaulby.

In 1991 I visited Marjorie Clark and her daughter Chloe in her basement flat in Edinburgh New Town, and was shown all Frank's papers loose in black bin-bags. A week later I at least had them sorted into 28 boxes which I am glad to say that Marjorie afterwards deposited with the Royal Commission on the Ancient and Historical Monuments of Scotland. Initial ideas included a Modernist reader based around the biographies of Tunnard and Clark, but that evaporated.

Years passed in teaching and other commitments till, in 2002, the Landscape Design Trust said it was interested in a monograph on Tunnard. I had long before become aware that Tunnard's career in America was of just as much interest as his career in England, and I drew in American authors with special knowledge of Tunnard to help round out the subject. On re-visiting Yale in 2003 I found that the Tunnard Papers had been recatalogued in 1991; all my earlier work had to be re-referenced, but I did get several images scanned. Some more recent authors may have wondered who had paid for this!

The project was put on hold by the Landscape Design Trust, but in 2007 I and a fellow Tunnard enthusiast, Jan Woudstra, decided to bring the book to completion anyway. Jan, as a student at Kew, had also been taken to St Ann's Hill by Alan Blanc, and latterly he had become a great expert in European Modernism in landscape. As presented, the book is the work of several contributors, and it has been a huge task to pull it together – no one's text has survived uncut, unspliced or unelaborated. The sheer volume of Tunnard writings whilst he was at

Yale has made it necessary to be selective, but the topics chosen were a sample of those which were at the time a challenge to conventional thinking. The result is a collaborative offering to mid-twentieth-century landscape theory as well as planning theory. It has shone light not just on Tunnard, and his close colleagues Frank Clark and Henry Hope Reed, but on the intellectual and academic context in which they worked.

David Jacques
Sugnall, Stafford, UK
October 2008

Foreword

by Christopher (Rusty) Tunnard

In a memorial to my father written almost thirty years ago, the Yale architectural historian Vincent Scully said this: '(Christopher Tunnard) was one of the true pioneers of contemporary architecture and city planning – an authentic prophet, seldom honored quite as much as he deserved to be but living on long enough to witness the decisive ascendancy of his ideas.'

In the years since then, I would receive periodic enquiries from scholars about my father's work, but these dwindled down to negligible until a few years ago, when multiple researchers informed me that there was a renewed interest in his early work as a landscape architect in England before the war. Then, in 2005, my father received the Distinguished Landscape Architect award from Sigma Lambda Alpha, a national honorary society for the profession. When I went to accept the award at a ceremony at Oklahoma State University, I was stunned at how many students were aware of both his work and his books.

I grew up knowing Christopher Tunnard as an American city planner and professor, but I was always curious to know more about his pre-war life as a Canadian-English landscape architect. Perhaps some of the mystery of my father's early life arose because he was a quiet and introspective man. My relationship with him was formed primarily in gardens and during travels. Dad spent hours in our gardens in the foothills of northwest Connecticut, and if you wanted to be with him, the best thing to do was to pick up a spade and start double-digging a perennial bed-to-be. Although these episodes were not full of talk, there was a sense of calm and order that he exuded, and I would feel close to him, which somewhat mitigated the absence of information about his pre-war life. (I still maintain these gardens, albeit not in the splendid state they once were, and they are a constant reminder of his influence on me and on others.)

On the last of our many European trips together, our family travelled through Italy looking for rare, lost, or just inspirational gardens for what was to become *World with a View*. A departure from his many books and articles on city planning, it is an essay that summarizes his many years of looking at gardens and designed or natural landscapes. He dedicated this, his last book, to me, using a compliment paid to me by a Sicilian taxi driver, who told him that his son was *molto studioso*.

So it was with great pleasure that I received the news that this book was in development, especially since it deals with that part of my father's life about which he rarely spoke. While reading the proofs, I have been alternately reminded of the father I grew up with and introduced to a 'new' Christopher Tunnard, a man of the future in 1930s' England. Those who knew him only during his life in the U.S. and at Yale will be amazed by the descriptions of this young, ambitious, dedicated Modernist who became known for creating 'gardens in the modern landscape' and later writing about them in articles and a book by that name.

From his postwar rejection of Modernism, to his pioneering exposition *Ars in Urbe*, to his ability simultaneously to help plan the new New Haven while helping create the New Haven Preservation Trust to preserve the old, my father was not shy of making strong statements about what he believed. Nor did he shun controversy, yet he always maintained his civilized demeanor and was the antithesis of a relentless self-promoter. About this, my father's old adversary Scully said that 'he was a stubbornly heroic figure who had braved misunderstanding, disappointment, and sorrow to stand up for what he believed in. And who happened, on the whole, to have been right.'

This book is a long-overdue and informative tribute, and I am indebted to the editors for their untiring efforts to get it published and to the authors for their contributions.

1   Prolegomena

('Prolegomena' was the term Tunnard used for his prologue to *World with a View*.)

Teachers of landscape architecture today may well have been taught by professors and lecturers who were themselves profoundly influenced by Christopher Tunnard. His early writings and brief teaching career at Harvard discredited earlier modes of thought and promulgated a Modernist mindset.[1] This is recognisable in its focus on the future, and privileged individual genius. Tunnard afterwards ploughed another furrow in urban planning, and the loss of his intellectual leadership of landscape architecture in the English-speaking world had repercussions on a whole range of issues. Not the least of these is that today practising landscape architects are often ignorant of the history of their own profession, and few have much perspective on the complex and nuanced intellectual traditions in which they work.

This was not so eighty years ago. The Arts and Crafts tradition dominated British practice, as the Beaux-Arts tradition did in North America. The latter, particularly, emphasised comprehensive knowledge of the achievements of the landscape design profession, and both traditions were largely resistant to Modernism throughout the 1930s. The wartime spirit during World War II and postwar reconstruction required forward-looking and optimistic approaches, and the design professions, by then convinced that Modernism was the way forward, expanded hugely as reconstruction, new towns, schools, hospitals and other public projects were entrusted to them. A younger generation of landscape designers on both sides of the Atlantic eagerly read Christopher Tunnard's *Gardens in the Modern Landscape* because it was the first book in English which crossed the boundary from traditional garden architecture and made links with Modernist architecture.

Modernism in landscape design had started in Continental Europe, but with postwar paper restrictions there were few publications on landscape design, and so Tunnard's book was also of significance in non-English-speaking countries. There were some, for example J.T.P. Bijhouwer, who were sceptical about the modern nature of Tunnard's designs.[2] Despite such doubts, the book was a most effective channel for promulgating pre-war Continental design philosophy to postwar English-reading professionals, and the ideas for communal landscape

Figure 1.1 The dustjacket of Christopher Tunnard's *Gardens in the Modern Landscape* (1938) which was the first book in English which crossed the boundary from traditional garden architecture and made links with Modernist architecture.

were consonant with postwar ideals. One author has even ventured that in the 1940s Tunnard was 'the world's leading theorist of modern landscape architecture'.[3] This might actually have been so, if the words 'English-speaking' had been prefixed. Furthermore, *Gardens in the Modern Landscape* remained the only text in English on modern landscape design till Garrett Eckbo's *Landscape for Living* (1950).

By then, however, Tunnard had altered his own views and interests significantly. Once he had been awakened to the social and broader environmental aspects of physical change, design gave way to planning. The vision of a new world held by Modernist architects was for high-rise dwellings, and the vision of engineers was for fast-flowing highways and multi-level intersections. Tunnard loved the city, and as he observed how these visions became reality in many public projects, requiring demolitions on a vast scale, and tearing the heart and soul out of communities, he was one of those who, against the flow, argued for alternative approaches. As a professor at Yale he argued ceaselessly for a humanist ethos to prevail in the reordering of cities. Hence the drive for reconstruction, which made his early book so influential with the new generation of landscape designers, became the force that he afterwards felt it necessary to curb.

This irony reveals the nature and temper of Tunnard's thought at various stages of his career, but also, when his shadow is cast against the backdrop of professional and academic norms, it provides deep insights into the conventional thinking of the time, and how radical and forward thinking Tunnard was.

This monograph does not seek to mythologise Tunnard as a genius or a hero, clever and profound as he was. He had mentors and collaborators that helped him shape his thoughts, and he was thereby no isolated loner. On the other hand, he faced a degree of scepticism or incomprehension from colleagues and contemporaries at almost all points of his career. Hence this monograph pursues the windings of Tunnard's intellectual journey in the fields of landscape and urbanism, highlighting the interplay between Tunnard on the first part, his mentors and collaborators on the second, and the prevailing orthodox view of the time on the third. In doing so, the rise of Modernist landscape architecture can be better understood, as can the emergence of counter-thought which would eventually go under the title of post-Modernism.

The determination and achievement of Tunnard and the small band of like-minded writers and practitioners can be appreciated when the prevailing conditions in Britain and North America are understood more fully. These are explained below prior to Tunnard's biography.

The landscape profession in Britain in the 1930s

When Tunnard was training to be a landscape designer in the early 1930s, English garden writing was still dominated by the work of two octogenarians, William Robinson and Gertrude Jekyll. Yet, while they carried out some designs (she with the much younger architect, Edwin Lutyens) and set the style, the majority of gardens were designed either by architects, or else by nursery firms.

Besides Lutyens, the best-known practitioners in landscape design were Thomas Mawson, Edward White and Percy Cane, and their firms had the bulk of the work. Mawson and his son Prentice and Edward White made their livings by designing very architectural gardens. In fact Thomas Mawson, who had been trained as an architect, referred to himself as a 'garden architect'. He was one of the few English landscape designers with an international reputation, cultivated particularly through his book *The Art and Craft of Garden Making* which appeared in five editions between 1900 and 1926 codifying the principles of Arts and Crafts garden style.

The up-and-coming architects who included gardens in their repertoire in the 1930s were J.C. 'Jock' Shepherd, Geoffrey Jellicoe and Oliver Hill.[4] Russell Page was another youthful designer setting out on the same course, having studied at The Slade and then drifted into garden design. Having worked briefly for one of the older generation, Richard Sudell, he had teamed up with Jellicoe by 1931.

Percy Cane was the most prominent early example of those who became a garden architect via the other main route besides architecture – horticulture.[5] He had previously been to art school, showed a talent for draughtsmanship, became a journalist, went to a school of horticulture and finally launched himself as a garden architect in 1919, aged 38. His successful practice was boosted by self-publicity, and by the 1930s he was known for a string of publications and projects in several countries. Madeline Agar, a horticulturalist, and her former pupil, Brenda Colvin, lacked the art training, but both had small practices, and were notable for incorporating sound ecological understanding into planting design.[6] Many horticulturally trained designers were salaried by landscape gardening contractors. George Dillistone had been director and manager of the landscape department at R. Wallace's. Stanley Hart, having trained at Cane's for three years, worked for En Tout Cas. Sylvia Crowe worked for Cutbush's.

In 1929 Sudell took the lead in founding an institute that he intended to be The Society of Garden Architects, but which adopted the American term of 'landscape architect' (see below), i.e. the Institute of Landscape Architects (ILA). It was envisaged that members would have the same professional relationship with their clients as architects had with theirs, working in their interests and taking full responsibility for any errors. Gilbert Jenkins, who had made some impressive topiary gardens in his time, and who was vice-president of the Royal Institute of British Architects (RIBA), wrote the ILA constitution. It shared the RIBA's ethos and many of its rules: for example, designers salaried by nurseries could join the ILA as 'trade associates' only, rather than as full associates or fellows.

Jellicoe proposed Thomas Mawson as President – 'the Institute must have a great name'.[7] Always the believer in organisation and education for the professions, Mawson accepted. White and Prentice Mawson were invited to join, and they accepted, becoming the next two presidents. Sudell accepted their pre-eminence with good grace, becoming the first editor of the ILA's journal, *Landscape and Garden* (*L&G*) in 1934.

The other profession closely linked to landscape design was town and country planning. The Town Planning Institute was founded in 1914. The congestion, pollution and squalor of older cities had led to the establishment of Garden Cities, new planned communities in the countryside. Town planning was seen principally in terms of spaciousness in layout for the sake of beauty and modern transport, and the implementation of building bye-laws for health and safety. The layouts chosen in the inter-war period tended towards stately geometry rather than the picturesqueness of nineteenth-century new settlements. Thomas Adams (1871–1940), who had been director of the Regional Plan of New York 1923–30, took a considerable interest in landscape after returning to Britain in 1936. Thomas Mawson had been a prominent member of the Town Planning Institute (TPI), as was the case with Thomas Sharp, President of the ILA after World War II.

There was no formal academic course in architecture in Britain till the twentieth century, but trainees, articled to established architects, had started the Architectural Association (AA) in 1847 to supplement their in-work training (Calvert Vaux, the co-designer of Central Park, New York, was an early member). The length of such training prior to acceptance into the RIBA had traditionally been set at two years. It was logical that the same should apply to those wishing to join the ILA. Educational provision in landscape design was generally lacking, but a few courses in horticulture gave some grounding in the subject, notably the female-only one at Swanley College, in Kent, which included some design teaching provided by Madeline Agar.[8] She wrote an instructional book on garden design, honed by her experience with pupils.[9] To the regret of many, the college economised by terminating the arrangement with her in 1921. However, the Royal Horticultural Society's course at Wisley, under its director, Frederick Chittenden, had an element of design, certainly in the late 1920s.

From 1930 the Faculty of Agriculture and Horticulture at the University of Reading offered Britain's first Diploma in Landscape Architecture. This was awarded after a three-year full-time course including some practical horticultural work. It was organised jointly by the Horticulture and Fine Art departments, which caused some friction, but meant that students were offered art (which included studio work) in all years, along with physics and chemistry, botany, horticulture, surveying and levelling, building construction, and bookkeeping. The literature available included Agar's *Garden Design in Theory and Practice* (1911), Richard Sudell's *Landscape Gardening* (1933), Percy Cane's *Garden Design of Today* (1934) and his quarterly *Garden Design*, to which may be added the ILA journal.

The Reading course was initially fairly dismal, with few students. No practising landscape designers were involved until Prentice Mawson became an external examiner in 1933. Arthur J. Cobb, the senior lecturer in charge of horticulture on the course, strove to improve matters. He edited *Modern Garden Craft* (1936), a substantial compilation of material relevant to the course in three volumes by himself, Dillistone and others. Geoffrey Jellicoe became the fine art lecturer two days a week in 1934 till 1937, after which Russell Page took over till the war caused the course to be suspended.

The poor start to the Reading course, and indeed the self-protectionism implied by the founding of the ILA, occurred in large part because confidence in the future of the profession was at a low ebb. The flow of lucrative private commissions had substantially dried up with the Depression of the late 1920s and early 1930s. A reviewer of the 1933 edition of *Gardens and Gardening*, The Studio's gardening annual, glumly stated: 'the great days of landscape gardening are over'.[10] The same reviewer despaired, too, of the decline in standards of design. He noted that Japanese gardens, artificial rockwork, and debased Arts and Crafts features remained the best that modern design could offer, and thanked The Studio for sparing him worse, 'the various hideosities of garden ornament, such as "crazy-paving", imitation and useless sundials and quaint "olde-worlde" little bunnies'.

The reviewer had in mind that the scale and excesses of Edwardian design had given way to the suburban garden. Increasingly, writers like Percy Cane and Stanley Hart were turning their attention to the problem of the smaller garden, providing plans for 'the garden of half an acre' and suchlike. Sir Geoffrey Jellicoe

Figure 1.2 'A plan for a one-and-a half-acre garden' by Percy Cane, 1936: a typical garden by Cane would be inspired by Arts and Crafts motifs.
(Source: Webber (1975), p. 48)

recollected that 'it was quite impossible to make money in those days because it was just domestic landscape'. Unsurprisingly, architects and garden architects tended to keep the expensive construction work for themselves, thereby taking the bulk of the percentage fee, and the horticulturally trained found that their staple diet was producing poorly paid planting designs to fit the architect's plans.

The 1930s, when the landscape profession was struggling commercially, and specialised education was only just emerging, was hardly an opportune time to re-imagine the identity of the client. Nevertheless whispers of change were audible. Prentice Mawson, a traditional Arts and Crafts practitioner, felt obliged to acknowledge in his presidential speech in 1934 that 'we stand at a transitional point in almost every sphere of human activity … We move ever forward from an aristocratic towards a democratic basis for society.'[11] His fear was that 'work which ought and does demand the highest skill is falling prey to the misdirected zeal of the improver, the nurseryman and the amateur' and also the highway engineer, and he pressed the claims of the professional designer in 'the successful planning of broad areas of open country, but still more in the creation of aesthetic settings for housing development, the laying out of public parks and recreation grounds'.

Then a more obvious radical, T.F. Thomson, a planner who was partner of Thomas Adams and the Modernist architect Maxwell Fry, observed that 'the whole country is chaotic in its unplanned endeavour to evolve a new social and economic order'. In his view that argued for a National Planning Board, and for 'a permanent panel of landscape architects to whom it could refer the projects of its several constructional Departments, which are of national or regional importance'.[12] Lady Allen of Hurtwood, in writing on 'The Future of Landscape Architecture', described the contribution that it should make to the seven stages of man.[13] She listed playgrounds, sports pitches, 'personal gardens' in city centres, public parks, holiday centres, roads, factory gardens, allotments and gardens of rest.

It was increasingly clear, too, that 'the great white bird of modern architecture has not yet found a secure and decorative perch'.[14] The Arts and Crafts tradition in garden construction was not only incompatible with the new architecture philosophically, but it was discordant in terms of the use of space and materials. Garden designers could clearly see that architecture was undergoing a metamorphosis. Oliver Hill's meretricious but eye-catching Joldwynds, Surrey, was perhaps the most publicised early indication of the architects' new aesthetic for the larger house. Simple settings, preferably with mature trees, provided a contrast of the natural to the bold artificiality of the building.

Landscape designers could have turned to continental examples, of which there were many in France, Switzerland, Austria, Germany, The Netherlands and Sweden. There were several leads that they could have followed, because the illustrated books on garden design, including The Studio's series, *Gardens and Gardening*, and the Country Life publication, *Modern Gardens* (1936), gave examples from these countries. For example, the stepping-stone path treatment using rectangular concrete slabs, favoured by the Austrian, Willi Vietsch, was illustrated in all such publications and in a review in *L&G*'s Summer 1937 issue.

The British gardening public was, though, stubbornly immune to influence from continental designers. When Willi Soukop, a Viennese sculptor, exhibited modern figurative pieces of reclining female figures and a donkey at the Chelsea Flower Show in 1936, the only sale was to his patron, Leonard Elmhirst of Dartington Hall. Meanwhile, the dispirited Soukop observed, the man at the adjacent stand was selling gnomes furiously, and went home relieved of all his exhibits.[15]

Sudell may have represented a generation of garden architects with new concerns in the age of the suburban garden, but he was not notable for bringing Modernism to the readers of *L&G*. The only pre-war landscape designers in Britain who could with justice claim that they had attempted to design by Modernist principles were Christopher Tunnard and his colleague Frank Clark.

The landscape architectural and city planning professions in the USA in the 1930s

Whereas the public parks of Britain had been started in the 1840s and were becoming repetitive productions by borough surveyors by the 1880s, the parks movement in the USA was then reaching its peak. The amazing success of the Olmsted firm of Brookline, near Boston, in providing for parks and other projects involving land planning (scenic reservations, parkways, park systems, residential communities, campuses, government buildings and country estates) meant that dozens of practitioners commenced their careers there and fanned out across the United States offering these skills.

Practitioners in this area of work perceived that they belonged to a definable profession with a separate identity from that of the architect on the one hand, and from the horticulturalist on the other. They adopted Calvert Vaux's and Frederick Law Omsted's self-description of a 'landscape architect', and some leading practitioners formed the American Society of Landscape Architects (ASLA) in 1899. The ASLA was thus formed 30 years earlier than the ILA, in a very different context of public and private investment, and because of vigour within the profession rather than depression. Formal education in landscape architecture likewise commenced 30 years earlier than in Britain, also a year after the founding of the professional body.

The earliest formal education for architects had been at the École des Beaux-Arts in Paris, and so when the Massachusetts Institute of Technology, Harvard University and other institutions devised architecture programmes in the late nineteenth century, they were usually closely modelled on that at the École.[16] The style of instruction was based on learning the lessons of history, and students were expected to have a comprehensive knowledge of all high architecture in the Western tradition. For those who could afford it, tours to study the monuments and gardens of England and France were integral to this educative process.

In the Department of Architecture at Harvard the École-trained Jean Jacques Haffner conducted advanced design with a courtly, military bearing from 1922 till his retirement in 1937.[17] Kenneth Conant, trained in the Department of Fine Arts and then as an architect, had achieved permanent tenure in the Department of

Architecture teaching architectural history through into the 1940s.[18] Furthermore, architectural preferences in the world outside the Department remained loyal to English and French models.

As far as landscape architecture was concerned, an undergraduate programme had been endowed and commenced at Harvard University in 1900, with Frederick Law Olmsted, Jr, as 'instructor'. He was assisted by Arthur Shurcliff and afterwards by James Sturgis Pray, both former employees at Olmsted Brothers. In 1908 the landscape architecture programme transferred to the Graduate School of Applied Science and became exclusively graduate, offering a Masters in Landscape Architecture (MLA). It was raised to the status of a Department, with Olmsted as professor and Pray as chairman, a position he held for 20 years. Most of the landscape faculty remained true to the Olmstedian mindset through the 1930s.

There had been a golden age of gardens and estates at great country places in the 1920s served by Marian Coffin, Beatrix Farrand, Bryant Fleming, Warren Manning, Ellen Biddle Shipman and Fletcher Steele.[19] The Depression and changes to the tax regime in 1933 shrank the clientele, but Coffin and Shipman were amongst those to survive by accepting more modest commissions and there was even a new recruit in the residential sphere, Thomas Church, practising in California.[20] Charles Gillette in Virginia and Loutrel Briggs in South Carolina worked on historical and historicist projects,[21] whilst Shurcliff, although from Boston, made a great name for himself in the restoration of gardens in the unique project at Colonial Williamsburg from 1928 into the 1930s. He was largely responsible for stuffing the 'colonial revival' garden with boxwood.

Increasingly the profession was contributing in new ways. For example, parkways were devised to provide attractive drives for motor vehicles. Gilmore David Clarke rose to the challenge, designing separated carriageways and diamond ramps and cloverleaves to grade crossings, and cladding bridges in weathered stone. His most famous schemes were those of the 1920s, in Westchester County, New York. He formed a famous partnership with Michael Rapuano in 1939. Wilbur Simonson, from Clark's office, designed the Mount Vernon Memorial Parkway in 1929, and Stanley William Abbott the Blue Ridge Parkway, a recreational route along several hundred miles of the Appalachians, in 1933.

Such was the prominence and confidence of the landscape profession in the United States in the early twentieth century that it spawned others – city planning and regional planning (in Britain the equivalent terms were 'town planning' and 'country planning', though the different problems of each country meant that the issues tackled were not exactly comparable). Residential subdivisions had been stock-in-trade for landscape architects, but more serious attention to planning the development of towns and cities as a whole had begun to be seen as a realistic possibility with the plan for Washington DC in 1901. A rush of 'City Beautiful' plans had followed in the 1900s and 1910s, artistic conceptions concerned with geometric physical layout, and light on social or economic analysis.

Daniel Burnham, Frederick Law Olmsted, Jr, and John Nolen had been at the head of this movement, and Olmsted was the first president of the American City Planning Institute in 1917. In Canada Thomas Mawson had been in demand at

Edmonton and elsewhere, whilst the United States had exported Walter Burley Griffin after he became Director of Design and Construction for Australia's new capital, Canberra, in 1913. Saco Rienk DeBoer in Denver from 1910, and Elbert Peets who designed suburban towns for the federal government during the Depression, were influenced by the Garden City movement in England as well as by the prevailing City Beautiful ethos in the United States. By the 1930s, city planning had become widely practised across the United States.

As in practice, so in education. Formal instruction in city planning had been offered within the landscape architectural programme at Harvard from 1909, and in 1923 the degree of 'MLA in City Planning' began to be awarded.[22] In 1929 Harvard obtained funding from the Rockefeller Foundation for seven years to establish a Department of City and Regional Planning. The leading lights were all landscape architects and former employees of the Olmsted firm.

The early twentieth century also saw the emergence of regional planning. Warren Manning was an early exponent, working on regional mapping projects in the 1910s, culminating in a 'National Plan' of the country's natural resources. The establishment of the US Forest Service in 1905 and the US National Park Service (NPS) in 1916 signalled many employment opportunities in this field. Benton MacKaye, trained as a forester, was an early employee of the Forest Service and proposed the Appalachian Trail in the 1920s. Earl Draper became the first planner of the Tennessee Valley Authority (TVA) in the 1930s, being joined by MacKaye. Daniel Ray Hull had a profound influence on the approach to the sensitive design of access and facilities to parks within the NPS in the 1920s, and on the development of the park system in California in the 1930s. The most prominent of all these public servants, though, was Thomas Vint who led the NPS Landscape Division, and whose initiative in the Depression years led to the Blue Ridge Parkway and the Historic American Building Survey to alleviate unemployment.

In the 1930s several academic bodies besides Harvard were offering qualifications in landscape architecture, including the University of California at Berkeley, Cornell University, University of Illinois, University of Michigan, Ohio State University, and the New York State College of Forestry.

At Pennsylvania State College most pre-war landscape students had graduated by 1943, and those who might have enrolled were joining the armed forces. The Dean of the School of Engineering thus conducted a postal survey about, *inter alia*, the future of the profession of landscape architecture.[23] There was consensus that the era of the great country place had ended. Educators, most from establishments that had formerly trained students to work on estate gardens, especially their decorative aspects, were irked by the continuing public perception that that was essentially what the profession did. They were anxious to distance landscape architecture from horticulture and claim it as a fine art. The ASLA had gone so far as to discourage the establishment of programmes of landscape architecture within horticultural establishments.[24] Like several other landscape architectural programmes, that at the University of Illinois had been established within horticulture but felt that through its move into the College of Fine and Applied Arts it had 'gained a greater respect for, and a better understanding of, our work'.[25]

On the other hand, the head at Illinois doubted the wisdom of transferring to a department of architecture:

> very few architects have much interest in, or sympathy for, the broad field of land planning. Most architects simply do not have the educational or philosophic background required ... they should not have a controlling or policy making part.[26]

Educators and practitioners alike emphasised that landscape architecture was the 'field of land development and utilisation in a broad sense'. They cited recent work on large-scale public works, including parkways and city and regional planning, as illustrations of how landscape architecture had broadened out into all forms of land planning. There was even optimism that these new directions had led to the maturing of the profession, which 'will now go on to establish itself, as have architecture and engineering, as one of the indispensable activities of our social structure'.[27] They saw an educational imperative of 'broadening out' from the formerly narrow scope of training for designing the gardens of the great country places.

There was a general feeling that broadening out had made the profession more useful to the nation. The various programmes saw landscape architecture as aligned with architecture, or even engineering, in the sense that they were all disciplines for the design of space and form, and some argued for interdisciplinary training to incorporate city planning, or highway design. Regional planning was seen as the wise use of natural resources, and Wilbur Simonson, then at the Public Roads administration of the Federal Works Agency, and Thomas Vint, then Chief of Planning at NPS, argued for the teaching of ecological conservation.[28] Most arguing these points were content that city and regional planning should remain as courses within landscape architecture.

A paradox may be detected underlying these viewpoints. On the one hand, the catastrophic decline in the private residential market had caused practitioners, in a post-mortem mood, to refute the close connection with horticulture, and to claim landscape architecture as a fine art, to correct public perceptions. On the other hand, the new areas of work were in planning and led to the promotion of conservation, if not horticulture itself, and to small-scale and ameliorative design as part of grander conceptions of highway, city and regional planning. How relevant, then, was the identification of landscape architecture with fine art? It must have seemed to many an outlandish and self-indulgent irrelevance to tackling the modern broad-scale issues.

Notes

1 'Modernism' as here understood refers to the ideological conception of architecture and landscape architecture developed initially in Continental Europe after the First World War, and afterwards adopted in the English-speaking world. It is thus more specific in ideas, time and place than being 'modern'.

2   Bijhouwer (1954), p. 119.
3   Pearlman (2007), p. 102.
4   For Jellicoe, see Harvey (1987), pp. 1–30.
5   Webber (1975), pp. 15–38.
6   Harvey (1987), pp. 139–40.
7   Ibid.
8   Amongst Swanley alumnae were Judith Eleanor Motley Low (founder in 1901of the Lowthorpe School of Landscaping, Gardening and Horticulture for Women in Groton, MS), Brenda Colvin and Sylvia Crowe.
9   Agar (1911), p. x.
10   Oldys (1933), p. 167.
11   *L&G* (Autumn 1934), pp. 17–19.
12   *L&G* (Autumn 1936), pp. 143–4.
13   *L&G* (Summer 1939), p. 73.
14   Tunnard, *Gardens in the Modern Landscape* (1938), p. 126.
15   Interview, David Jacques with Willi Soukop, 24 February 1989.
16   Floyd (1989) describes this general background extensively, also the rôle of schools for women designers.
17   Ibid., p. 97.
18   Ibid., p. 61.
19   Griswold and Weller (1991).
20   Imbert (2000).
21   Gillette replicated the 'Tudor Garden' at Hampton Court at Agecroft Hall, a genuine Tudor mansion transported to the United States in the 1930s; Briggs worked on more than 100 gardens in the Charleston area.
22   Floyd (1989), pp. 30–1.
23   Miller (1975), pp. 5–6.
24   Ibid., p. 17.
25   Ibid., p. 19.
26   Ibid., p. 20.
27   Ibid., p. 20.
28   Ibid., p. 31 and 34.

Part I
Biography

2   Britain

Tunnard's background and character

Christopher Tunnard outwardly maintained a flawless composure. He managed to be unfailingly polite. As a young man he was slim and good looking, well groomed with well-cut suits, giving the impression of being well-to-do. He was organised and articulate, always seeming to be on top of the situation. For example, his talks were all exactly on target, with just the right amount of dry humour, and he never ran out of time. He was very professional in his behaviour, and initial contact was usually quite impersonal. American acquaintances could find him slightly reserved, austere, even aloof. They thought of him as very English. When, however, they were able to overcome first impressions they found he was thoughtful, gentle and shy, and always a gentleman. He had great humanity, being always kind and considerate, and made a pleasant, diligent and stimulating teacher and colleague.

For him, the ideas, not the drama of presentation, counted. His ego was subordinated to his aim of fairly and honestly articulating his thoughts. Hence he displayed little vitriol, and he eschewed histrionics. Tunnard's early colleagues noticed a hint of nervousness. However, no one doubted that he was an altogether serious, cerebral young man with a fine intellect and clear aims. He was certainly hard working, and could be tough in pursuit of his intellectual convictions, sometimes to the point of being difficult. He could be fearless, opportunistic and eager to please for the sake of promoting an idea.

Tunnard might have been regarded as an Englishman, but then he was also Canadian and American. Although his later career was to be at Harvard and Yale, he was born and brought up in British Columbia before spending his formative professional years in Surrey and London. His father, Christopher Coney Tunnard (1879–1939), was from landed gentry, being the second son of Charles Thomas Tunnard of Frampton House, near Boston, Lincolnshire.[1] He had gone out to Canada as a young man, and at the time of his marriage in 1906, he was in Winnipeg, Manitoba.[2] Probably he was a bank employee at the time.[3] His wife, Madeleine Kingscote (1881–1977), was likewise from a gentry family from Kingscote, Gloucestershire, though she was born in New South Wales.[4] Christopher and Madeleine moved to Victoria, in British Columbia, where, on

7 July 1910, Arthur Coney (the subject of this book) was born.[5] He had a brother, Peter, nine years his junior.

Christopher Tunnard senior was in the Canadian army during World War I, and during the 1920s was employed by the Department of Soldiers' Civil Re-establishment, a Canadian Government organisation formed following the war to help soldiers re-enter civilian life, and for the care and retraining of the wounded. In 1920 he was the organisation's representative on Victoria Island, and by 1923 was the Deputy Director of Administration, presumably for the whole province.[6] The Tunnards lived in the pleasant Oak Bay district, and Arthur Coney attended schools in the area,[7] and then, in 1927/8, studied 'Liberal Arts' at Victoria College,[8] which meant English, Mathematics, Chemistry, History and French.[9] During this schooling he seems to have converted his second name 'Coney' to 'Christopher', his father's name.[10]

The landscapes of the Pacific coast left a lasting impression on Arthur Coney. Writing in 1960 about his childhood remembrances of San Francisco, he recalled 'my earliest visit forty years ago when my grandmother brought me here for a day or two on our way to spend the winter in Santa Barbara'.[11] He also seems to have been impressed by Japanese gardens,[12] of which there must have been many until internment and dispersal of those of Japanese descent during the Second World War.[13] In 1928 his parents moved back to the United Kingdom, taking a house called 'Scava', near Portadown, in County Down, Northern Ireland.

The course at Victoria College thus had to be abandoned and Tunnard chose to enrol on the horticulture course run by the Royal Horticultural Society (RHS) at Wisley, in Surrey. Nearly 50 years later he recalled the teaching methods of Frederick Chittenden, the director.[14] This included plant ecology, which meant a few pleasant Saturday morning rambles on Wisley Common. The botanical books he took out from the RHS's Lindley Library were presumably in preparation for his final exams in 1930.[15]

Armed with a National Diploma in Horticulture he undertook a two years' apprenticeship with Sharp and Company, seed merchants in Sleaford, only 15 miles from Frampton.[16] About the time this was completed, his parents moved to Great Canfield, by Dunmow, Essex.

Working with Percy Cane and Frank Clark

In September 1932 Tunnard was articled to Percy Cane.[17] The latter was the leading garden designer in London with a flourishing business located in Westminster and well known for his publications.[18] Cane posed as the thoroughly professional man, taking 'briefs' as a barrister would. He was a perfectionist, and a demanding employer. Whilst at Cane's Tunnard undertook a six months' course in sketching and perspective drawing with Harold White, an illustrator whom both Cane and Prentice Mawson used, and enrolled at the London County Council's Westminster Technical College to study building construction.[19] He was once more borrowing books from the Lindley Library, mainly on design.[20]

Thus far he was pursuing a conventional course, but at Cane's he found himself

Figure 2.1 From 1932 to 1934 Tunnard was first articled to and later employed by Percy
Cane, then the leading garden designer and well known for his publications.
(Source: Webber (1975), *frontispiece*)

TERRACE GARDEN FOR A MODERN HOUSE

Figure 2.2 Percy Cane attempted to update his garden designs to suit 'modern'
architectural design in the 1930s.
(Source: Cane, *Garden Design of To-Day* (1934), p. 11)

alongside the radical, if quiet and sensitive, personality of Herbert Francis (Frank) Clark. At first sight they made an unlikely pair. To begin with, Clark was eight years older, and Tunnard was, at 6' 1", considerably taller. However it was their temperaments that were the real contrast. Clark had a relaxed, expansive view of life. He had shown little inclination to seek a career, and had been a constant source of anxiety to his indulgent mother. In later life he could be late, was careless of his personal appearance and let his in-tray build up to alarming heights. His colleagues would not have been surprised to see sticking plaster holding together broken spectacles. Even his friends characterised him as an amiable bumbler.

However, appearances can deceive. He was intelligent and idealistic, someone who really felt and understood the artistic process, and no mean artist himself with a pen, on both writing and drawing paper. Friends knew him as calm and gentle, diffident and unassuming, only too ready see the other person's point of view. He was generous with his time and in his assessments. He had very considerable charm; Percy Cane, Brenda Colvin and Susan Jellicoe all adored him. However, he lacked the drive to capitalise on his qualities.

Clark had been in rebellion against his stern and demanding father, a jute and copra exporter in Manila in the Philippines.[21] Aged 14, Frank followed his father to Marlborough College in 1916.[22] He enjoyed the rugger and evidently did enough work to go up to Clare College, Cambridge, in 1921.[23] Finding that architecture was not on offer, he chose economics. He did very little work, and later claimed that he had contrived to spend two years at Cambridge seeing his tutor but once. He joined the wine society and sought the company of radical poets. When he took Part I of the Economics Tripos in 1922, he did sufficiently badly that his pass result was not 'classed', i.e. counted amongst the honours passes.[24]

Clark was recalled to Manila to work in the family business. However, he was no supporter of the expatriate community, becoming friendly with Philippinos and buying several native carved figures. His fellow British regarded such general behaviour as strange, and an increasingly uncomfortable atmosphere led to him leaving the English Club. He was by then estranged from his father, who did not speak to him for years afterwards.

Clark moved on to America in steerage accommodation. In about 1925 he drifted to the West Coast, taking a variety of jobs. He was at times a ship's steward, a worker in a department store, and a counter of salmon in Alaska.[25] While he was a lumberjack he became interested in plants, and, although not a trained botanist, gathered the native flora. After a few years he obtained some more respectable jobs with travel agents. Meanwhile his interest in avant-garde poetry and art flourished. He made a collection of poetry pamphlets, and wrote some poetry as 'Frank Halliday' (Halliday being his mother's maiden name). In 1930 he married another radical called Felice.[26]

He returned to England about Christmas 1931 with her. There was then the question of what this unqualified young man should do. His first inclination was to write, and he did offer some of his poetry free to newspapers, but this was not going to make him a living. Clark then declared his desire to be a landscape designer, and his father paid for him to be articled to Cane.

Figure 2.3 Herbert Francis (Frank) Clark met Tunnard whilst articled to Percy Cane: chalk portrait by Kenneth Martin (1905–1984), first shown at Agnews Gallery in 1940.
(Source: Private collection)

Cane gave Clark some basic horticultural knowledge and some skills in garden design, insisting on a rigorous approach to detailing such features as paving patterns. Cane also used him to promote and distribute his quarterly journal, *Garden Design*. For the evenings, Clark enrolled on a still-life art course at the St John's Wood School of Art in order to improve his drawing and colour wash technique.[27] Clark was broadening himself by reading too. He visited the Royal Horticultural Society's library, and borrowed books on historic designs and plant collecting.

Tunnard continued with Cane as an employee and applied for student membership of the Institute of Landscape Architects (ILA) in December 1934.[28] Soon he started freelancing, operating from his house at 'Salcott', on Fairmile Park Road, in Cobham, Surrey.[29] Clark was probably freelancing too.

Articles in *Landscape and Garden*

Tunnard supplied the ILA journal, *Landscape and Garden*, with a series of articles from 1935. His first was 'The Influence of Japan on the English Garden', developing themes found in Percy Cane's *Garden Design of To-day* (1934) and Raymond McGrath's *Twentieth-Century Houses* (1934). His next article was on 'Interplanting'. This concerned the ecological difficulties of mixing plants, and revealed him as an obviously keen plantsman who was building up his practical knowledge of which species coexist satisfactorily. He also wrote of a visit to the French Riviera, probably in the autumn or winter of 1935/6, particularly a villa at Eze, residence of Colonel Jacques Balsan.[30] A charismatic aviation pioneer, he had married Consuelo, Duchess of Marlborough, in 1921, the same year that he built the Château Balsan in Eze. Achille Duchêne had been the landscape designer.[31] Tunnard illustrated his piece with his own photographs, so had already bought the camera which served him well in the coming years.

As if to mark the arrival of a new-found persona, Tunnard dropped his first name 'Arthur' in the early part of 1936 and was thereafter always just 'Christopher'. Some of his growing confidence as a critic of the old ways in landscape design can be seen in his report on the May 1936 Chelsea Show to *Landscape and Garden*.[32] 'This Royal Academy of Garden Architecture appears to be fast approaching the moribund state of its prototype, so little can be found of evolution, originality or evidence of a well-balanced sense of values among the exhibits', he declared. The deficiencies of the designs stemmed from their being by the garden contractors who were principally interested in promoting expensive construction, he claimed. He wished that the future should belong to 'the landscape architect proper, who deals not in materials but in ideas'.

St Ann's Hill and the landscape garden

One of Percy Cane's jobs was for A.L. Schlesinger at 21 Addison Road, Kensington.[33] This may have been how Tunnard came to be acquainted with Gerald L. Schlesinger, a prosperous lawyer who purchased the St Ann's estate in Chertsey when in 1935 he and his wife separated. The house was in poor condition, and it was decided to pull it down and build afresh. Tunnard became very involved in Schlesinger's project, and moved there from Salcott, his house in Cobham, in September 1935. He gave 'Aldbury', in Chertsey, as his temporary address to the RHS, but from January 1936 his address changed to 'The Studios, St Ann's Hill House'.[34]

McGrath was the architect, and he used Gordon Cullen (1914–1994) as draughtsman for the drawings.[35] Tunnard effectively became the client, and took a very close interest in the designs. McGrath designed in a studio for Tunnard on the top floor, opening out onto the roof garden over the first floor.[36] The structure was in reinforced concrete – very innovative for the time – with L.G. Mouchel and Partners acting as engineers. The house was under construction when the snow came in early 1936.[37] Works continued throughout that year. Designs for the swimming pool had been drawn up in October 1935 and the working plan for the contractor a year later.[38] The sculptor Willi Soukop, originally from Vienna but then residing at Dartington Hall, was commissioned to provide a fountain for it. Early in 1937 the finished work on the house was ready for photography and publicity.[39]

Once the design for the house and immediate surrounds had solidified, Tunnard could turn his thoughts to the garden. In order to seek inspiration he made 11 visits to the RHS Lindley Library between November 1935 and January 1936.[40] At that time the Keeper of the Library was Tunnard's old tutor, Frederick Chittenden. The books that he borrowed during 1936 included Hubbard and Kimball's *Introduction to Landscape Design* (1917), Madeline Agar's *Garden Design* (1911) and George Taylor's recently published *The Modern Garden* (1936),[41] all books that he must have carefully perused for design ideas.

Figure 2.4 Stable block at St Ann's Hill, shortly after demolition of the main house.
(Source: English Heritage)

He thanked Chittendon for 'permission to photograph illustrations in old horti-cultural works', and his assistant William Stearn for 'assistance with references and the bibliography'.[42] He had been reading much about English garden history, and it was not long before he became quite knowledgeable on the landscape garden.[43]

Figure 2.5 Eighteenth-century pavilion with grotto at St Ann's Hill, c. 1936.
(Source: English Heritage)

Figure 2.6 View to south-east from position of house at St Ann's Hill.
(Source: Tunnard, *Gardens in the Modern Landscape* (1938), p. 137)

It struck him that at St Ann's, as at other Modernist houses such as Joldwynds and Wentworth, the eighteenth-century natural style, with its irregular 'atmospheric' planting, was proving peculiarly appropriate as an adjunct to the architecture: 'those eighteenth-century landscapes which remain will suffice for most of us and can be adapted for our needs'.[44]

McGrath had been compiling a book on glass, *Glass in Architecture and Decoration* (1937), and was able to include two photographs of St Ann's Hill. One was the mirror wall in the hallway onto which Tunnard's plan of the garden had been sandblasted. The other was an assistant's impression dated 1936 of what the enclosed garden and its 'winter garden' (i.e. conservatory) would look like. Tunnard supplied material for a lengthy passage on greenhouses: 'Our indebtedness … to Mr Christopher Tunnard for valuable data on early horticultural buildings.'[45] The historical research had come in useful, as he was able to cite J.C. Loudon's *An Encyclopaedia of Gardening* (1850 edn), Alicia Amhurst's *The History of Gardening in England* (3rd edn, 1910), Christopher Hussey and Gertrude Jekyll's *Garden Ornament* (1919), and Hussey's *The Picturesque* (1927).

Christopher Tunnard, landscape architect

This was to be an enormously important time for Tunnard. In June 1936 Tunnard applied and was accepted as an Associate Member of the ILA.[46] His connections brought him commissions at some notable Modernist houses. In spring 1937 he attended an international congress in Paris that opened his eyes to landscape Modernism in Europe. Last, he started the series of articles in *AR* that were to conclude with *Gardens in the Modern Landscape*.

His practice was operated from his studio at St Ann's Hill. Most jobs were in Surrey and the other Home Counties. The job numbering commenced in early 1936 and was discontinued after number 27 at the same time that he left St Ann's Hill for Mount Street in London at the very end of 1937. Clark was frequently taken on as an assistant.[47] Clark was generally responsible for ordering plants and implementation. The ledger and plant orders folder gave details, some very sketchy, on 33 schemes.[48]

Clearly Tunnard was ambitious, if his recollection of job hunting was accurate:[49]

> Many years ago a young landscape gardener drove through the Reptonian Park of the largest estate described in this book to be interviewed concerning its restoration. In spite of a devotion to eighteenth century principles, a fairly extensive acquaintance with county psychology, and a Rolls Royce complete with driver especially hired for the occasion, he was dismissed as being 'too inexperienced'.

Most jobs, though, seem to have been in suburban developments, or in old farmhouses in the countryside. His early schemes up till spring 1937 were not so different from what might have been expected from Percy Cane. At his former home, 'Salcott', in Cobham, Tunnard had devised traditional flower borders in a walled garden with a sundial at the centre of a York stone cross path.[50] One of the paths went to a wooden round-headed door in a brick garden wall.[51] Printstyle

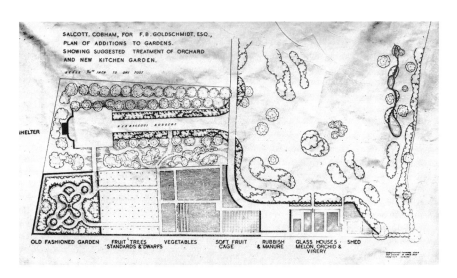

Figure 2.7 At his former home at 'Salcott' on Fairmile Park Road in Cobham, Surrey, Tunnard continued to extend the gardens for a new owner in a manner reminiscent of that of Percy Cane.
(Source: Clark Papers)

Figure 2.8 Walled garden at Salcott with centrally placed sundial and traditional flower
borders, designed by Tunnard in an Arts and Crafts manner.
(Source: Mercer (1937), p. 119)

Place, in Bidborough, Kent, was also traditional, consisting of a small enclosed
garden with a wooden seat and a lily pond, flanked by an oak-beamed pergola
which led to a formal herbaceous garden and a rose garden with a shelter by
McGrath. Paths were of self-faced York stone.[52] McGrath received a commission
for a private house in Gaulby, Leicestershire, from Charles Robert Keene (b. 1891),
the managing director of a clothing company. He was a Methodist and a Labour
member of Leicester City Council, his main interests being in education, culture
and town planning. This project was slow to mature, but meanwhile his brother
W.D. Keene went ahead with a garden scheme provided by Tunnard in 1936
for a house not far away called Ravenhead, at Ingarsby.[53] He showed a straight
drive from the north between hedges to a square 'forecourt', a large rectangular
lawn below the south front terrace, and a 'topiary walk' running east from this
lawn.[54]

   Hoping to learn more about Modernism in gardens, Tunnard attended the four-
day International Congress of Garden Architects hosted by *La Société Française
des Architectes de Jardins* in Paris in the spring of 1937.[55] This was to coincide
with the *Exposition Internationale des Arts et Techniques dans la Vie Moderne* which
included landscape design drawings. Tunnard specially noted the work of Walter
Mertens and Gustav Ammann from Switzerland. He must have submitted some
plans or photographs in advance, for he later recalled receiving a 'silver-gilt medal
for landscape design'.[56]

   The president of the Congress was Achille Duchêne, well known in Britain for
his parterres at Blenheim, but in France for his restoration of Vaux-le-Vicomte.

Figure 2.9 (a, b) 'Rose garden and shelter, Printstyle Place, Bidborough, Kent': Tunnard's
design for this garden included a traditional rose garden and a small enclosed
one. Photographs by Tunnard.
(Source: *L&G* (Spring 1938), p. 43)

Figure 2.10 'Paris Exhibition: Garden of the Swiss Pavilion … ' at the *Exposition Internationale des Arts et Techniques dans la Vie Moderne* in Paris in the Spring of 1937; this coincided with a landscape exhibition and a four-day International Congress of Garden Architects, which opened Tunnard's eyes to landscape Modernism. Photographs by Tunnard.
(Source: *L&G* (Summer 1937), p. 81)

Each country was supposed to send reports and representatives to the Congress, though Russia and the United States had done neither. Nevertheless, Tunnard thought that the Congress was extremely valuable in order to compare notes with practice abroad. One contact was Baron Sven A. Hermelin from Sweden who espoused functionalism and free planning. Another was Jean Canneel-Claes of Belgium, who had designed some interesting functional gardens near Brussels,[57] including, in 1931, his own. In their simple planning, by the rational allocation of areas to sand-pits, tulips or vegetables, and in their economy of materials, Canneel-Claes's designs agreed in practice with Hermelin's guidance.

Tunnard thought that:

> when all talk of styles and traditions is done, there remains a technique which is international, which rejects the old ways and looks forward to the new, unfettered by restrictions of fashion or of academic theory, yet adapting itself to the conditions of the day by the use of logic and sanity and a poetic

Figure 2.11 The architect Jean Canneel-Claes's design for his own house and garden, near Brussels, made a great impression on Tunnard and completed his rejection of the Arts and Crafts style. Also see Figure 4.3.
(Source: Tunnard, *Gardens in the Modern Landscape* (1938), p. 64)

interpretation of the needs of civilisation … The planned landscape and garden will be works of art as well as social amenities.

Tunnard's rejection of the Arts and Crafts tradition of Thomas Mawson, Edward White and Percy Cane was complete. From spring 1937, when given the opportunity, his designs reflected his new adherence to the Modernist standpoint. When Tunnard did become involved in McGrath's scheme for Charles Keene at Gaulby in 1937, his layout showed the influence of Canneel-Claes.[58] There were also several further schemes with McGrath, including two probably unexecuted designs for the Surrey commuter belt,[59] one for the garden of a weekend house at Cobham, and the other for a one-acre garden in Walton-on-Thames.

McGrath's connections soon introduced Tunnard to the fashionable modern architectural scene. McGrath's work in 1931 with Serge Chermayeff and Wells Coates on the interiors of the new British Broadcasting Corporation (BBC) building in Portland Place had been a landmark in the acceptance of Modernist style. Another fashionable architect at the time was the flamboyant and eccentric Oliver Hill.[60] He was initially an ardent follower of Lutyens, then tried his hand with equal panache at the Modern Movement style at new country houses in Surrey, and it was he that had designed Joldwynds, at Holmbury St Mary, and Wentworth, near Virginia Water. At a time when many architects considered that garden layout was part of their remit, Tunnard's usual role in selecting plants to flesh out the bare outlines and in specifying and organising the garden construction was in this respect traditional.

Chermayeff was also interested in Tunnard's services. In 1935 he had designed a house for himself to be built on the edge of a coppice woodland called Bentley Wood, near Halland, Sussex. Tunnard was recommended by McGrath and was involved by June 1937. His work was on devising clearance, establishing areas of daffodils, and advice on plants for the terraces by the house and the kitchen garden.

Tunnard's ambition of creating a landscape architectural practice was on the wane during 1938, partly perhaps because of the general economic conditions, and partly because he was increasingly interested in town planning and writing. Nevertheless Clark continued making calculations and ordering plants for further jobs in 1938 and into 1939. These were mostly in London, and were mainly private homes except for the Ideal Home Exhibition, 'Springfield Park', and a garden in Battersea Park, all in 1939. The more significant designs are described more fully in the section on 'Landscape Design' in Part II.

The *Architectural Review* articles

The English press was slow to report on landscape and garden design abroad. The best source was *The Studio* which provided a rather intermittent and selective view of modern garden design concentrating on the artistic and architectural gardens. By the time it started a regular annual report in 1932, the political circumstances in central Europe were changing and the first generation of Modernists were leaving.

Figure 2.12 (a, b) Joldwynds, Surrey, designed by Oliver Hill, was one of the most publicised Modernist houses and defined the new aesthetic for the larger house in the country.
(Photographs: Jan Woudstra)

On the other hand, the magazine *Architectural Review* (AR) monitored the latest events in the European architectural scene.

McGrath was well known to *AR*, for he had supplied it with many articles. The editor, Hubert De Cronin Hastings, was an intuitive and sophisticated journalist, well able to spot a good topic to explore. His interest in promoting Modernist architecture led to his strong support of Coates, McGrath and Chermayeff who were amongst its more ideological and articulate advocates. Hastings's assistant editor until 1935 was John Betjeman, and then it was James (Jim) Richards who had written a few pieces for *AR*, including a long article on Henry Moore in 1934. Richards's interest had been in Moore's reference to pre-Columbian art. In Richards, *AR* got a protagonist for the Modern Movement with a political commitment to the Left and a concern for the social function of architecture.[61]

There had not been much in *AR* on landscape except a series of articles in 1935 on changes in the English countryside by William Arthur Eden, a young architect who lectured at the School of Planning at Liverpool.[62] Hastings and Richards were conscious that landscape design was too thinly represented. McGrath thus acted as go-between. Probably in early 1937 McGrath took Tunnard to *AR*'s offices in order to introduce him. The suggestion that Tunnard might contribute a series of articles on Modernist landscape design came out of the ensuing discussion.

He had made extensive historical researches from which he could, like W.A. Eden, deduce some of the lessons of history including the processes by which appropriate forms have been selected in various epochs. His first articles on 'Landscape into Garden: Reason, Romanticism and the Verdant Age' and 'Pictures versus Prospects: The Evolution of the Nineteenth Century Garden' came out towards the end of 1937. He could also nominate a number of lines of thought that should be relevant to modern gardens. There was the Japanese approach, and his observations on the English landscape garden. On his return from Paris he could elaborate on the functionalist continental style of Canneel-Claes. Finally, his and Clark's strong mutual interest in contemporary art remained a powerful bond between the two men and provided inspiration for their joint exploration of new thinking.

Tunnard worked hard on composing the articles, visiting the RHS library 13 times between June 1937 and April 1938. He always knew what he wanted to research, and showed himself as diligent at it.[63] There came the question of how to depict Tunnard's ideas. Fortunately, from about 1934 *AR* had its own illustrator, Gordon Cullen. He had met Hastings at the Café Royale in connection with a competition sponsored by Venesta, a plywood manufacturer, in which Cullen had come third, and he started illustrating for *AR* as a sideline thereafter.[64] Sometime prior to February 1938 he was turning plans and photographs of Tunnard's schemes into illustrations which appeared in March. Tunnard asked Chermayeff for permission to illustrate Bentley Wood:[65]

> Cullen has made a pleasant sketch of Bentley which I will send to you. It is at present with the Arch. Press. May I have your permission to use it with

four others in a series showing the modern garden in the April issue of the Review?

The 'Gardens in the Modern Landscape' series for *AR* came out between October 1937 and May 1938. Jim Richards, who had taken over from Hastings as full editor in 1937, found Tunnard very ambitious, and keen to please. He was a conscientious researcher who always took a lot of trouble. He used to come in with finished text and his own illustrations.[66] Richards was very happy with the series.

Clark could write well, so could have helped Tunnard generally with the text. One section that was perhaps Clark's rather than Tunnard's was that on planting design called 'The Planter's Eye'.[67] This revealed knowledge of Impressionism and contemporary art. They found fault in Gertrude Jekyll's work in that she merely replaced one type of colour gardening, the Victorian bedding schemes, with another, though admittedly better. Furthermore her technique was based on the lessons of Impressionism, 'fifty years old and being discarded by painters'.[68] The theoretical flaw they said they found in Jekyll was that she 'failed to recognise the Impressionists' chief discovery that the earth was lit from the sky; in other words, that light was the main factor and the key to the whole situation'.[69]

Their ideas for garden planting sought to allocate colour to its proper role in order to 'remove the necessity for consideration of colour planning as an end in itself and substitute an ideal for colour in which this factor could play a functional part in garden planning'. They pointed out that English landscapes are predominantly green, and that the quality of light varies so greatly. Colour, they thought, can have a structural function in garden planning; it can

> revivify these tones and renew the structural life of the landscape (a) through concentration of purely physiological colour in architectural surroundings which nourish it and lessen the devitalising power of light in a heavy northern atmosphere, (b) through employment of the methods of chiaroscuro (light coming out of darkness) or of illuminative backgrounds in the open garden or larger landscape compositions.[70]

Some plans for the shrubbery at Gaulby by Clark were included in order to illustrate these precepts.[71]

Clark, with his understanding of painting and poetry, was beginning his quest, which he maintained for the rest of his life, to find modern forms and means of expression that would bring landscape design into the fold of the contemporary arts. *Gardens in the Modern Landscape* commenced by asserting that 'A garden is a work of art', a motto that Clark stood by. The necessity of landscape design being an art is explained by his underlying belief in the 'Zeitgeist', the spirit of the times. He wrote in his diary in November 1940 that

> Artists … express the culture of their day – not only individual sensibility. Tomorrow will certainly change and artists will as certainly express that

change. Each kind of artist cannot escape the ideas of his generation and because he is sensitive he again must express either the anger + disillusionment or the hopes or the fears which most generally are part of the consciousness of himself and of his neighbours. I find this so obviously true + so well illustrated in reading 18th century writers'.[72]

As the last remark makes clear, Clark gained more than a brief acknowledgement from Tunnard in return for help on the book. He had immediately absorbed Tunnard's interest in the eighteenth-century landscape garden.[73] It fascinated him because the creators of the landscape garden had achieved the goal of finding forms expressive of their philosophical ideas. Their new landscape was an expression of ideals of freedom, and thus achieved 'the close connection between those political ideas and their expression in the arts'[74] – something that the politically radical Clark would have dearly loved to establish in his own day.

London life

At the very end of 1937, Tunnard took part of 115 Mount Street, in Mayfair, just the other side of Berkeley Square from McGrath's office at 38 Conduit Street.[75] It was not a propitious time for relaunching a business in landscape design, for the general downturn in construction work was dire. In 1939 Serge Chermayeff went bankrupt and left for America.[76] This meant, for example, that the Henry Moore figure at Bentley Wood had to be returned to the sculptor.[77] Some, but very few, jobs in London did fall to Tunnard, such as The Hill House, 87 Redington Road, Hampstead, where Schlesinger was installing his wife and daughter, and an apartment block in Kensington.[78]

Clark found himself moving to Hampstead and working simultaneously on Tunnard's remaining jobs and in Russell Page's office. Page asked him to produce a design for Barbara Hutton's garden, but every time that he saw the drawings he became less responsive. The disconcerted Clark went to Geoffrey Jellicoe. Jellicoe said that the answer was to work in his office. This he did, as the only landscape architect there.

What Jellicoe perhaps did not fully appreciate was that he and Clark were on quite different wavelengths philosophically. Jellicoe found Clark to be an incurable romantic, with his mind in the eighteenth century. Indeed, Clark did admire the English landscape garden tradition that he knew from Claremont and that had served Oliver Hill so well at Joldwynds and Tunnard at St Ann's Hill. Conversely he found that the Italian garden tradition in which Jellicoe worked a complete anathema to his Modernist principles.[79] Despite these differences, though, the two men had a mutual respect and liking for each other.

The move to London enabled Clark and Tunnard to pursue their interests in contemporary art by visiting the galleries around Bond Street and Cork Street, whilst in Hampstead Clark met with the avant-garde.[80] They came to know Paul Nash (1889–1946), the sculptor, surrealist landscape painter and photographer, and planted his garden.[81] Clark was also acquainted with John Hutton, Barbara

Hepworth and Erno Goldfinger. Ben Nicholson gave him a small print.[82] Tunnard later recalled meeting Nash and being shown his collection of *objets trouvées*.[83] He also met John Piper (1903–1972), Henry Moore, Nicholson and Hepworth, with whom he carried out 'experiments in relating her sculpture to certain forms of landscapes'.[84] However, he had a further connection, his cousin John Samuel Tunnard (1900–1971), an avant-garde surrealist painter with ties to the Bloomsbury group.[85] John inherited the family home, Frampton House, which he later sold. He went to the Royal College of Art and made a reputation undertaking Impressionist still lifes, before turning to abstracts in about 1935. He moved to Cadgwith, Cornwall, in 1933. In 1938 Peggy Guggenheim exhibited his work in her gallery in Cork Street, an occasion for the two Tunnards to meet up.

This was the time when Tunnard became active with the MARS Group, the English wing of CIAM (*Congrès Internationaux d'Architecture Moderne*). Progressive architects and planners came together in order to show how contemporary social and economic forces could be translated into buildings and towns. This was Tunnard's introduction to the social purposes of landscape architecture, and led him to write of the 'social landscape', and to develop ideas on communal gardens and the 'minimum garden' for families. He was horrified by the break-up of the historic Claremont estate, in Surrey, and he chose it as a case study to argue for communal gardens. A new article went to *AR* about June 1938.[86]

In the summer of 1938 the ILA put on a small exhibition at the showrooms of Gordon Russell, a furniture maker, at Broadway, Worcestershire. Tunnard contributed some material, and might have been expected to be glad that the ILA planned to take the exhibition to the second international congress in Berlin. His membership of the MARS Group, and his acquaintance with German émigrés, had evidently politicised him, though. He wrote to the ILA's Secretary, as a member of MARS, objecting strongly to any dealings with the regime in Germany, and asking that none of his material be in the British exhibit at the congress.[87]

Gardens in the Modern Landscape

An early spinoff from the *AR* articles was the invitation to Tunnard to make a BBC programme with Jim Richards at Alexandra Palace on 7 March 1938.[88] Probably this was the first broadcast on the subject of landscape design. Two models were designed especially for television. One bore a resemblance to Canneel-Claes's model of the Heeremans garden at Liedekerke, and it is probably no coincidence that while the caption to the Liedekerke picture in *Gardens in the Modern Landscape* went 'a garden ... planned for economy of upkeep', he was photographed at the BBC 'arranging the suburban garden for minimum upkeep cost'.

The next move was to turn the articles into a book by the Architectural Press. Tunnard managed to have the Claremont article included, as well as some additional material on civic planning, the Amsterdam Bospark, and the piece on the planting design at Gaulby. The changes to the plan of Gaulby were not caught, but the setting up of the Soukop fountain to the conservatory garden at St Ann's

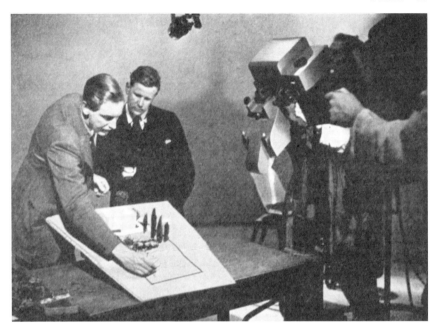

Figure 2.13 'Garden Lay-out by Christopher Tunnard, A.I.L.A., and J.M. Richards, A.R.I.B.A.': an early spinoff from Tunnard's series of articles in *Architectural Review* was a BBC television programme, broadcast on 7 March 1938; Christopher Tunnard is shown with Jim Richards in the background. (Source: *L&G* (Summer 1938), p. 118)

Hill was.[89] The frontispiece was a photograph of the recently completed house at Bentley Wood, and the book would have been put to bed editorially in the late summer of 1938.

Gardens in the Modern Landscape was published in December 1938, and advertised in *L&G* at the cost of fifteen shillings.[90] Tunnard's writing style was often so didactic as to be pedantic, and many readers found it a confusing and difficult read. A common complaint was that the book looked and read like the series of articles from which it was derived. Geoffrey Jellicoe justly informed readers that Tunnard himself had called it a scrapbook,[91] and Russell Page thought it 'difficult to review as a complete book as it has no consistent theme'. Some reviewers acknowledged that the book was an important statement of the Modernist position. Richard Sudell thought it was a 'thought-provoking book, and as such is a welcome addition to landscape literature'. Jellicoe pronounced that 'it is certainly the first serious contribution for many years to garden literature … This new landscape is so exhilarating and so convincingly described.' Page found the book to be 'highly stimulating and very controversial'. He thought the section on 'Oriental Aesthetics' was a 'solid contribution towards garden design', and praised the study of Claremont.[92]

W.A. Eden considered the book to be 'provocative of thought', and particularly liked 'The Planter's Eye', written, he felt, from direct experience.[93] Eden felt that: 'As one reads, one is gradually permitted to see with his eye, and at the end one is conscious that one's own experience has thereby been broadened … It is real theory.' Eden would have liked more of this type of investigation: 'The problem of seasonal changes is one that many people find extremely tantalising, and a fuller treatment of this and other aspects of planting would have been useful.'

However, almost all reviewers found something that they did not like. Page complained bitterly about the page layout, as did W.A. Eden.[94] Page also made a sustained attack on Tunnard for 'drag(ging) in that King Charles' head called "functionalism"', and objected to Tunnard writing that, with the demise of the axial vista 'that most snobbish of all forms of Renaissance planning, has the cult of symmetry begun to suffer a deserved eclipse'. 'Why, Mr Tunnard, is the axial vista snobbish?' Eden picked up on 'modern' in the title, and supposed that the book would turn out to be a 'period piece', such that 'the student of 2038 may look back with the same sort of amusement as is derived by Mr Tunnard from the perusal of the theories of the English Landscape School'. Bradford Williams, Managing Editor of the ASLA's *Landscape Architecture* magazine, was sceptical that the 'new technique' would produce worthwhile results (see below in 'The Artistic Approach'), although he was amused by the reintroduction of Brownian landscapes to solve modern social problems: 'in the words of the author, "the Brownists are at large to-day, grading and contouring, and smoothing and shaping." Read and increase your capabilities!'[95]

Jim Richards wanted *AR* to continue to include material on landscape design and invited Tunnard to contribute a series called 'Garden and Landscape'. It was left to Tunnard to decide what he what he wanted to provide. Richards also asked Gordon Cullen to make sketches of architectural plants so that one could be printed in association with Tunnard's text in each issue.[96] Tunnard took the opportunity to develop his interest in housing layout and the planning of small gardens. His interest in 'minimum gardens' was continued in his designs for the 'All-Europe House' for the Ideal Home Exhibition in 1939.[97] This and his ideas for the 'small garden' were illustrated by ink sketches by Clark.[98] Others were illustrated by photographs of models. That of 'The Suburban Plot' was the one that he had shown on television. The 'country acre' was in fact the Walton-on-Thames scheme that had not gone ahead.

The ILA and the offer by Harvard

Tunnard became more involved in the affairs of the Institute of Landscape Architects. He was on the Council from August 1938, and placed on the Exhibitions Committee. He was put in charge of a more ambitious exhibition than that in 1938. It was called 'Garden and Landscape: an Exhibition of the work of the Landscape Architect'.[99] He designed it, helped by Clark.[100] It was 'arranged' by Susan Jellicoe. The exhibition was held once more at Broadway, from 12 May to 3 June 1939, and the ILA held a weekend meeting on 13–14 May

THE SUBURBAN PLOT
A STANDARD GARDEN PROBLEM

A narrow rectangle of ground, perhaps 40 feet wide and 120 feet long, is the raw material from which the suburban householder has most commonly to contrive his garden. The illustrations below build up in model form a garden that aims at providing what is required in a simple way. It is assumed that the owners of such a garden would keep no gardener and might occasionally want to leave it altogether unattended.

1

It is assumed that the plot runs north and south, with the road at the north and a slight slope at the southern end. The house, as is customary, is placed a little way back from the road, leaving the usual small front garden, in which stands an existing tree. There is a passage through at one side.

2

The front door is at the side of the house, so as to leave the front garden free of paths and so that the living-room windows in the front of the house are not overlooked by callers. A stone-paved path leads to the front door, which is flanked by small flower-beds, suitable for rose bushes.

3

The front garden, being rather public, is not used for recreation and is planted with a simple lawn and a hedge that can easily be kept tidy. As no gardener is kept only one small herbaceous border (which is a form of planting needing considerable attention) has been provided alongside the path.

4

The stone-paved path is continued along the garden side of the house to form a terrace on the south side, on which side it is presumed that the principal living-room windows would open. The terrace terminates in a shelter for out-of-door meals. At the other end is a sand-pit for children.

5

Immediately in front of the terrace is a small lawn, large enough for recreation and for sitting out-of-doors but not so large as to be a nuisance to look after. The lawn is framed by beds of flowering shrubs which serve as a windscreen. These have the advantage that they need little attention and provide something to look at in winter as well as summer. Stone flags preserve the edge of the lawn.

6

A double row of trees continues the axis of the path from the front gate and leads to the far part of the garden. Poplars have been chosen because they are quick growing and their regular vertical form provides a useful contrast to the low planting elsewhere.

7

The end of the garden, down the slope, is planted with grass that can be left rough, being only occasionally scythed, and with fruit trees, arranged geometrically. Daffodils and other bulbs can grow in the grass in the spring. If the owner wants to cultivate vegetables a kitchen garden can be dug here.

Figure 2.14 The 'standard garden problem' as represented in the suburban plot was shown on television and later illustrated in *Architectural Review*. (Source: *AR* 85 (1939), p. 41)

Figure 2.15 One of Tunnard's models for a garden shown on television bore a
           resemblance to one of Canneel-Claes's of 1936 or 1937 for a garden at
           Liedekerke in the Valley of the Dendre, Belgium.
           (Source: Tunnard, *Gardens in the Modern Landscape* (1938), p. 80)

at Broadway to coincide with it.[101] Afterwards the exhibition moved to the RIBA
building at 66 Portland Place, from 21 June to 1 July.[102] Besides having the Henry
Moore sculpture from Bentley Wood in front of a huge blow-up photograph of the
place, and photographs lent by Paul Nash, most of the exhibits were photographs
supplied by members of the Institute.

The printed catalogue had an introduction by Tunnard.[103] As he explained,
the purpose of the exhibition was to show that: 'in one way or another landscape
architects play a part in every form of out-of-door planning and fulfil a function
which is as vital to the community as that of their collaborators, the architect and
the engineer'. The theme was recreation: 'Providing facilities for rest and play is
perhaps the most important sociological function of landscape architecture, for
to-day the need for "common pleasures" makes the problem of the use of leisure
more important than it has ever been.'

The material was divided into three sections – garden, decoration and landscape. The first explored the relationship with architecture, and the second the
use of plants and architectural materials. Tunnard emphasised that the landscape
architect was more concerned with 'contrasts of form, subtle gradations in colour,
and sensitive associations in group planting' than with the decorative qualities of
individual plants only. 'Man-made order in the landscape in the face of increasing

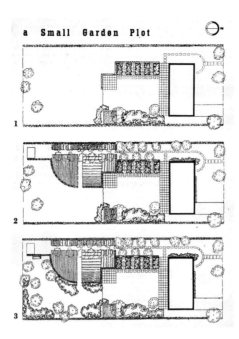

Figure 2.16 (a, b) Tunnard's proposals for a small garden plot shows the idea of the gradual development of the gardens; it was illustrated with ink sketches by Frank Clark.
(Source: *AR*, 85 (1939), p. 199 [plan and perspective])

destruction and irresponsibility in planning' was the theme of the 'Landscape' section. New areas of concern for the landscape architect – playgrounds, holiday camps, factory sports grounds, and landscape associated with hospitals, factories, trading estates, roads and airports – showed the profession's relevance in the modern world. The role of regional plans and planning schemes in directing the form of development was emphasised.

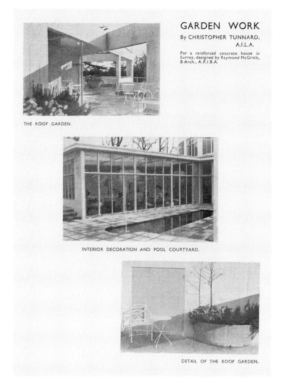

Figure 2.17 The initial exhibition, 'Garden and Landscape: an Exhibition of the Work
of a Landscape Architect' held in Broadway in 1938 included illustrations of
'Garden work' by Tunnard at St Ann's Hill.
(Source: *L&G* (Autumn 1938), p. 163)

The 'Common Pleasures' theme of the Broadway exhibition was Tunnard's next
venture in *AR*. He must have been trying to explore why one designs at all, and
what benefits gardens confer on people. The first pleasure was that of simply being
in open space as a walker, bather or rider.[104] Tunnard also had time to give a lecture
to the ILA at the Royal Horticultural Society Hall on 7 June on the subject of 'The
Modern Movement in Landscape Architecture'.[105] When Thomas Adams stepped
down as ILA President during 1939 he handed over to the Honorary Secretary,
Geoffrey Jellicoe. Tunnard then became the Honorary Secretary.[106] The Institute
wrote in June 1939 commiserating that his father had died.

In the spring of 1939 the Architectural Association (AA) had beckoned to
Jellicoe. The students were agitating to be taught the International Style in architecture, and Maxwell Fry was strongly supported as the choice for Principal,
whilst Jellicoe was also nominated as a compromise candidate.[107] Jellicoe got the
job and was appointed at £1,000 for four days per week.[108] He was glad to accept
because practitioners like himself were feeling the cold financially. Towards the

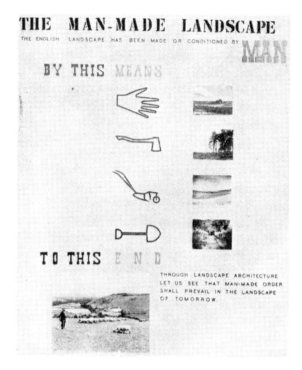

Figure 2.18 'The Man-Made Landscape', one of the panels designed by Tunnard and Clark for the Institute of Landscape Architects exhibition of 1939, held at Broadway and later at the RIBA building in Portland Place, London. (Source: *L&G* (Summer 1939), p. 104)

end of the year he was obliged to let Frank Clark go from his practice, but in his AA guise he was anxious to recruit Tunnard as representing the modern thinking. Unfortunately he could offer only a meagre £400 per annum.

Tunnard had meanwhile received a more attractive proposition from Harvard University. A number of landscape students there were keen to follow the trend in the architecture department towards Modernism. The Dean of the Graduate School of Design at Harvard University, Joseph Hudnut (1886–1968), ordered Tunnard's book in March 1939.[109] Three students in particular, Garrett Eckbo, Dan Kiley, and James Rose, read and cited it in May.[110] Kiley was later to recollect that he and these fellow students requested Hudnut to invite Tunnard to Harvard.[111]

In June Tunnard wrote to the ILA secretary apologising for having to miss a general meeting at the end of the month, but saying that 'I am sailing tomorrow for a flying visit to the US, … I may say that until this morning I had no idea or intention of paying this sudden visit but a cable I just received has made this imperative.'[112] The purpose of the visit was not stated, but may well have been an interview at Harvard. His boat would have docked in New York, and he took the

Figure 2.19 The 1939 ILA exhibition, held at the Royal Institute of British Architects, Portland Place, included a large photo mural of the end of the terrace at Bentley Wood, with the Henry Moore sculpture positioned in front on a zinc container dressed with turf, one architects' plant and a large tree trunk positioned in a separate flowerpot (detail of undated sketch). (Source: LI Archive)

opportunity to visit the New York World's Fair on Flushing Meadows. Amongst the many exhibits it was the 'Pool of Industry' that seems to have inspired him the most. This was an early notable example of a series of fountains choreographed to music by the fair's band. There were 1,400 nozzles in the gigantic pool, as well as coloured flames and fireworks that created a nighttime spectacular. A few months later his 'The Adventure of Water' followed in *AR*.[113] This was an historical exploration of the use of fountains culminating in his appreciation of the New York World's Fair.[114]

Meanwhile there was a debate at Harvard as to whether to take Tunnard on. Henry Vincent Hubbard, the chairman of Regional Planning, and Bremer Pond, the Chairman of Landscape Architecture, were planning to appoint Norman Newton, a Cornell graduate who had won the Rome Prize in 1929 for his design of a country club. However Hudnut wrote to them about Tunnard:

[T]he Department of Landscape Architecture needs a man of his qualities – not because he is a great landscape architect, but because he represents a view toward the modern movement in the arts which alone can bring our two departments into a spiritual harmony'.[115]

Hudnut also wrote to Walter Gropius, the Professor of Architecture, that 'What we really want is that Tunnard should come to Harvard. Once he is here we will keep him, no matter how many Newtons come along too.'[116]

Walter Gropius, famous as the founder of the Bauhaus school, in Weimar and then Dessau, Germany, was quite likely to have agreed. When the Nazi regime closed the Bauhaus – Modernism had been rejected as being Bolshevist, and modern art was considered as degenerate[117] – he moved to London and had formed a partnership with Maxwell Fry. Tunnard was part of Fry's circle in the MARS Group, and this would have established Tunnard's credentials in Gropius's eyes. In Tunnard's own recollection of events:

> Gropius started me on my teaching career when he and Dean Hudnut brought me over from England to work in the department of Landscape Architecture at Harvard. I had just been a member of a design team which produced the M.A.R.S. plan for London. This team was headed by Gropius's former partner Maxwell Fry with whom he had worked in England.[118]

Tunnard's departure was evidently pretty sudden.[119] He announced to Jim Richards at short notice that he was to leave for America and would not be available as an *AR* contributor any more.[120] Richards encouraged him to supply material from America, but didn't hear any more from him and so the 'Gardens and Landscapes' series dried up. Jellicoe cabled Tunnard virtually as he was boarding the boat but to no avail. Hence it was that Tunnard arrived at Harvard at the onset of the war in Europe in September 1939. His mother came with him, and for a while lived in Cambridge.

Notes

1 Burke (1921), Tunnard pedigree. Charles Thomas (b. 1843), Christopher Tunnard's grandfather, lived at Frampton House. His eldest son was John Charles (b. 1873), who had an only son, John Samuel, the surrealist painter (1900–1971). The second son was Christopher Coney (1879–1939), the father of the subject of this monograph and of Peter Kingscote (1919–1940). The fifth son was Thomas Monkton (b. 1882), who became vicar of Birtles, Cheshire, married Grace Cook, and was father of Viola Mary (1916–1974), a pianist, Thomas Newburgh (b. 1919), and Peter Humphrey (b. 1920) who became a gallery owner.

2 Archives of British Columbia, O'Reilly Collection. Settlement on the marriage of Christopher C. Tunnard Esquire with Miss Madeline Kingscote, 7 November 1906.

3 Winnipeg business directories, 1907 and 1908; 'Clifford (sic) C. Tunnard' was listed as a bank clerk.

4 Madeleine Kingscote was a daughter of William Anthony Kingscote (1848–1900), who was married in 1872 to Catherine Jeanette Pringle (d. 1923), of Bective, New South Wales. Catherine Pringle was rich and cultured. Madeleine was a free spirit, artistic and literary. She helped Republicans out of Franco's Spain.

5 Marquis (1957); also Victoria College, Tunnard's student record card. The Archives and Records Service of the Province of British Columbia has no birth record for Arthur Coney, though registration of births was not then required by law.

6 *Wrigley's British Columbia Directory* (1920) lists the elder Tunnard for the first time

as of 620 View, Victoria City, and as Assistant Director's Representative and Island Representative to the Soldiers' Civil Re-establishment; *Wrigley's British Columbia Directory* (1923, 1926), gives the address as 1265 Roslyn Road in Oak Bay, Victoria City.

7　St Michael's School and Oak Bay High School.

8　In the 1920s Victoria College was affiliated with the University of British Columbia (UBC), and offered courses towards a degree granted by the UBC. The college became an autonomous degree-granting institution as the University of Victoria on 1 July 1963. It was from the University of Victoria that Tunnard received an honorary doctorate in 1970.

9　Victoria College, Tunnard's student record card; copy provided by Christopher Petter, University Archivist, University of Victoria, 20 October 1989.

10　'Coney' was an old Tunnard family name, and his family and very close friends called him this. Peter Tunnard pointed out that it opened Arthur Coney to ridicule at school. Victoria College knew him as 'Arthur Christopher' in 1927.

11　Tunnard Papers, Box 32, folder 513. Journal of a visit to Japan, India and Persia (1960).

12　Tunnard, in 'The Influence of Japan on the English Garden', *L&G* (Summer 1935), p. 50, stated that 'the only specimens of these transplantations with an authentic air which the present writer has seen have been made by the Japanese themselves, in this country and in Western America, where there are large native settlements'. In addition, the young Tunnard might have known the Japanese garden begun in 1908 at the eclectic Butchart estate gardens on Victoria Island.

13　Streatfield (1995).

14　Tunnard, *A World with a View* (1978), p. 107 and 182–3.

15　Lindley Library, Loan Register, Volume 7 (1924–34); borrowings occurred between January and May 1930. The topics including general botany, mosses, physical geography and the geography of plants, and books on design included Viscountess Wolseley's *Gardens: Their Form And Design* (1908), and Hubbard and Kimball's *Introduction to Landscape Design* (1917).

16　David Mulford, editor of the *Wisley Garden Club Journal*, kindly supplied the information from it that in 1931 Tunnard was 'seed testing for Messrs Sharpe, Sleaford'. Tunnard Papers, Box 15, folder 235, contains manuscript notes recording that he was 'apprenticed to Sharp and Company, Agricultural Supplies, 1930–32'.

17　Marquis (1957); also *Wisley Garden Club Journal*.

18　Cane (1934), Chapters I and II, provides a statement of Cane's approach at this time. Tunnard Papers, Box 15, folder 235. Manuscript notes.

19　Tunnard Papers, Box 15, folder 235. Manuscript notes.

20　Lindley Library, Loan Register, Volume 7 (1924–34); borrowings in April 1932 were George Tansley, *Practical Plant Ecology* (1923); Alicia Amhurst (the Hon. Mrs Evelyn Cecil), *History of Gardening in England*, 3rd edn (1910), and Marie Luise Gothein, *A History of Garden Art* (1928); in late November books on town gardens; in December Thomas Mawson, *The Art & Craft of Garden Making*, 5th edn (1926).

21　Interviews, David Jacques with Marjorie Clark, 15 March 1989 and 30 June 1989, and with Laurence Fricker, 3 January 1990; Fricker was his student at Reading and colleague at Edinburgh.

22　Information from E.J.P. Hardman, the Bursar of Marlborough College, 11 July 1989.

23　Interview, David Jacques with Marjorie Clark, 15 March 1989.

24　Information from P.N.R. Zutshi, Keeper of the Archives, Cambridge University Library, 11 July 1989.

25　Typescript of the final rehearsal of the BBC Home Programme 'In Town Tonight', 16 March 1940; Clark Papers, 758/1.

26　Felice was active in British organisations supporting the socialists in the Spanish Civil War of 1936; never a very constant companion, she returned to America after the Munich crisis in 1938.

27 Marjorie Clark went to the St John's Wood Art School in about 1933, aged 16, for a general art training. She liked to attend the evening classes because, although she ended up making the tea, some famous names would come in to teach. It was here that she first met Frank Clark.

28 Application form in LI archives; *L&G* (Spring 1935), title page.

29 *Wisley Garden Club Journal* gives 1934 for when he declared that he was in practice as a landscape architect; Marquis (1957) likewise gives 1934.

30 Tunnard (Spring 1936), 'Garden-making on the Riviera'.

31 Information from Michel Duchêne, his grandson, via Pierre Bazin of the *Institut pour le Développement Forestier* in Rennes.

32 Tunnard (Summer 1936), 'Garden Design at Chelsea Show, 1936'.

33 Cane (1934), '21, Addison Road, Kensington'; see also Cane (1934), *Garden Design of To-day*, pp. 156–64.

34 *L&G* (Summer 1936) listed Tunnard as an associate member as from 'The Studios, St Ann's Hill House, Chertsey'.

35 Interview, David Jacques and Gordon Cullen, 11 February 1989. Cullen worked freelance in Raymond McGrath's office, undertaking most of the drawings for McGrath's *Twentieth-Century Houses*, and he also made many of the drawings for St Ann's Hill. He did not, however, visit there till the date of this interview.

36 Anon. (October 1937), 'House in Surrey'.

37 Photographs in the National Monuments Record, part of English Heritage.

38 Information from Mr Chapman of L.G. Mouchel and Partners.

39 Anon. (Spring 1937), 'Garden Work by Christopher Tunnard A.I.L.A.'.

40 Lindley Library, Visitor Book, 14 June 1935 to 27 May 1940.

41 Lindley Library, Loan Register, Volume 8.

42 Tunnard, *Gardens in the Modern Landscape* (1938), 6.

43 Ibid., p. 183, i.e. the bibliography, shows that he had read many of the classics in the original.

44 Ibid., p. 126.

45 McGrath and Frost (1937), p. xi.

46 LI membership files; amongst the plans he sent with his application of 8 June 1936 were his own for The Hooke in Chailey, Salcott in Cobham and Printstyle Place in Bidbrough, and he sent photographs of Salcott and St Ann's Hill House.

47 Interview, David Jacques with Marjorie Clark, 15 March 1989.

48 Christopher Tunnard AILA, ledger and 'plant orders' folder; Clark Papers, 758/69.

49 Tunnard (December 1949), 'Unmodern County'.

50 Mercer (1937), p. 116.

51 *L&G* 2/1 (1935), p. xix; 2/2 (1935), p. x.

52 Anon. (Spring 1938), 'Garden by Christopher Tunnard, A.I.L.A.: Printstyle Place, Bidborough'.

53 Clark Papers, MS/758/69; these were job numbers 10 and 11.

54 The bones of this layout remain in 2008.

55 Tunnard (Summer 1937), 'Landscape Design at the Paris International Congress', pp. 78–83.

56 Tunnard Papers, Box 15, folder 235.

57 Tunnard, *Gardens in the Modern Landscape* (1938), p. 80 – photograph of a model of a garden by Canneel-Claes at Liedekerke; pp. 64–5 – illustrates Canneel-Claes's own small suburban garden near Brussels.

58 Ibid., p. 75. Some drawings by McGrath are in the RIBA Drawings Collection.

59 Ibid., pp. 72–3, line drawings by Gordon Cullen. An exhaustive search of the Ordnance Survey plans for Cobham and Walton-on-Thames have failed to reveal any sign of these two designs.

60 For example, Dorothy Stroud remembered him keeping marmosets in his shirt.

61 Richards (1980).

62 *AR*, 77 (March 1935), pp. 87–94; (April 1935), pp. 142–52; (May 1935), pp. 193–202.
63 Dr William Stearn, the Lindley Librarian between 1932 and about 1957, remembered this about him.
64 Interview, David Jacques and Gordon Cullen, 11 February 1989.
65 Tunnard to Serge Chermayeff, 19 February 1938: Christopher Tunnard AILA, 'plant orders' folder; Clark Papers, 758/69.
66 Interview, David Jacques with Sir James Richards, 27 July 1989.
67 Interview, David Jacques with Laurence Fricker, 3 January 1990. Fricker recollected that Clark had identified 'The Planter's Eye' section as one by himself.
68 Tunnard, *Gardens in the Modern Landscape* (1938), p. 57.
69 Ibid., p. 109.
70 Ibid., p. 123.
71 Ibid., pp. 118–22.
72 Frank Clark, notebook and journal (1940–3); Clark Papers, 758/38.
73 Clark carried out historical research of his own in 1942–3 which bore fruit in several articles and his *The English Landscape Garden* (1948).
74 Clark (1943), 'Eighteenth Century Elysiums', p. 186.
75 Christopher Tunnard AILA, 'plant orders' folder; Clark Papers, 758/69. This folder indicates the change of address. Marquis (1957) states Tunnard dated his move into London as 1937.
76 Powers (2001), 143.
77 Sir James Richards has said that this was never paid for, and so when Chermayeff left for America in 1939 it was returned.
78 Anon. (1939), 'Flats in Palace Gate Kensington', pp. 173–84.
79 Interview, David Jacques with Sir Geoffrey Jellicoe, 19 September 1989.
80 Marjorie Clark, who had first met Clark at the St John's Wood School of Art about 1933, remembered encountering him in galleries later on.
81 Christopher Tunnard AILA, 'plant orders' folder; Clark Papers, 758/69. This cites the client as Paul Nash, Esq., at 3 Eldon Road, Hampstead: Nash lived at this address from 1936 till August 1939.
82 Marjorie Clark kept the Nicholson print until the late 1980s.
83 Tunnard, *A World with a View* (1978), p. 52; his encounters with Nash was when he was painting 'root-monsters', which would have been in 1938 and 1939.
84 Tunnard (May–June 1956), 'The Conscious Stone', p. 22; his experiments with Hepworth would have been in 1938 or 1939 when she was in Hampstead but having difficulty selling work; in September 1939 she left for St Ives, Cornwall, where she made a garden attached to her studio.
85 Glazebrook (1977). See also the catalogue of the Bloomsbury Group show initiated by the Yale Center for British Art (2000).
86 Tunnard (September 1938), 'The Case for a Common Garden – Claremont, Surrey'.
87 Tunnard to Loftus Hare, 7 May 1938; LI files.
88 Anon. (Summer 1938), 'Television of Garden Planning', p. 118. Sir James Richards remembered the occasion well. The go-ahead producer was called Wyndham-Goldie. Tunnard was very articulate, but not very outgoing. This did not matter because the recording took the form of a conversation.
89 Soukop had made his sculpture for the swimming pool, and there are photographs of it there in the National Monuments Record, and photographs of the enclosed garden without it in Tunnard, *Gardens in the Modern Landscape* (1938), p. 104.
90 *L&G* (Winter 1938), p. 238, for the review by Sudell; p. 239 for the advertisement.
91 Jellicoe (1939).
92 Page (23 March 1939).
93 Eden (6 March 1939) p. 464.
94 Ibid.
95 Williams (April 1939).

96 Cullen related that he never saw them in actual gardens – only in nurserymen's windows. Sir James Richards thought it was wonderful how he evoked the character of the plants.

97 Anon. (26 June 1939), 'The All-Europe House', pp. 813–19.

98 Tunnard (1939), 'The Sectional Layout of a Small Plot'.

99 *L&G* (Spring 1939), p. 9 and 31.

100 Interviews, David Jacques with Professor Peter Youngman, 15 February 1989, and with Sir Geoffrey Jellicoe, 19 September 1989.

101 Jenkins (Summer 1939), 'Cotswold Gardens', p. 74.

102 Anon. (Summer 1939), 'An Exhibition of the "Work of the Landscape Architect" at the Royal Institute of British Architects, 66, Portland Place, W.1, June 1939'; besides the illustrations with this article, the panel on water was illustrated in Tunnard (September 1939), 'The Adventure of Water', p. 101.

103 LI archives, Box 6; Christopher Tunnard (ed.), 'Garden and Landscape' (printed catalogue of ILA exhibition held in June 1939), pp. 4–7.

104 Tunnard (March 1939), 'Common Pleasures'.

105 *L&G* (Spring 1939), p. 58.

106 Marquis (1957).

107 Interview, David Jacques with Sir Geoffrey Jellicoe, 19 September 1989.

108 Harvey (1987), p. 9 and 13, supplemented by Sir Geoffrey's recollections.

109 Joseph Hudnut to the Harvard Cooperative Society, 27 March 1939, sent clipped to an order form to the Architectural Press; Harvard University Archives, UAV 322.7xxx, subseries I, box 5.

110 Eckbo, Kiley and Rose (May 1939), 'Landscape Design in the Urban Environment', quoting Tunnard, *Gardens in the Modern Landscape* (1938), p. 62 and 67.

111 Interview, Lance Neckar with Dan Kiley, 11 November 1988; they were not actually taught by Tunnard who arrived in the next academic year after Eckbo left.

112 Tunnard to Miss Heckford at ILA, 9 June 1939; file on Tunnard in LI archives.

113 Tunnard(September 1939), 'The Adventure of Water'.

114 Tunnard's visit to the World's Fair in New York in June 1939 may possibly have been connected with the British Pavilion garden, designed by Percy Cane on the lines of the college quadrangles in Oxford and Cambridge; Webber (1975), pp. 118–21.

115 Joseph Hudnut to Henry Vincent Hubbard, 13 July 1939; Harvard University, UAV 322.7, subseries I, box 3.

116 Joseph Hudnut to Walter Gropius, 22 July 1939; Harvard University, Houghton Library, Walter Gropius Papers, 85.

117 Lane (1985).

118 Talk on 'Walter Gropius at Harvard' to the Society of Architectural Historians in Boston, 27 June 1962; Tunnard Papers, Box 33, folder 542.

119 Tunnard (September 1939), 'The Adventure of Water'; 'on a warm June evening, I and about fifty thousand others stood at Flushing Meadow (the site of the New York World's Fair, 1939).' He was back in Britain on 25 July when he visited the Lindley Library. His final departure must therefore have been in August or September 1939.

120 Interview, David Jacques with Sir James Richards, 27 July 1989.

3 America

The ethos of Harvard GSD

The Graduate School of Design that Christopher Tunnard joined in 1939 was undergoing a radical conversion to Bauhaus thinking at the time. The two leading figures in this were Joseph Hudnut and Walter Gropius.[1] The former had been dean of the architectural school at Columbia University, and in 1936 he succeeded George Harold Edgell, the Dean of the School of Architecture at Harvard University. Whilst Edgell had been thoroughly supportive of the historically based tradition of Beaux-Arts design, Hudnut had showed himself to be a vigorous proponent of what in America was dubbed The International Style.

Hudnut wrote the introduction to an American edition of Gropius's *The New Architecture and the Bauhaus* and sponsored Gropius's appointment as Chairman of the Department of Architecture in 1937 accompanied by considerable publicity. They were at first a formidable team, and set about dismantling the Beaux-Arts tradition of design instruction at Harvard.

The Bauhaus model of teaching differed from this tradition in many ways. New social and economic imperatives and new technologies were emphasised. Amongst the social purposes of architecture were adequate living conditions, to be achieved efficiently through technical standards for structure, light and air. Hence high-rise buildings could have sufficient light, air and greenery to each dwelling provided they were properly arranged and spaced. Furthermore, structures needed to express themselves honestly.

To the Bauhaus proponents, the Beaux-Arts academic concern for architectural style was a tyranny to be overthrown. The ability to design was what Gropius wanted to bring out of his students. Design was seen as a general skill, a function of inner genius, applicable across scales, materials and systems, as long as the basic principles and method were understood. Architects were seen as the leaders of collaborations. Gropius and his close adherents had the zeal of missionaries, and were impatient with those who stood in the way of their version of progress.

The fate of the teaching of architectural history was symptomatic. Kenneth Conant, the historian within the Department of Architecture, was offering a comprehensive view of all high architecture in the Western tradition. Gropius had

Figure 3.1 In 1936 Joseph Hudnut had become Dean of the School of Architecture at
Harvard, and was to be a significant influence on Tunnard.
(Source: Harvard GSD, 200)

a reputation for being hostile to the teaching of history in such a traditional way.
He retorted that he was not averse to the subject, as long as it included vernacular
architecture and the achievements of non-Western societies. Nevertheless there
was in practice little scope for teaching on the great monuments of Western culture. Consequently those interested in architectural history felt so alienated from
the mainstream at the GSD that in August 1940 some former students of Conant's
formed the (American) Society of Architectural Historians. Conant was present
at the gathering and approved.

By contrast to the Department of Architecture, the ruling creed within the
Department of Landscape Architecture remained traditionalist.[2] The chairman
from 1938 was Bremer Pond. He had worked at Olmsted Brothers and been on
the Harvard faculty since 1914. He vehemently refuted the close connection with
horticulture, and persevered in upholding landscape architecture as a fine art, as he

saw it, till retirement in 1950.[3] He supported the practice of collaborative working between architects, engineers and planners, but said far less about Bauhaus methods, or about broad-scale land planning, than he might, and questioned how involved in highway design the landscape architect should become. The architects looked upon him and his department as 'old-fashioned', and his relationship with Hudnut and Gropius had its tensions.

Whilst the chair of Tunnard's department maintained his Beaux-Arts inclinations against the odds, Tunnard's position within Landscape Architecture also had its difficulties. His colleagues must have been acutely aware that he had been employed for his avant-garde writings, which he continued in the radical architectural magazine, *Task*, founded by the Cambridge Discussion Group, and in the *Bulletin of the Garden Club of America*, examining the fundamentals of landscape architecture. His affinity with Hudnut and Gropius would have led Tunnard's closest colleagues to regard him as a cuckoo in the nest. Eckbo later recalled how Tunnard found himself at odds with many of the old guard of the landscape architectural profession.[4]

However, there were further tensions in the department. Norman Newton, who joined Pond's department at the same time as Tunnard, saw landscape architecture neither in a Beaux-Arts way, nor as fine art, but as land planning in a broad sense.[5] Newton considered that the day when landscape architects should have been trained for the gardens of great houses was over, and recollected 'the course of action we had agreed upon … when I joined him at Harvard after two decades of practice: to drop all residential problems and to concentrate on large-scale public works'.[6] Newton had followed this up by setting a state park problem to the students in 1941.

Hudnut and Gropius decided to bring together the three departments of Architecture, Landscape Architecture and City and Regional Planning under one name, the Graduate School of Design. This may have been partly pragmatic, because the Rockefeller Foundation funding for planning had expired, but the stronger argument, sufficient to override Pond's objections,[7] was that collaborative working was a fundamental of the Bauhaus educational approach. The union was thus immediately cemented by collaboration between first-year students on large-scale design problems.

The landscape students themselves were much more ready to adopt this style of teaching than were their professors. In many ways Garrett Eckbo, Dan Kiley and James Rose, mature students in landscape architecture in the previous several years, had been among the earliest Modernists in the school.[8] Rose was an extreme case who had been expelled for (he claimed) refusing to design in a Beaux-Arts manner, and conducting design experiments instead.[9] These experiments were written up by Rose in the magazine *Pencil Points* in 1938 and 1939, and together Eckbo, Kiley and Rose produced short articles for *Architectural Record*, as a manifesto for a new approach to landscape design.[10]

Teaching at GSD

Hudnut and Gropius had desired to appoint Tunnard from the date of his arrival in late 1939. However, they were committed to Norman Newton already, and initially the offer to Tunnard could only be as a visiting lecturer and critic. Nevertheless he was evidently given a quite full teaching load in both the undergraduate Architectural Sciences programme (for Harvard College 'interdisciplinary' design majors) as well as in the Department of Landscape Architecture and City and Regional Planning. His classes in plant materials and courses on 'Site Planning' meant that he taught most of every day.

He could not, of course, complete the jobs that his practice was responsible for, but he had left the ledger and plant orders folder with Clark for him to carry on.[11] In the spring of 1940 Tunnard attempted to bring Clark over to give a lecture course.[12] Clark's topics were to be the English pastoral tradition, including painterly compositions from Claude and Poussin, Japanese gardens, and Swedish landscape design. He accordingly prepared many glass slides for the mission.[13] The scheme fell through when he was refused exit because of war restrictions.[14]

Tunnard remained at first more closely attuned to events in England than to the unfamiliar American scene. He wrote to Marcus Brumwell, a patron of the work of Ben Nicholson, Naum Gabo and other modern artists, in 1940, bemoaning his increasing dislocation from the British modern art scene. He remarked that it had been a 'nice surprise to get the Ben (Nicholson) lithographs'.[15] He added that one was hanging in his office, and one was at Henry-Russell Hitchcock's in Middletown, CT. On the other hand he evidently took great delight in his new surroundings: 'I am in love with the USA and hope I don't have to leave it soon.' This was a reference to his reluctance, through an inclination to pacifism, to become enmeshed by the war. Brumwell was disappointed by Tunnard's apparent lack of patriotism, as he annotated the margins of the letter: 'Why doesn't he pay us poor men from his opulence. Isn't it time he came home to fight?' Maxwell Fry wrote in a gentler tone to Gropius in January 1941: 'Tell Christopher Tunnard that he should come back to take up where he left off because we shall not see his like again, and would prefer to see him.'[16]

However, Tunnard was becoming entrenched at Harvard. He had been officially appointed as 'Lecturer on Landscape Architecture' for the summer session of 1940, and was reappointed for the full academic year 1940/1.[17] Collaborative working being fundamental to the GSD concept of the design process, Tunnard was involved in interdisciplinary site design studios.[18] Housing design tended to dominate at the GSD. The pattern for projects seems to have been that Gropius and Martin Wagner, who had been Berlin's city planning director during the Weimar Republic, would set the projects, then Tunnard, as landscape critic, amongst others, would assist the students in their work, and finally Gropius would view the completed work. Alongside Tunnard serving as a critic was Hugh Stubbins, an architect originally from Birmingham, in England, who had trained at Harvard and then joined its faculty in 1939.[19]

The collaborative project in 1940/1 was a case study on the town of Ware, particularly on the relationship that planning might forge between landscape resources, growth and cycles of development. Tunnard's course on 'Site Planning' was initiated to help students with their studio work on this project. The term 'Site Planning' had been used in a discussion in *AR*, probably by Tunnard, of the garden at Bentley Wood to mean the process of deriving a layout responding to the needs of the human occupants and the site opportunities and constraints.[20] His course at Harvard by this name was a Modernist and socialist embrace of a humanised landscape. It was a composite of urban design and planning analysis with an introduction to modern landscape architecture at the civic and regional scale.[21] Tunnard admitted that the subject matter was rather rambling, though his analytical method of site planning is one that most subsequent practitioners would recognise.

His lecture on the landscape of the new towns revealed his enthusiasms for science, technology, and the application of a socialist understanding of accessibility as the contexts for modern living.[22] Among the twentieth-century American projects discussed were Frank Lloyd Wright's Broadacre City and the Hutchinson Parkway in New York State. However, the lecture was essentially about trends then current in England. Tunnard did not mention that many American landscape architects were already engaged in land planning in a broad sense (highways, parks and reservations, subdivisions, etc.), and that they had, in fact, founded the professions of city and regional planning in America. John Nolen, the most prolific planner in American history, was not mentioned. The lecture omitted the pioneering examples of planning for American towns in the late 1920s, as well as the current American federal projects for new towns.

Tunnard's slides for his course depicted the forms of ditching and contour ploughing that characterised the then new methods of soil conservation. Industry would frame a new aesthetic for functional recreation, and the picturesque and nature would fall away as the language of parks. The text fused issues of agriculture and the provision of electrical power to farmers, with visual ideas that included apartment living illustrated by Le Corbusier's work and his own scheme for the Claremont landscape garden, and a verbal image of factories in fields designed by Gropius. The thrust of his lectures was that the landscape needed to be redesigned across all scales from the garden to the region.

The course's factual deficiencies seemed not to matter; in the GSD it was method rather than mere knowledge that mattered. In 1941 Gropius congratulated Tunnard on one exercise: 'we find this kind of work very encouraging. In my opinion, the main force in education is to get the students enthusiastic. If that is achieved, students will rush forward by themselves.'[23] Tunnard was placed on the faculty at the start of the 1941/2 academic year. The collaborative project in 1942/3 was a new town scheme on green fields for Weston and Wayland, MA, then on the outskirts of the Boston metropolitan area. The student work from this design studio was featured in *Architectural Forum* in July 1943 and later in Sigfried Giedion's book on Walter Gropius.[24]

Tunnard was learning about the American background; for example, the work of the Tennessee Valley Authority (TVA) which interested progressive thinkers because it represented the idea of a comprehensive design and planning approach that could only be achieved in democratic settings through a regional authority. He later recalled:

> I was giving (under the expansive climate of the Gropius regime) a course called 'Site Planning', which covered everything from the T.V.A. to residential densities. I am horrified to think now how disorganised it must have been then. Yet these were exciting days'.[25]

This was the time when women's education in landscape architecture began to be integrated with that for men. The traditional rôle of women on both sides of the Atlantic was to provide the horticultural, decorative aspects of gardens, and it was served by the women-only schools for women designers. Meanwhile the men provided the structure and architecture, and that was served by male-only programmes at the universities. This division of labour had nowhere been more clearly expressed than in the partnership of Edwin Lutyens with Gertrude Jekyll, and was normal if not universal in the boom following World War I. Nevertheless the Reading course was open to both sexes from its start in 1930, as Frank Clark, who helped Geoffrey Jellicoe out with the teaching sometimes in 1938/9, would have discovered.

In the United States, though, with the changing rôle of landscape architecture, members of the ASLA desired intensely to alter the public perception of the profession as mere prettifiers. The need for a new image thus militated against the integration of the sexes in landscape education during the 1930s. However, in the summer of 1940 the Harvard GSD (men only) collaborated for the first time with the Cambridge Graduate School of Smith College (women only) in a six-week summer school for 50 students.[26] Tunnard was one of the four teaching staff. The others were Walter Bognor, Carol Fulkerson and Albert Simonson. In 1942, as a consequence of 'the present emergency', Harvard GSD decided to admit women students to its courses in architecture, landscape architecture and regional planning in order to eliminate unnecessary duplication in teaching. The Cambridge students transferred to the GSD, and that school then closed.[27]

What kind of new landscape?

The tensions in Harvard's Department of Landscape Architecture between the Beaux-Arts approach to garden and civic design on the one hand, the Modernist approach on another, and Norman Newton's public works ideals on the third, gave rise to considerable debate.

The call for a Modernist approach to landscape architecture in the United States was being demanded by younger practitioners and students from 1938. Eckbo, Kiley and Rose had published their own thoughts, quoting 'the English landscapist' in their pleas for the introduction of scientific issues into the design of gardens.[28]

Tunnard himself continued to theorise in print. He wrote two articles on the issue of agricultural production in *Task*. The first, 'What Kind of Landscape for New England?' appeared in *Task* 1, 1941. His contention was that in the winning of the war were the forms and societal changes needed to win the peace. The perception arose, at least in the ASLA journal, *Landscape Architecture*, that there were serious planning problems to be addressed after World War II, and that the Modernist approach would be having an influence on postwar residential development. It therefore printed an article on 'Modern Gardens for Modern Houses' by Tunnard in its January 1942 issue.[29]

In this piece Tunnard pointed out that numerous houses of modern design had been built throughout the USA, yet 'people who are used to the conventional methods of axial composition or of naturalistic arrangement of plant material just haven't the right approach to the problem of the modern garden'. Clichés which had been accumulating through the centuries had become 'part and parcel of the garden planner's technique'. He delivered a sustained ridicule of the Beaux-Arts tradition of garden design which he characterised as 'picture-book planning' and 'pattern-making for the sake of picturesque or romantic effect'. Unfortunately, Tunnard felt, 'there is at the present time an almost complete lack of designers skilled in the technique of planning for modern architecture'.

Tunnard believed that humans must order the natural environment, and shape – humanise – rather than merely follow wild nature. On the other hand, this should not be achieved by imposing an unproductive or wasteful design. The general approach was to attend to method and utility and not some garden style: 'The right style for the twentieth century is no style at all, but a new conception of planning the human environment.' Hence site planning to provide space for people and plants together with outdoor activities, and to integrate the place into its environment, was needed. Professionals were not necessary, as this skill had always been a folk art, and in direct contradiction to the views of the chair of his department, and his own in *Gardens in the Modern Landscape*, he stated that: 'Gardening is not a fine art; it is an art of the people.'

He recommended experimentation with new materials, such as plywood, asbestos sheeting and glass. Planting should be seen as serving some functional purpose, not just providing a decorative effect. There should be communal facilities like swimming pools under 'group control' and a sharing of as much outdoor living space as feasible. Garden planning, Tunnard summarised, 'is about to change, and change rapidly from its archaic methods and sentimental attachment to the past to something contemporary in spirit, a manifestation of the times in which we live'.

The west coast was perhaps more fertile ground for a Modernist approach to landscape architecture than the east coast. This showed itself both in the design of private gardens and in the planning and design of suburban communities. Although Thomas Church made many traditional gardens, his design for the 1939 San Francisco World Fair developed the forms and materials that would characterise his well-publicised Modernist work. Redwood paving in two forms, i.e. cut sections and sawn blocks, a 'transite' fibreglass screen, modern art and furniture were seen in combination with biomorphic and constructivist geometries.[30]

Eckbo had returned to California in 1940 and began undertaking community and recreational design work for the Farm Security Administration (FSA).[31] In the summer of 1940, Telesis, an environmental research group composed of architects, landscape architects, industrial designers and planners in the Bay Area, mounted a show at the San Francisco Museum of Art. Initiated by Eckbo and Vernon DeMars with Burton Cairns, Francis Violich and Phillip Joseph, the show attempted to meld an interdisciplinary approach to the making of the city, suburb and the region.[32] Eckbo kept in touch with Tunnard, and provided a photograph of his 1939 design for the FSA Welasco Unit in Texas. Tunnard used this in his 1942 article on 'When Britain plans …', and also in the 'Community Gardens' section of the 1948 edition of *Gardens in the Modern Landscape*.[33] Nevertheless the review of the 1938 edition in the *California Arts and Architecture Quarterly*, possibly written by Eckbo himself, demonstrated that differences as to the application of Modernist ideals existed, even if Eckbo and others were in broad support of Tunnard.[34]

Indeed, to many Americans it appeared that modernity of a sort had already arrived in gardens and civic design. For example, Marjorie Sewell Cautley, a landscape architect who had worked with Henry Wright and Clarence Stein on American housing reform schemes such as Radburn, NJ, and Sunnyside Gardens, NY, had anticipated several of Tunnard's views. Her book focused on compositional techniques for the private home and for collective housing, though her solutions were more conventional than Tunnard's.[35] Others took the observation further, and felt that the form of modernity described by Tunnard was unnecessary and perhaps not the American way.

Some others took the opportunity of 'Modern Gardens for Modern Houses' to question Tunnard's suppositions. Fletcher Steele, widely acknowledged to be the doyen of the modern American garden, wondered what the 'modern' way of life might be.[36] He observed that, in gardens, at least, 'people … are about the same as they were fifty years ago'. The communal spirit had always been evident, and 'the description of the modern method of design for landscape architecture might have been expounded by any pre-Revolutionary farmer'. When 'Mr. Tunnard has been longer among us', he would appreciate that the average American built gardens 'because we like them one way or another, not to be old-fashioned, or axial, or modern'. In fact 'most of them would sound very modern to those who read Mr Tunnard's article'. The implication was that Tunnard's approach was more clever propaganda for a foreign style, and less the common sense that he claimed.

William Strong, another established member of ASLA, also disliked the alien style of Modernism and he set out to dismiss Tunnard's various points.[37] Strong defined 'Modernism' as a 'practical solution of a given problem', producing a design that was useful, safe, low in cost and aesthetically satisfactory, and argued that the modern American design already had such qualities, even if owners insisted upon decorative effects. A Canadian was even more dismissive of the claims of Modernism in gardens:[38]

> We need only to glance at the modernist's pitiful attempts out of doors to know that he is stuck. In most cases he has thrown up his hands and done

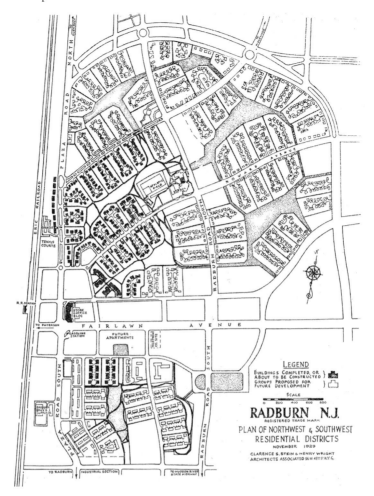

Figure 3.2 American Housing Reform schemes such as Radburn, NJ, designed by Henry Wright and Clarence Stein in 1929 anticipated several of Tunnard's views. (Source: Stein (1951), p. 41)

nothing. The few examples where any serious effort has been made are of such severity, or of such grotesqueness, as to have little resemblance to anything we should recognise as a garden.

However, not all comment was adverse. Geoffrey Baker, architectural critic for *The New York Times*, was a self-confessed fan, and provided a sympathetic review. Noting that Modern architecture was principally 'a sophisticated art for the upper middle classes', he wondered how the 'folk art' for gardens advocated by Tunnard could be given wider exposure.[39] Overall, though, Tunnard, faced with hostility by those resentful of being told they were old-fashioned, and handicapped by his lack of familiarity with the American scene, found that preaching Modernism there was a somewhat more uncomfortable experience than it had been in England.

The shift to city planning

Thirty years on, Tunnard recalled that his interest in American cities 'began in London in 1938, when [he] first opened a copy of Lewis Mumford's *The Culture of Cities*'.[40] He saw it just in time to include it in his bibliography for *Gardens in the Modern Landscape*. When at Harvard he found that Gropius, and even his students Eckbo and his friends, had all been enthused by the same book.[41]

Mumford (1895–1990) was a journalist, but one that had a huge following through his writings for magazines, especially his column 'Skyline' in *The New Yorker* from 1931. He cared deeply about cities as places where people gather to exchange goods, ideas and culture and thereby establish complex networks of human relationships, with cities indeed becoming the summit of human achievement. His early role model had been the Scottish biologist turned town planner, Patrick Geddes, especially for his advocacy of direct observation. Mumford regretted the spread of suburbs, as, in his view, they sapped strength from the city, but he acknowledged the problems of overcrowding and advocated the 'regional city', the American equivalent of the British garden city, for example Radburn. In his panoptic view of human life, with discourse ranging across several academic disciplines, and in his belief that society could be enhanced by intelligent rational planning, he provided an optimistic view of the future of cities.

Dean Hudnut also had a strong interest in city planning. As a young architect he had been profoundly impressed by the German planner Werner Hegemann, and worked with him till Hegemann returned to Germany in 1921.[42] Unusually, at a time when civic design was dominated by the Beaux-Arts approach, Hegemann believed that the pattern of the city should be an expression of the lives and aspirations of its citizens, and so should be in constant flux. Architecture and planning should employ both art and science to enable an efficient, aesthetic and humane environment. Hudnut developed into a complex individual, highly cultivated, and far from being a blinkered supporter of the International Style. He had an ironic humour, breadth of sensitivity, and a clear and elegant way of expressing his ideas.[43] He saw cities as places made by and for people, and believed that interventions in their form should respect their history and should stem from democratically born ideas. He interested himself in civic design and taught on the history of cities, using the examples of older European cities.[44]

Whereas Walter Gropius pursued his Bauhaus idealism unswervingly, Hudnut's thinking unfolded subtly in different directions. He saw dangers in Gropius's impersonal approach to architecture, relying on method, materials and technique, and a GSD conference on urbanism in 1942 may have provoked Hudnut's misgivings of Gropius's ideas for the city. The latter was still advocating the ideas of Le Corbusier and CIAM, namely clearing away slum housing in favour of high-rise dwellings for the proletariat, set in an open landscape, with free-flowing highways leading to other zones where employment, shopping and other land uses could be accessed. Hudnut, who, like Mumford, loved the city for its street life, spontaneous interactions and the symbolism and memories invested in its fabric, considered that Gropius's approach was anti-city, authoritarian and destructive of everything that was positive about cities. He started with the wishes of the population, and saw planning and architecture as 'political arts' that should enable the city to be kept and adjusted better for twentieth-century life. By 1943 it was clear to all that the two men disagreed fundamentally on the teaching of history and on the approach to civic design.[45] The all-too-evident conflict between Hudnut and his former protégé led to confusion and decline in the GSD.[46] This ended only with Gropius's resignation in 1952 and Hudnut's retirement the following year.

Despite being made to feel an outsider within his own school by Gropius's coterie, Hudnut pressed on with developing his ideas on city planning. In 1941, when Henry Hubbard retired, Hudnut took on John Gaus, an admirer of Lewis Mumford, as Chair of the Planning Department. He was not a designer, but taught political science, and had a compendial knowledge of American geography and institutions. Gaus wrote a paper on the education of planners in order to shape a new curriculum.[47] He argued for courses on the role of government in policy making, and for social analysis as a necessary precursor to physical design. Hudnut's humanistic approach, and Gaus's educational prescriptions, attracted some adherents at Harvard. Hugh Stubbins, for example, took Hudnut's position in preference to Gropius's: 'I admired Joseph Hudnut's views about the form of cities and never agreed with Gropius about abandoning the study of history.'[48] Eventually Hudnut's views were expressed in *Architecture and the Spirit of Man* (1949), half of which was on the 'architecture of cities', i.e. civic design.

Tunnard's Harvard career came to an abrupt halt when he was conscripted into the Royal Canadian Engineers in December 1942. Hudnut was sorry to see him go: 'You may be sure that you will be tremendously missed at Robinson Hall, and of course we expect you to take your job back and carry on as soon as the war is ended.'[49] There was also a complimentary goodbye from Gaus:[50]

> While I have been here only a short time, it has been long enough for me to see how generous you have been with the students and how much they have responded; and I realize too the reasons for the high repute in which you and your work are held by your colleagues.

An embolism caused Tunnard to lose sight in one eye during 1943, and he consequently obtained a medical discharge.[51] The war had meanwhile meant rapidly falling student recruitment, so Hudnut found that he could not offer Tunnard his job back after all, but 'I have requested the President to award to you an Arthur W. Wheelwright Fellowship for the academic year 1943–44, the stipend to be $3,500.'[52] Tunnard must have expressed his interest in planning by this time, for the purpose of the award was 'in order to make it possible for you to complete the researches in city planning which you are making … the facilities of the School of Design will be available to you for this undertaking'. Tunnard had evidently been drawn to Hudnut's, rather than Gropius's, viewpoint, and provided sketches for Hudnut's article on 'The Political Art of Planning'.[53] Certainly he was offended by Gropius's phrase 'city desert': 'they are still warm and plastic', he wrote, 'they are the focal points of a nation'.[54] Tunnard was afterwards grateful to Hudnut, and wrote that he owed 'him his introduction to a new field of activity'.[55]

During the 1943/4 academic year, Tunnard went to live with his mother in Greenwich Village.[56] Madeleine's move there in early 1940 may have been to be closer to Peter who was in Michael Chekhov's Theatre Studio at Ridgefield, CT, 40 miles away, from the end of 1938 when war with Germany threatened.[57] Peter had composed poetry and atmospheric short stories whilst at Dartington, and in New York and the coastal islands of South Carolina and Georgia. However, his career was cut short by his death in mid-1940.[58] During his own time in New York City, Christopher became closely associated with Henry Hope Reed who had assumed the editorship of *Task* and taken it to New York in 1943. He became familiar enough with Tunnard to use his earlier name, 'Coney', as shown by correspondence in 1949;[59] presumably this was through knowing Madeleine.

Reed, in *Task* 4, 1943, attacked the role of real-estate investors, front men and speculators, especially in New York. This broadside was not only an attack on the establishment but the first of the magazine's attacks on Robert Moses, the regional commissioner of parks in New York, also a target of Mumford's for his emphasis upon infrastructure development at the expense of community planning. A similar view was held by Tunnard, who emphasised that architecture and physical planning 'have never shaped society'.[60] He wrote the second attack on Moses, and it appeared in the next issue (5) of *Task*, in 1944, as part of a critique of Moses' consultancy with the city of Portland, Oregon. This was followed by a more public exchange between Moses and Hudnut in *The New York Times*.[61]

Unfortunately, as Hudnut had emphasised, the Wheelright Fellowship did not 'imply a reappointment either as lecturer or instructor in the School of Design. It is my understanding that your appointment in the School is definitely terminated.' After it ran out, Tunnard worked for a short spell as associate editor of an influential magazine, *Architectural Forum*, from September 1944 into 1945. The editorial position of the magazine was broadly progressive, but this did not prevent searching critique of books extolling Modernism. Tunnard's work seems to have been principally on these book reviews.[62] In February 1945 the magazine reported that he had accepted a job at Yale, as a Visiting Lecturer in Architecture.[63]

This connection with Harvard's old rival does not seem to have affected Hudnut's and Tunnard's admiration for each other. Tunnard's debt was partly repaid when he referred to Hudnut in the Introduction to the second edition of *Gardens in the Modern Landscape*: 'Architects and designers in America have gained much from his generous support; not least amongst them the author.'[64] This Introduction espoused views that Tunnard shared with Hudnut, even though this meant rejecting many of the key ideas that he had held ten years before. Tunnard afterwards continued to cite Hudnut, as in his *The City of Man*:[65]

Why are we lacking in what Joseph Hudnut has called the 'homely ordinance' of architecture in our city streets – an architecture which has the power to give them life and to create an atmosphere of urban charm?

The City Planning section at Yale

The year 1945 was a pivotal one, both for personal reasons – Tunnard married Lydia Evans in Dover (MA) where her mother had a summer house – and academically, for he was appointed as Assistant Professor in City Planning in the Department of Architecture in the School of Fine Art at the University of Yale. This was the formal commencement of his long association with Yale. During his time there he wrote five books and more than 40 articles in an attempt to control and reshape the forces generated in the 1930s and unleashed in the postwar frenzy of construction.

He made an extended visit to England in the summer of 1947, visiting some of the great landscapes of previous centuries, and also revisiting his own landscape designs, many of which he found had become jungles.[66] In July he gave a talk to the ILA which was a history of the profession in America, with a brief summary of current work.[67] A list of people to invite to an event, perhaps this lecture, included Arthur Ling, Maxwell Fry, Jim Richards, Sir Leslie Martin, H.T. Cadbury-Brown, Sir Hugh Casson, Sir William Holford, Geoffrey and Susan Jellicoe, Colin Rowe, Dorothy Stroud (of Sir John Soane's Museum and later, the biographer of Capability Brown), Nikolaus Pevsner, John Betjeman, Henry-Russell Hitchcock, Ian Nairn (then of the *Sunday Telegraph*), Reyner Banham, James Lees-Milne (The National Trust), and Sir Herbert Griffin (Council for the Preservation of Rural England).[68] Whilst he clearly retained many friends and acquaintances in the UK, Tunnard was at this time committing himself to planning and the American scene, becoming a US citizen in 1949. About that time his membership of the MARS Group lapsed, and by the late 1950s he had ceased to pay subscriptions to the ILA.

Tunnard's conversion to Hudnut's approach was complete by the time that he moved to Yale. He was amongst those with serious misgivings about the ability of Modern Movement practitioners and academics to develop new lines of thought. Tunnard was increasingly alarmed by unrestrained development in and around American cities and realised that conventional planning in the USA was not equipped to deal with the phenomenon.[69] He argued that large tracts of old cities were becoming an 'urban wasteland', while their outskirts sprawled out in low-density development over vast areas, eroding the distinct nature of cities. Rampant urbanisation had become a visual and planning disaster, and he criticised the lack of effective controls that allow 'the richest country in the world to become the ugliest'. He attributed many of the causes to 'public indifference to public beauty'. Tunnard may have been committed to the social aspects of city planning, but was just as dedicated to cities being places that could uplift the spirit through art and design.

His immersion in the academic planning community led to articles in *AR* on 'The American planning tradition' in 1945 and 'Planning in the United States' in 1946. He lectured and led studio work. In the classroom Tunnard called for the intelligent integration of man-made interventions and the natural environment. He called for civilised standards of design which were somehow tied to the human being's responsiveness to his surroundings. The project in 1946/7, for example, was an expansion plan for Westport, Connecticut, that did not 'disturb its pleasant bucolic atmosphere'.[70] It involved siting of a new shopping district, pedestrianisation, a civic centre and beach development. Tunnard had involved sociology students in the exercise, and they noted that part of the town was inhabited by well-to-do commuters who desired to keep industry out of the town, and part was for industrial workers who consequently had to travel long distances for their work. Radical zoning changes were proposed so that light industry could be located in Westport in isolated places that 'would not be noticed by the casual summer visitor'. His 'City Planning Section' within the Department of Architecture was evidently considered a success, and his reward came when he was appointed Associate Professor of City Planning in 1948.

He was active outside Yale. By 1947 he had joined the American Society of Planners and Architects, a radical group which Hudnut, its first president,

Figure 3.3 In the classroom Tunnard called for the intelligent integration of man-made and natural environments. The project in 1946/7 was an expansion plan for Westport, CT.
(Source: 'Yale students have plans for Westport, Conn.' *New York Herald Tribune* (8 May 1947): Yale, Tunnard Papers, box 15, folder 236)

launched in 1944.[71] He spoke at the conference on 'What is happening to Modern Architecture?' at the Museum of Modern Art (MOMA) in 1948, and the same year he gave a talk to a conference on aesthetic evaluation at Ann Arbor on the subject of 'Art and Landscape Design'. The next year he wrote on 'Modern Landscape Design: The growth of a new art form', for the *Journal of the Royal Architectural Institute of Canada*. He was meanwhile in demand as a visiting lecturer to MIT in 1948/9 and to North Carolina State College 1950/1, and he lectured very widely elsewhere.

The results of several years' teaching on site planning and civic design problems began to be reflected in contributions to various journals. His piece on 'The American planning tradition' in 1945 was followed the next year by 'Planning in the United States'. The *Magazine of Art* published a piece in 1947 on 'The romantic suburb in America' and two years later 'Westport improved', based on a student project. 'A city called beautiful' went into the *Journal of the Society of Architectural Historians* in 1950. Tunnard wanted to write a book on his humanistic approach to city planning. He applied for and was granted a Guggenheim Fellowship for the study of American Cities which enabled him to visit places later discussed in the book from July 1950 till June 1951.[72]

The Graduate Program in City Planning

In 1950, during his fellowship, the School of Architecture appointed Tunnard to be Director of a new Graduate Program in City Planning, and he thus became responsible for a separate graduate programme in that subject for the next

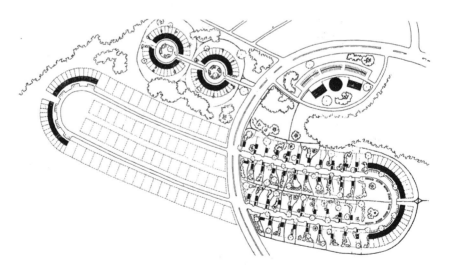

Figure 3.4 Yale students explored the viability of historical typologies, such as the crescent and circus, instead of the American ideal of detached housing. (Source: Tunnard, *The City of Man* (1953), p. 90)

decade. Nevertheless, Tunnard's position was far from secure. The issue of his reappointment brought a letter in 1954 from the Provost asking Dean Charles Sawyer about the 'experimental' status of the City Planning Program and stating no permanent commitment.[73]

Fortunately, or perhaps in anticipation of this issue, Tunnard could by 1953 show a remarkable output of publications stemming from the Guggenheim Fellowship. This had culminated in a book, *The City of Man* (1953). He also assembled enough material from his graduate programme to capture some of the more ephemeral aspects of his programme's groundbreaking work. Printed works included a booklet entitled 'City Planning: A Pictorial Compendium of Examples and Designs'. The next year the programme produced 'City Planning at Yale: A selection of papers and projects'. As the following passage from the latter illustrates, Tunnard's approach to the curriculum was interdisciplinary and humanistic:

> [The student] is encouraged to develop a concept of the city in all dimensions and to present his solutions in a clear, an imaginative and graphic manner, backed up by the techniques of survey and research essential to all city planning activity. The valued cooperation that public and private agencies afford us from time to time teaches him to understand the needs and demands of other people and to realize that the city must always reflect the work of many hands. It is hoped that this broadly humanistic attitude to the city and its problems is brought out …
>
> We are in the fortunate position of being able to draw on the resources of a top-rank Department of Architecture and of the School of Fine Arts as a whole, as well as on the University Departments of Sociology, Engineering, Political Science, Public Health, the Bureau of Highway Traffic, and many others. Through these other departments the student is able to acquire the techniques and background knowledge of subjects important to the city planner, while in our own courses he develops the skills and philosophy of city planning, per se.

During the early years of his time as Director of the Graduate Program he underwent another conversion. Although he had formerly not imagined that anything was missing from his Modernist position, he later realised that it had serious deficiencies. Now he pinpointed the knowledge and skill that had been neglected: they were in appreciations of the past and in a sense of relative values in works of art of earlier times. He explained:[74]

> by the time I came to the School of Fine Arts at Yale, I was beginning to learn how to fill the gaps … it was a case of being introduced to quality and value through art criticism and I learned this from association with Yale's art historians … an ability to analyze and enjoy a work of art in its social context … an exclusive diet of contemporary works and personalities was like being handed a plate of broken glass and sawdust – as J.B. Priestley has put it.

In his credits to *The City of Man* he was specific about these fine art colleagues. He thanked Betsy Chase (1906–1996), a docent at the Yale University Art Gallery; George Howe (1886–1955), Chair of the Architectural Department at Yale University 1950–4; George Kubler (1912–1996), professor of the history of art at Yale; C.L.V. Meeks, architectural historian at Yale; and Charles Sawyer (1906–2005), Dean of the School of Fine Arts. No longer did he despise art and ornament in the city. In 1952 he and Lamont Moore of the Yale University Art Gallery staged an exhibition, 'Ars in Urbe', that was a reminder of the value of Classical design and motifs in the civic scene, and which appeared to many architects and planners as discordant and provocative in the face of their work in urban renewal.

Tunnard's friend Henry Hope Reed Jr had joined him as an Assistant in City Planning at Yale, and a fruitful partnership of like minds was initiated, reminiscent of that with Frank Clark 15 years before. They were close enough in 1951 to create Christopher Tunnard & Associates, with Reed and James Henry Ward as associates, partly with the prospect of a consultancy project for a city plan for Barranquilla, Colombia, in mind.[75]

Reed's interests and credentials say much about Tunnard's allegiances at the time. Reed was a graduate in history from Harvard in 1938, and subsequently went to Paris to study at the École du Louvre. Initially he had little interest in architecture. However, in the early 1940s he joined with Wayne Andrews, architectural writer and photographer, in driving around the older parts of New York City, looking at old buildings, and admiring those decorated with sculpture, mural decoration and Classical elements. In *Task* 5, of 1944, Reed had written perhaps the first article in America advocating preservation of fine old buildings.

Reed wrote 'Monumental Architecture – Or the Art of Pleasing in Civic Design', for the Summer 1952 edition of *Perspecta*, the Yale architecture magazine. This went against everything that Modernism had stood for in eliminating decoration and style:

> We have sacrificed the past, learning, the crafts, all the arts on the altar of 'honest functionalism' … In so doing we have given up … the very stuff which makes a city beautiful, the jewels in the civic designer's diadem.

America's cities needed decoration, murals, domes and interesting skylines, not flat roofs and glass boxes. The United Nations building, he wrote, had 'the same attraction as the inside of an empty icebox,' in that it was 'mercilessly and savagely clean, a debauch of uncompromising cleanliness'. Unsurprisingly, the architectural establishment, by now committed to Modernism, regarded Reed as a crazy maverick, hardly worth responding to.

Evidently passions were running high. *Progressive Architecture* magazine was provoked in 1956 into asserting that Tunnard's and Reed's preference was for 'a way of building ludicrously out of character with contemporary life'. In return, William Foster, editor of *American City Magazine*, irritated Tunnard to a rare display of anger: 'You are insufferably obtuse ….'[76]

Reed had introduced Tunnard to Wayne Andrews and the New York Historical

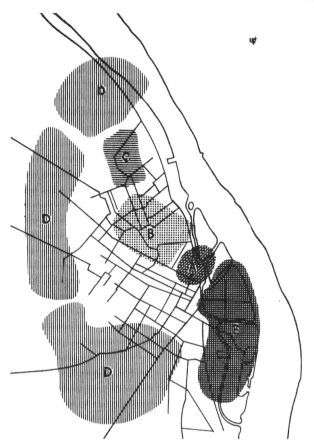

Figure 3.5 Zoning plan for large-scale planning proposals for Barranquilla in northern
Columbia by Christopher Tunnard & Associates, 1951, which encourages
finance (A), new housing (D) and industry (E).
(Source: Tunnard, *The City of Man* (1953), p. 382)

Society, and worked on the text of Tunnard's researches and conclusions into
American cities and sourced illustrations, of which there were a great number.
Tunnard began testing his ideas by means of lectures at various universities,
and then by publishing them in numerous articles in the *Journal of the Society of
Architectural Historians*, *Magazine of Art*, *AR*, *The Journal of the American Institute
of Planners*, *Town Planning Review*, *Community Planning Review* and Brinkerhoff
Jackson's *Landscape*. At length *The City of Man* (1953) was the outcome, in which
the special debt to Reed was prominently acknowledged. The first half of the book
was largely historical, looking at the forces and processes that had shaped urban
growth. The second answered the book's subtitle: 'the recovery of beauty in the
city – a new approach'.

It preceded some other important books on urban aesthetics over the next decade. Kevin Lynch's *Image of the City* (1960), a more technical analysis than Tunnard's, written after five years' study, of how the city is perceived and remembered by its citizens, did not acknowledge Tunnard. Nevertheless its emphasis on human perception, especially of landmarks, had an obvious lineage from *The City of Man*. *Townscape* (1962), from Tunnard's old collaborator, Gordon Cullen, sought to alert architects and planners to the aesthetic benefits of historic and newly planned spaces, with incident and surprise gained by movement through them.

Tunnard and Reed continued to collaborate. In the same year as *The City of Man*, an article, 'The Temple and the City', was published in *New World Writing*, and two years on, their *American Skyline: The Growth and Form of Our Cities and Towns*, came out.[77]

In 1953 Tunnard went as a critic to the School of Architecture at the University of Minnesota where he was introduced as a classicist by the Modernist university architect Winston Close.[78] This was perhaps understandable in view of the exhibition the year before at Yale, but it was not quite on the mark. Both Tunnard and Reed may have shared historical insights into city development, were passionate about the role of art in promoting meaning and grandeur in the public realm, convinced that Modernism as a creed would soon be recognised as bankrupt, and content to be bedfellows when both felt disapproval from the architectural establishment. However, Tunnard's approach did differ from Reed's. He was concerned about modern art and design in new or renewed urban areas just as much as he appreciated the beauty and worth of many older towns and cities, whilst Reed was chiefly fanatical about old buildings, glorying in nineteenth-century decoration, and arguing for their protection.

Reed became well known for his advocacy of tradition in civic design, and remained in the public eye for 30 years, being throughout a thorn in the flesh of the architectural establishment. Realising that Reed was by then a force to be reckoned with, its mouthpiece, *Progressive Architecture*, lambasted his 'necrophiliac architectural leanings' and 'blood-curdling desires for American architecture' in 1962. Nevertheless Reed and his ilk made preservation a permanent force within city planning.

Keen to gain a constituency amongst a wider public for his interest in New York City's buildings, he had initiated architectural and historical walking tours for various organisations from 1956. These were popular and successful. In 1960 *The New York Times* reported that 'The most ardent fans of Manhattan's newest outdoor sport, the architectural tours of the Museum of the City of New York, are women.' Reed's walking tours engendered a pride of ownership amongst New Yorkers in their own city, and this shaped the popular support for the preservation movement, an essential ingredient in the campaign for New York City's landmarks legislation passed in 1965.

Reed expanded his ideas with an article in *Harper's Magazine* in 1957 called 'The Next Step Beyond "Modern"'. He said that so-called functional architecture had 'run its course' and made an impudent prediction: 'the architects who now call themselves Modern will come to see their work derided and replaced'. In his 1959

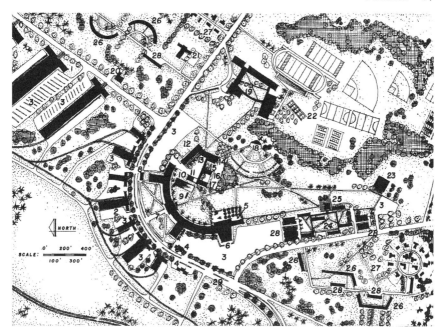

Figure 3.6 Proposal for a new type of industrial town designed at Yale in 1953. One
        of the aesthetic considerations was that industry (1 and 2) need not be
        considered objectionable and could be placed close to shops (7). Drawing by
        Marvin Goody.
        (Source: Tunnard, *The City of Man* (1953), p. 176)

book *The Golden City* he juxtaposed pictures of classical and modern buildings,
such as the old and new wings of the Yale Art Gallery, or the flagpoles of the New
York Public Library and of the Seagram Building, asking readers to make their own
choices. It was a powerful indictment of a decade of the destruction of beautiful
older buildings in favour of lesser modern works, and an outright challenge to the
pre-eminence of Modernism.

A year after the landmarks legislation was passed, Reed was appointed 'curator' of Central Park by its Commissioner. He knew the park intimately, and was
keenly aware of the intentions of the park's designers Calvert Vaux and Frederick
Law Olmsted. His publications on the park, his challenges to uses and building
that would lead to its degradation, and his walking tours of it, helped build the
constituency that would press for its restoration in the 1980s at the hands of the
Central Park Conservancy.

The simplicity and single-mindedness of Reed the outsider was not Tunnard's
way. His mission was to define a rationale for a synthesis of the new with the old,
and of art with science, in a world in which decision making has to reconcile
competing and contradictory viewpoints.

He joined several advisory boards in order to test his views. He was appointed

Figure 3.7 A brownstone house in New York City was the sort of property given new
public esteem through the campaigns by Henry Hope Reed and other
preservationists. Drawing by John Cohen.
(Source: Tunnard with Reed, *American Skyline* (1955), p. 105)

a member, and from 1957 till 1962 chairman, of the City of New Haven
Planning Commission. He was also appointed a member of the Advisory Board
of Connecticut Commission on the Arts, and of the Regional Planning Authority
of South Central Connecticut. He commenced local activism in New Haven
and Connecticut planning and preservation matters in the 1950s, and from
1963 he was President of the New Haven Preservation Trust, a group dedicated
to the preservation of houses and buildings of a historic nature. He was a guest
speaker at the World Design Conference in Tokyo in 1960. He even had time
to carry out some planning consultancy work with faculty member Walter D.
Harris.[79]

After writing *The City of Man*, Tunnard had time to expand his interests into
some major problems of city form. He remembered that in 1938 Lewis Mumford, in

The Culture of Cities, had christened the rapidly advancing coalescence of eastern seaboard cities from Boston to Washington as 'Megalopolis'. In its sheer scale lay the seeds of its own collapse into 'Nekropolis'.[80] Tunnard mentioned these ideas in *The City of Man*,[81] and from the time of its publication, and until 1961, his research time in urban aesthetics was joined by a growing interest in regional growth. It led to his conference at Yale in 1955 on 'The Urban Atlantic Region'. Conceiving that the topic might be expanded into a book, a Rockefeller Foundation grant was obtained in 1957, and case studies began. Tunnard's article on 'America's Super Cities' in *Harper's Magazine* in 1958 coincided with publication of *The Exploding Metropolis* (1958) by William H. Whyte and his collaborators at *Fortune* magazine. Meanwhile, in the British context, Ian Nairn's *Outrage* (1959) fulminated against the swallowing of countryside by suburbia.

Tunnard's synthetic leanings were also seen in his establishment, with the Bureau of Highway Traffic (BHT), of a Joint Program for Master's students from 1958. The proliferation of highways was one of the more obvious manifestations of ugliness in and around American cities. State highway departments made many insensitive decisions, and urban communities and planners quickly found how devastating the impact of highway construction could be. Tunnard reasoned that professional viewpoints were generally imprinted by early training, and so the benefits of engineers appreciating their work from a planning and amenity perspective were obvious. The programme became one year at the BHT and a second one at City Planning, and it lasted for about a decade. Tunnard had thus organised a faculty that exposed City Planning and Joint Program students to the humanistic approach and encouraged them to see that planning was about making choices.

Case studies for the book were completed in 1961, and the text of *Man-Made America: Chaos or Control* was co-authored with Boris Pushkarev, formerly a graduate of the City Planning Program and then of the Yale city planning faculty. Pushkarev dealt with more technical topics like regional planning, infrastructure in the landscape, housing density and freeway aesthetics. Tunnard wrote on open space and historic preservation. It brought together many themes: the concert of art and beauty, the blending of old and new and natural and man-made. It rested on Tunnard's thesis that 'through planning it should be possible to make our physical surroundings attractive, so that community beauty is the rule rather than the exception'.[82] And for him community beauty encompassed not only the significant buildings and landscapes, but a great variety of structures and landscapes, including the vernacular.

The text was delivered in 1962, and *Man-Made America* was published in 1963. Its subject was highly topical. Jean Gottmann described the dynamics of *Megalopolis: The Urbanized Northeastern Seaboard of the United States* (1961). Peter Blake charged that these dynamics were turning the country into *God's Own Junkyard: The Planned Deterioration of America's Landscape* (1964). This book was highly acclaimed by both critics and by the planning profession. American planners hailed it as a statement of what planning should involve. The media critics also liked it: it was the winner of the 'science, philosophy and religion' category of the National Book Awards – the USA's pre-eminent literary prize – in 1964.

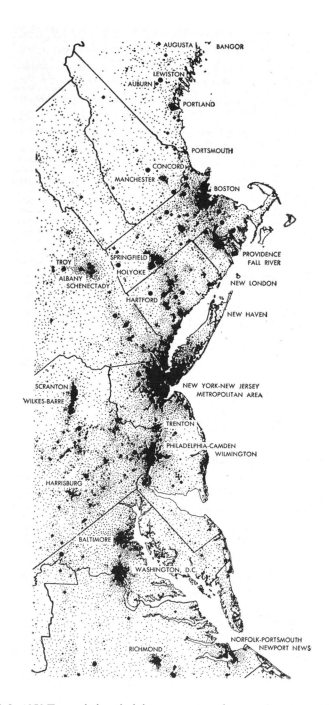

Figure 3.8 In 1958 Tunnard identified the aggregation of eastern American cities as a
super-city.
(Source: Tunnard and Pushkarev (eds.), *Man-Made America* (1963), p. 37)

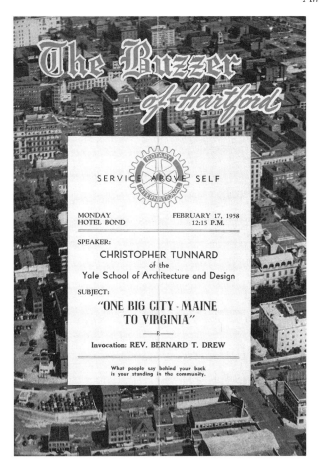

Figure 3.9 The super-city was subsequently a topic of a lecture for Rotary International
'One Big City – Maine to Virginia', on 17 February 1958.
(Source: Yale, Tunnard Papers, box 11, folder 162)

The Department of City Planning

Yale decided to establish a new Department of City Planning, distinct from the
School of Architecture, and Tunnard was appointed the professor to head it up
in 1962. This was perhaps in response to an offer of a full professorship from
Harvard.[83]

   This was a pivotal time for planning. Intense discussions and bitter confronta-
tions raged within the planning profession in professional journals such as the
Journal of the American Institute of Planners, and in planning schools and planning
conferences, but also with the public at large, which became incensed by the
grandiose plans of Urban Renewal. Its problems were discussed in newspapers and
respectable magazines like *Fortune* and *The Atlantic Monthly*. Planning decisions

Figure 3.10 One of Tunnard's projects at Yale was the Monroe Planning Study c. 1955.
(Source: Yale, Tunnard Papers, box 42, folder 700)

received unprecedented attention. Urban Renewal became a lightning rod for a widespread anti-planning movement, and American planning has never fully recovered from its stigma.

A series of stimulating books provided food for thought. Besides *Man-Made America*, J.K. Galbraith pointed out the creases in *The Affluent Society* (1958), whilst Michael Harrington marshalled the shocking evidence for extensive inner-city poverty in *The Other America* (1962). Lewis Mumford's *City in History: Its Origins, its Transformations, and its Prospects* (1961) provided insights into urban ecology and inspirational arguments for continued urban living. Tunnard reviewed it for the *Journal of the American Institute of Planners*. Jane Jacobs, in her *The Death and Life of Great American Cities* (1962) made a persuasive case that the true life of cities springs from their old, richly textured if loose-fit, neighbourhoods, and argued that urban renewal, as conceived by over-efficient modern architecture and planning, was squeezing the spontaneity out of cities. A greater awareness of the politics, economics and sociology of cities was forced upon the planning profession. Academic planning theory consequently went through a remarkable period of development mainly, in the USA, though the pages of the *Journal of the American Institute of Planners*.[84]

The 1960s were a time when awareness and interest in environmental and preservation issues became widespread. At that time not many planners became advocates of these new initiatives, and it was left to concerned citizens to voice their opinions and organise. Tunnard, who had early realised the dangers of Urban Renewal, thus stood out as an advocate of both historic preservation and the environment as critical elements within a balanced and humanised conception of planning.

At Yale he was respected as an original thinker in civic design and planning, but never accorded sufficient administrative and financial support. He spent some time housed in the Department of Architecture. Even though he assumed more and more administrative responsibilities, he received only minimal administrative and other assistance from the university. While managing all the administrative details – from personally ordering desks to dealing with electricians – Tunnard taught a full load of courses and was able to build a planning programme with mostly part-time faculty into a full-fledged department in the 1960s. With few resources and little encouragement from above he nevertheless created an extraordinary place of learning for students preparing for the profession of planning.[85]

The main members of the faculty of the Department of City Planning were Tunnard, Arthur Row and Harry Wexler. Row had been Edmund Bacon's deputy in Philadelphia when the famous renewal plans were drafted. He chaired the department and became instrumental in the Joint Program. He had a good overview of the basic parameters underlying redevelopment, such as land use activities, demographic change, property values, economics, urban renewal and infrastructure. He seemed to understand how to deal with planning theories and planning practice. Wexler was an attorney with an acute social conscience. He taught a land-use regulation course. He and Tunnard saw the need for more community-oriented courses for which he lured some of the country's leading advocate planners like Paul Davidoff. When Row left for India in 1966 Wexler and Tunnard became the co-chairs of the department and were in that position when the programme was closed.

Being professor gave Tunnard much freedom to pursue his interests. He continued to lecture at numerous universities, including being Visiting Professor of City Planning at Harvard (1960–1), University of California at Berkeley, and the University of Rome, Italy. In the USA he participated on innumerable national public and private committees and organisations like the National Trust for Historic Preservation. In 1964 he attended the meeting of the International Congress of Restoration in Venice to which he made a presentation on the movement for historic districts in the United States.[86] This conference was a landmark in preservation/conservation terms, for the Venice Charter, the internationally accepted foundation charter for the conservation of monuments and sites, was ratified during its proceedings, and there was also a resolution to create the International Council on Monuments and Sites (ICOMOS). Tunnard was a member of the US Provisional Committee of ICOMOS from its inception in 1965 and although he was not often able to attend meetings, was one of the 12 'active members' into the 1970s. Following up on the Venice Charter, ICOMOS in the Spanish- and Portuguese-speaking countries of the Americas held a meeting in 1967 in Quito (Equador) to coordinate and stimulate efforts to protect their cultural heritage. Tunnard was one of the 20 'Participating Experts' that produced the 'norms of Quito'.[87]

By the mid-1960s he was moving in the highest circles in the preservation world in the USA. He was invited to the White House Conference on Natural Beauty in Washington, DC, in May 1965, at which the First Lady – Lady Bird Johnson – opened the proceedings. He made suggestions on decaying urban waterfronts and education.[88] Nearly concurrently he was connected to the campaign that led to the National Historic Preservation Act. In response to some well-publicised losses of historic buildings brought about by urban renewal and interstate highway construction, the US Conference of Mayors and the National League of Cities set up a Special Committee on Historic Preservation, chaired by Albert Rains (1902–1991), a lawyer and recently retired Democratic representative on Congress from Alabama. The committee visited Europe and took expert advice at home. Carl Feiss, an architect and urban planner with experience in historic preservation, and one of the prime movers of the initiative, put together a book containing essays on the physical heritage of America, eye-catching photographs, the committee report and a foreword by Lady Bird Johnson. Tunnard contributed an essay which ranged over the reasons for preservation, the rise of the preservation movement, in particular that for historic districts, landmarks and landscape preservation.[89] The publication, *With Heritage So Rich*, was out at the end of January 1966, and it attracted immediate public attention.

This provided the impetus for the legislation enacted by Congress into law in October 1966. The National Historic Preservation Act was the most far-reaching preservation legislation ever enacted in the USA, and vital to instilling a preservation ethic across the United States. It established several institutions: the Advisory Council on Historic Preservation, the State Historic Preservation Offices, the National Register of Historic Places, and the Section 106 review process. The National Register of Historic Places was to be compiled by the National Park Service of districts, sites, buildings, structures, and objects significant in American history, architecture, archaeology, engineering and culture. Meanwhile the State Historic Preservation Offices were to conduct statewide inventories of historic properties and to nominate properties to the National Register.

The Advisory Council on Historic Preservation consisted of 20 members from both public and private sectors, met four times a year, and reported to the President and Congress on historic preservation issues and the development of policies and guidelines in handling conflicts between federal agencies. In 1967, along with his old student Lawrence Halprin, Tunnard was in the first tranche of ten 'citizen appointments' to the Council. One early case, brought before the Council in 1968, was the siting of a nuclear power plant on the opposite side of the Hudson River from the Saratoga battlefield.[90] Proposals for a six-lane riverfront expressway through the Vieux-Carré in New Orleans, declared a 'National Historic Landmark' in 1965, were brought before the Council in 1969.[91] The level of damage ensured that funds were not approved.

Tunnard's last civic design book was *The Modern American City* (1968). Its first part lays out the origins of American cities, their downfalls, and the direction Tunnard would like to see them follow. The second half contains 41 short readings by Tunnard, Thomas Jefferson, Edgar Allen Poe, Andrew Jackson Downing, and Lyndon B. Johnson. In 1968 he was a 'Distinguished Visitor' to the Department of Architecture at the University of New South Wales. During his time in Sydney he ran a seminar on 'Planning for future leisure: Sydney, 2000', the papers to which were published in 1971.

He was travelling and consulting ever more extensively for both public and private organisations in North America and around the globe on United Nations Economic, Social and Cultural Organisation (UNESCO) missions. UNESCO's Division of Cultural Heritage asked him and John C. Pollacco to conduct a technical assistance mission to Jamaica between September 1968 and April 1969. They carried out a survey of historic buildings and sites in order to make recommendation for their development and presentation particularly in reference to the development of tourism.

Meanwhile, though, his Department's position within the University was unravelling. The lesser problem was that BHT relocated to Penn State University in 1968. Tunnard's department had had some success in 1966 when it received support from the Bureau of Public Roads to the amount of $165,000 for a study of the highway as environment, including the aesthetic aspects of highway design.[92] Drivers were interviewed and asked to describe what was seen and how it made them feel to provide quantitative data on the subjective aspects of travel. However, Yale had been putting pressure on the BHT either to upgrade to a Master's Degree programme or to relocate. There were strong ties with the Engineering faculty at Penn State, and the BHT's Director, Fred Hurd, arranged the transfer. Hence the Joint Program in City Planning and Transportation Engineering terminated.

The more serious threat was that Yale's President and senior administrators felt that the University should address the 'urban crisis' that was beginning to be perceived and for which new legislation was constantly being enacted. Apparently, in about 1966 Yale received offers of significant funding. The intention was to give support to the Law School and a Masters programme in urban design within Architecture, rather than to the Department of City Planning, which would be phased out after commitments to current students had been met.[93] City Planning was in a weak position as it no longer had significant external funding.

During the academic year 1967/8 the City Planning programme moved to a considerably more activist position. Under Wexler, the students were behaving as though they were already advocate planners. Bearing in mind the problems of inner-city areas, Tunnard and Wexler thought that they should encourage more black students to attend. In the 1968/9 academic year they invited city planning students to participate in the admissions process and sought to recruit minority students to fill up to 12 of the 24 places in the incoming class.

Only when this process was well underway did the Provost's Office focus on the implications of a far greater demand for financial aid. The Provost may also have suspected that this admissions policy was a ploy to extend the life of the Department, because any subsequent decision to eliminate a Department with a significant ethnic minority student body would be viewed as racist. The response was to cut the incoming class in 1969 by half. The students did indeed view this as institutional racism, and the Department decided to proceed with admissions anyway. This resulted in draconian action by the authorities. Tunnard was removed as Chair and contracts were not renewed to the rest of the faculty after the end of the 1968/9 academic year.

When these problems occurred, Tunnard maintained his support of his Department's actions and his staff. He was no university politician. In retrospect, instead of pursuing his numerous worthy causes outside the Department it would have been more politic for him to attend to issues like his programme's future support and funding. City Planning was not a traditional discipline or profession, and needed constant protection and nurturing within the university system. Whilst Tunnard was himself a prominent figure, and probably unassailable in his professorship, the administrative tactics of his Department lost friends within the system, the radicalism of his students came at an unfortunate time – student unrest in Europe and America was peaking in that very year of 1969.

These were 'tumultuous years,' as Tunnard wrote to his friend, Harvard city planning professor Reginald Isaacs.[94] Tunnard continued as a full professor, but had no department. Honours continued to be heaped upon him for his writing. In 1966, he had been made a Fellow in the Royal Society of Arts. In 1970 he was awarded an honorary degree of Doctor of Letters (LL.D.) at the University of Victoria in British Columbia. Yet at his place of work he was an ambassador without portfolio; like a ghost around the Art and Architecture Building. His administrative isolation was only the final stage of a long, lonely period at Yale.

It is no wonder that his life outside the university, his wide-ranging correspondence, his fellowships and travels, his consulting, his speaking engagements, his writings and his appointments to national public and private committees assumed such importance as these outside contacts no doubt provided him the intellectual stimulation and professional support he missed at Yale. For example, he continued his work for UNESCO. The Division of Cultural Heritage asked him to conduct technical assistance missions to the Kathmandu valley in Nepal, and the stupas at Pramanan and Borobudur in Indonesia.[95] He was co-author of the ensuing report on cultural tourism in Central Java, and contributed to publications on conservation in cities and of cultural landscapes.

He became professor emeritus in 1975 on his retirement. At the end of his career Tunnard returned to his point of beginning. In his inquiry into the nature of scenic values in landscape, in *World with a View* (1978), he circled back to sharawadgi, to John Piper and Paul Nash, and to the moral visions of the landscape from Gilpin to Ruskin and to the Council for the Preservation of Rural England. He argued for aesthetic sensibility to be allowed to assert itself in the care and development of the landscape and drew on his experiences with the Advisory

Figure 3.11 In 1970 Tunnard was awarded an honorary degree of Doctor of Letters (LL.D.) at the University of Victoria, British Columbia.
(Source: Yale, Tunnard Papers)

Council on Historic Preservation and UNESCO. At his death from cancer in 1979 friends and colleagues at Yale collected funds for an annual Christopher Tunnard Memorial Fellowship.

Notes

1 Pearlman (2007), pp. 1–2.
2 Simo(2000); see esp. pp. 21–34.
3 Miller (1975), pp. 17–18.
4 Interview, Lance Neckar with Garrett Eckbo, 23 January 1989.
5 Norman Newton was later to write the comprehensive history of landscape architecture with *Design on the Land: The Development of Landscape Architecture* (Belknap Press, 1971).
6 Miller (1975), p. 10.
7 Mary F. Daniels, 'Pond, Bremer Whidden (1884–1959)', in Birnbaum and Karson (eds) (2000), p. 300.

8 Conversation between Lance Neckar and Edward Larrabee Barnes, 24 April 2002.
9 Dean Cardasis, 'Rose, James C. (1913–1991)', in Birnbaum and Karson (eds) (2000), p. 318.
10 Treib (1993), pp. 68–77 and 78–91.
11 Christopher Tunnard AILA, ledger; Clark Papers, 758/69. Clark used it for calculations when he was commissioned to redesign Bloomsbury Square, Russell Square and St Giles's Churchyard in 1945.
12 Typescript for final rehearsal for the BBC programme 'In Town Tonight', 16 March 1940; Clark Papers, 758/1. The announcer said 'Mr H. Frank Clark is in town tonight. We've caught him before he returns to America shortly'.
13 Information from Laurence Fricker and W.A. Brogden. Clark never had a camera of his own and these slides would have been commissioned. They were 2" x 2" black-and-white, and used by Clark in all his subsequent teaching at Reading and Edinburgh.
14 Information from W.A. Brogden on 15 December 1989, who was told this whilst a student of Clark's in Edinburgh.
15 Tunnard to J.R.M. Brumwell, 21 May 1940; Tate Gallery Archive, Hyman Kreitman Research Centre, TGA 20046. Alan Powers kindly supplied a transcription to Lance Neckar, 20 March 1997.
16 Maxwell Fry to Walter Gropius, 9 January 1941; Harvard University, Houghton Library, Walter Gropius Papers, 85.
17 Official Register of Harvard University, 1940–41.
18 Talk on 'Walter Gropius at Harvard' to the Society of Architectural Historians in Boston, 27 June 1962; Tunnard Papers, Box 33, folder 542.
19 Floyd (1989), 97.
20 Tunnard (attributed) (Summer 1938), 'Modern Architecture in the Sussex Landscape'.
21 Tunnard, 'Site Planning Course' (3 October 1940); Tunnard Papers, Box 37, folder 599, labelled 'Landscape Architecture 1'. The notes were typed onto 115 Mount Street paper, and were delivered in nine meetings between 8 October and 31 October 1940.
22 Tunnard Papers, Box 32, folder 515.
23 Walter Gropius to Tunnard, 27 November 1941; Tunnard Papers, Box 37, folder 599–601, labelled 'Landscape Architecture 2'.
24 Walter Gropius and Martin Wagner, 'A Program for City Reconstruction', in *The Architectural Forum*, July 1943, pagination missing. Tunnard and Stubbins are mentioned as critics. See also Giedion (1954), pp. 226–7 for illustrations of the same work.
25 Talk on 'Walter Gropius at Harvard' to the Society of Architectural Historians in Boston, 27 June 1962; Tunnard Papers, Box 33, folder 542.
26 Anderson (1980), p. 138.
27 Henry A. Frost to the Editor, *Landscape Architecture*, 42 (1942), p. 119.
28 Eckbo, Kiley and Rose (1939–1940), 'Landscape Design in the Urban Environment', 'The Rural Environment' and 'The Primeval Environment'.
29 Tunnard (January 1942), 'Modern Gardens for Modern Houses'.
30 Tunnard, *Gardens in the Modern Landscape* (1948), p. 172.
31 Treib and Imbert (1997), pp. 42–7.
32 Telesis Environmental Research Group, catalogue of the 'Space for Living' exhibition, July–August 1940, San Francisco Museum of Art. Eckbo mentioned in conversation with Lance Neckar a relationship between Telesis and the journal *Task*.
33 Tunnard, *Gardens in the Modern Landscape* (1948), p. 142.; see also Treib and Imbert (1997), Fig. 97.
34 'Books in Review', *California Arts and Architecture*, 57 (May 1940), p. 36.
35 Cautley (1935).
36 Steele (1942), '"The Voice is Jacob's Voice, but the Hands …"' (review), pp. 64–5.
37 Strong (1942), 'It is modern if it cares well for basic necessities', pp. 66–8.

38 Dunington-Grubb (1942), 'Modernismus Arrives in the Garden – To Stay?'
39 Baker (1942), 'Equivalent of a Loudly-Colored Folk Art is Needed', pp. 65–6.
40 Tunnard (1968), *The Modern American City*, p. 3.
41 Pearlman (2007), p. 94 and 119.
42 Ibid., p. 25.
43 Floyd (1989), p. 62.
44 Ibid., p. 62 and 110.
45 Pearlman (2007), Chapter 5.
46 Lynn Miller of Penn State University remembered these conflicts well. At the beginning of a semester Hudnut would address the school on the work ahead, to be followed by Gropius who would inform the students that they would not be undertaking such work at all.
47 Gaus (1943).
48 Floyd (1989), p. 99.
49 Joseph Hudnut to Tunnard, 22 December 1942; Tunnard Papers, Box 8, folder 129.
50 Tunnard Papers, Box 6, folder 92: Tunnard evidently reciprocated these feelings, later citing Gaus's 'Education of Planners' (1943), p. 7, in *The City of Man*, p. 307.
51 Wartime Journal of the ILA 4 (October 1943), p. 3; Marquis (1957).
52 Joseph Hudnut to Tunnard, 15 July 1943; Tunnard Papers, Box 7, folder 108.
53 Hudnut (October 1943), 'The Political Art of Planning'.
54 Tunnard (1953), *The City of Man*, p. 43 and 48, quoting Gropius (1945), p. 53.
55 Tunnard, *Gardens in the Modern Landscape* (1948), p. 8.
56 This was at 56 West 11th Street.
57 Dartington Hall Trust Archive, ref. MC/S7/1: audio tapes including 'Oral History', on the Chekhov Theatre Studio with Madeleine Tunnard, Mary La Hainsworth and Deirdre Hurst du Prey, recorded 07 April 1974. One fellow student at Ridgefield was Yul Brynner.
58 Dartington Hall Trust Archive, box MC/S4/43, Deirdre Hurst de Prey General Files, Travel to Tunnard.
59 Tunnard Papers, Box 16, folder 253.
60 Tunnard, *Gardens in the Modern Landscape* (1948), p. 7.
61 Hudnut, Joseph (22 July 1944), 'A "Long-haired" Reply to Moses', p. 16, 36–7; see Pearlman (2007), p. 193.
62 Some of the titles reviewed were: Fran Violich, *Cities of Latin America* (1944); Julian Huxley, *On Living in a Revolution* (1944); and *Art in Progress*, a book illustrated by Henry Moore's 'Recumbent Figure'.
63 'Appointments', *Architectural Forum*, 82 (February 1945), 72.
64 Tunnard, *Gardens in the Modern Landscape* (1948), p. 8.
65 Tunnard, *The City of Man* (1953), p. 333, citing Hudnut (1949) p. 116.
66 Tunnard (April 1949), 'Art and Landscape Design', p. 109.
67 LI archive, box 6; Christopher Tunnard, 'Town and Country Landscape, U.S.A.' (text of lecture to the ILA, 1 July 1947).
68 Tunnard, list of invitees (c. 1947); Tunnard Papers, Box 1, folder 4.
69 Tunnard, 'Our exploding cities demand new planning concepts' (radio broadcast) (2 January 1949); details held by Yale University News Bureau.
70 'Westport gets Yale Students' Expansion Plan', in *New York Herald Tribune* (8 May 1947).
71 Pearlman (2007), p. 150.
72 John Simon Guggenheim Memorial Foundation to Tunnard, 19 May 1950; Tunnard Papers, Box 10, folder 153. The Guggenheim offered $5,500 over 12 months to enable the preparation of a book on the American tradition in city planning.
73 Provost to Charles Sawyer, 24 May 1954 (carbon copy directly to Tunnard); Tunnard Papers, Box 25, Folder 381.
74 Tunnard (May–June 1956), 'The Conscious Stone', p. 23.

75 Tunnard Papers, Box 2, folder 21; Ward obtained his B.Arch. in 1948, and his MCP in 1951; his thesis was on a modernist 'redevelopment of the center of New Haven'.

76 Tunnard to William Foster, April 1959; Yale University, Tunnard Papers, Box 4, folder 71.

77 The 'Skyline' title may have been a tribute to Lewis Mumford's column in the *New Yorker*.

78 Interview, Lance Neckar and Winston Close, January 1989.

79 Tunnard and Pushkarev (eds), *Man-Made America* (1963), p. 154 and 437. The partnership was dissolved in 1965 and Harris afterwards wrote *The Growth of Latin American Cities* (Ohio University Press, 1971).

80 Mumford (1938), pp. 291–2.

81 Tunnard, *The City of Man* (1953), p. 256.

82 Tunnard and Pushkarev (eds), *Man-Made America* (1963), p. 406; the other contributors to *Man-Made America* were Geoffrey Baker, Dorothy Lefferts Moore, Ann Satterthwaite, and Ralph Warburton.

83 Tunnard to Reginald Isaacs, 29 March 1961; Tunnard Papers, Box 7, folder 108.

84 Faludi (1973), p. vii.

85 Warburton (1991), 'Christopher Tunnard …'.

86 Tunnard, 'Historic Districts: Ghosts and Intruders', in ICOMOS (1964).

87 ICOMOS, *Final Report of the Meeting on the Preservation and Utilization of Monuments and Sites of Artistic and Historical Value held in Quito, Ecuador, from November 29 to December 2, 1967*.

88 Tunnard (1965), 'On Education' and 'On Water and Waterfronts'.

89 Tunnard (1966), 'Landmarks of Beauty'.

90 Tunnard, *A World with a View*, (1978), pp. 153–6.

91 Ibid., pp. 136–41.

92 'Highway as Environment', Yale University Department of City Planning Highway Research Project (New Haven, CT: Yale University, 1971).

93 De Angelis (1991), endnote 24.

94 Tunnard to Reginald Isaacs, 10 January 1971; Tunnard Papers, Box 10, folder 147.

95 Tunnard, *A World with a View* (1978), pp. 168–78. See also Tunnard Papers, Box 20, folder 310.

Part II
Landscape and urbanism

4   A technique for the twentieth century

Tunnard clearly had a mind for theorising.

Constructivism was given much publicity in the mid-1930s, and the very notion of a changepoint in landscape style inspired this freshly qualified landscape architect to greater and wider ideas. His thoughts were given added direction and urgency as he perceived that the essential conditions for the creation of the eighteenth-century landscape garden were once more in alignment. His general design approach notably rejected the separate enclosed spaces of the Arts and Crafts garden to a more expansive look inspired by the landscape school, and as he came to be involved in planning he experimented with interconnected realms merging into each other from private to communal into public, without boundaries.

His arguments had to rest on more than a presumed similarity of appearance, though; it would require philosophic underpinnings. He set about identifying the aspects of garden planning that would make the landscapes of his day the works of art he desired. When Tunnard came to articulate the principles of a new landscape architecture in *Gardens in the Modern Landscape* he gave prominence to three themes: the 'Functional Approach', the 'Empathic Approach', and the 'Artistic Approach'. These were the principal strands to the 'new technique' that he sought (he could not use the word 'style' for reasons that will be apparent).

Not all Tunnard's theorising bore fruit. His earliest and his last attempts at re-thinking modern landscape design were, respectively, in planting design and in applying space theory to landscape. Whilst in Tunnard's hands these stems withered as his mind took different turns, offshoots were to flourish in the hands of others. At least it can be said that Tunnard previsioned the postwar interest in architectural plants and in spatial design.

Constructivism and the landscape garden

The constructivist movement found a footing in London in the mid-1930s amongst sculptors and artists who were self-consciously aware that they stood at a momentous turning point in the means of artistic expression, away from representation and towards abstraction and significant form. The Russian sculptor, Naum Gabo, explained the origins and purposes of the group:[1]

Constructive ideas … always appear on the borderline of two consecutive epochs at the moment when the human spirit, having destroyed the old, demands the creation and assertion of the new. All great epochs have always depended on one leading constructive idea. It has always given the art of the time a social power and ability to rule and direct the spirit of the age.

The art of our own generation was born on such a borderline; it was born on the ruins of all previous artistic traditions. The revolution in art which took place at the beginning of this century proved that it was impossible to impose on a new epoch the artistic forms and aesthetic ideas of the old, and that it is impossible to build up a new creative art upon the caprice or temporary moods of the individual artist. In order to do this it is necessary to have new, stable principles and new constructive elements; these principles must be closely bound up with the social and psychological spirit of our epoch and they ought to be sought for not externally, but in the realm of plastic art itself.

Constructivists were convinced that great ideas can be conveyed by symbolic form. The prehistoric Men-an-Tol stone ring in Cornwall, the works of the cubist painters and recent extreme geometric sculptures by Barbara Hepworth were examples. Figurative painting and sculpture no longer had a place; the great works of the past retained their power not because they were figurative, but because of their form and line:

It is the lines themselves, with their rhythms, it is the colours with their tones of light and shade, it is the sizes and shapes with their order in space, their scale and their relations to each other, it is these elements which keep these creations effective and still alive for us and which form the substance of art through the ages. Having realised this fundamental truth all the constructivist has to do is to deliver these vital and independent elements from all their outlived and temporary images and by freeing them to convey the spirit and impulses of our own time.

(Ibid.)

This was as true for architecture and other plastic arts as it was for sculpture. Shared concerns for contemporary thinking, truth to material, and social imperatives seemed to confirm the new alliance between the arts and painters, sculptors, and architects, represented respectively by the editors (Ben Nicholson, Naum Gabo and Leslie Martin) who compiled *Circle* (1937), a manifesto for virtually every progressive person in these fields.

Christopher Tunnard read *Circle*, and was fired by the idea that 'the significant forces which find liberation in painting and carving or modelling shall also be expressed in the complex technical achievement which is the garden artist's manipulation of living and natural forms'.[2] When he came to write the 'Foreword' to his book, he declared that 'we are faced with the task of creating a new landscape for the twentieth century'.[3]

His historical researches had indicated to him a previous constructivist moment in the history of garden design – the landscape garden of the early eighteenth century.[4] The strong connections to painting and literature, the employment of imagination, and the resultant revolution in gardening taste all served to confirm this.[5] Tunnard knew the landscape garden well through St Ann's Hill and the Surrey landscape gardens, and the dawning of their significance must have provided the frisson of excitement; no wonder that the new landscape garden would have strong affinities with the previous one.

It is worth noticing that Tunnard was not alone in his fascination with the landscape garden. Christopher Hussey, author of *The Picturesque* (1927) and a writer for *Country Life*, also perceived that the gardens appropriate to modern architecture, at least in England, had precedent: 'The type of garden that is developing in connection with modern architecture is largely a reversion to the landscape design of the great eighteenth-century practitioners.'[6]

The Functional Approach

Percy Cane had written extensively about garden planning, and emphasised that gardens needed to reflect changing lifestyle. Hence Tunnard was merely repeating such observations when he wrote that the parts of a garden 'which are designed for use are the most important and in some ways the most interesting parts of the garden of today. Perhaps this may be a clue to our enjoyment of the gardens of the future.'[7] He anticipated that some traditional components would be displaced as new ones emerged:

> If, then, a new garden technique is to be evolved, it need not necessarily reject the traditional elements of the garden plan, although it is the author's opinion that necessity will drive us to find new forms in which those elements will largely be discarded.

For example, the croquet lawn would fade away, he thought, in favour of the more fashionable tennis court and swimming pool.

However 'functional aspects', together with the rejection of useless stylistic detail, and a reliance on creativity to produce relevant forms, had been elevated to the level of a creed amongst Modernist European landscape designers, as Tunnard found for himself when in spring 1937 he attended the four-day International Congress of Garden Architects in Paris, organised by *La Société Française des Architectes de Jardins*. Brenda Colvin was there too, though her findings served to support the ecological lesson that gardens varied from country to country according to climate and the temper of the people.[8] For Tunnard, however, this was a great opportunity to explore Continental Modernism in the landscape design profession, and he reported on the event in *Landscape and Garden* and *AR*.[9]

Impressions of modern European garden design

He described how his information was mainly gathered through 'many agreeable social encounters', at which it had been possible 'to catch something of the spirit which animates the attitude of each country's delegates towards design, to learn something of the difficulties, political, economic and climatic, which have to be overcome'. The conference was leavened by garden visits. Colvin's photographs were of Château de Champs, Vaux-le-Vicomte and a small Parisian garden by André Véra in Rue Quinault, St Germain-en-Laye. Tunnard also included photographs of the garden of the Swiss exhibition.

Tunnard thought he could detect three tendencies in French garden design. The most traditional was exemplified by the president of the Congress, Achille Duchêne, who was well known for his restoration work at Vaux-le-Vicomte and in England for his water parterre at Blenheim, but who had also produced 'a Utopian conception of the garden of to-morrow which accords but strangely with the ideas of some of our modern designers'. Tunnard considered the work of 'modern' designers far removed from that of Duchêne, and in this category he grouped André Véra with his brother Paul, H. Gonse, Jean-Claude Nicolas Forestier, Albert Laprade and Jean-Charles Moreux, who would come to be thought of as cubist designers. Tunnard found at the garden in Rue Quinault that 'the parterre treatment directly in front of the house had lately been removed and the pattern considerably simplified'. Only the gardens of Le Corbusier were seen as a 'direct challenge to the order obtaining in France to-day', but they were just

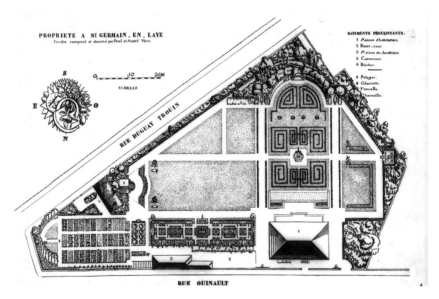

Figure 4.1 Garden at Rue Quinault, St Germain-en-Laye, designed by André and Paul Véra for themselves from the 1920s onwards.
(Source: Shepheard (1953), p. 107)

Figure 4.2 In spring 1937 Tunnard visited the Véra garden during the International
Congress of Garden Architects.
(Source: *L&G* (1937), p. 79)

'small and fragmentary', and mostly concerned with roof gardens. It is appears that
at this stage Tunnard did not fully appreciate Le Corbusier's significance in city
planning.

Tunnard considered that 'the French remain true to a principle – that of the
necessity of order and a strict conformity to axial and symmetrical arrangement'.
This was a quote from André Véra on the aim of the modern garden, who considered it to be 'explicit in the provision of regularity and order, by means of formal
arrangement, as an antidote to the shifting sands of political change'. In finding
an explanation for the formal French response, Tunnard opined:

> One of the most interesting ideas put forward at the Congress by delegates of
> France and Belgium was that of the strong appeal of the 'natural garden' for
> the primitive mind and though this theory does not bear close examination,

it explains a good deal of the attitude of the Latin races towards gardens of this type.

Tunnard found that French influence in Belgium was strong, and while noting Jules Buyssens's talk to the Congress, he singled out Jean Canneel-Claes's functionalist work as being 'extremely interesting'. An architect by training, Canneel-Claes's earlier designs showed a similarity in plan with the French cubist designs of the 1920s, including Villa Noailles. Perhaps he realised that such designs were neither humanised, nor did they encourage use or outdoor life, for he afterwards pleaded for a 'humanised garden', requiring 'less objectivity and a greater sociability'.[10] He became a proponent of the functional garden in the 1930s, and by 1935 was producing the schemes that so impressed Tunnard.

The Netherlands was noted, without explanation, as being inclined to the English taste in garden design. The Swiss were noted for their achievements in having 'adapted the art to local conditions and materials' and the 'high standard of work attained by designers'.

> The Swiss have a strong feeling for the homogeneity of their landscape and the necessity for preserving its features; their gardens therefore are usually extremely well merged into their surroundings and the liberal use of indigenous plants ensures that they shall not seem incongruous in the magnificent scenery which is the nation's chief pride.

The work of Walter Mertens and Gustav Ammann was considered to exemplify this. Italy was noted as a country where landscape architecture had had little influence, though the work of Maria Parpagliolo (later Shepherd) and Pietro Porcinai was selected for mention.

To Tunnard, the Scandinavian approach to landscape architecture was represented by the Swedish: he did not distinguish Danish design, for example.[11] Baron Sven A. Hermelin, President of the Swedish Garden Architects' Association and Professor of Garden Architecture at the National School of Horticulture, read a report on the garden of the future, which 'had proved extremely interesting'. Hermelin said that his country's motivating principle of landscape architecture was the idea of gardens for the people.[12] This appealed to Tunnard, and he spoke to Hermelin afterwards. The report was later quoted more fully in Tunnard's *Gardens in the Modern Landscape*, and it 'considered how gardens of the future would be simple in design and a mere framework for the display of plants and the provision of health-giving amenities such as swimming pools, sand pits for children, tennis courts and arbours for rest'. The Swedes preferred to group their plants in simple natural arrangements rather than to confine them to severe geometrical patterns.[13] They were opposed to the idea of symmetrical and axial planning, indeed preferred working on sites with irregular boundaries in contrast to the French. Tunnard used this to illustrate a rational architecture, where 'styles, axial and symmetrical planning' and 'ostentatious decoration' have been 'discarded to make way for the simple statement'.[14]

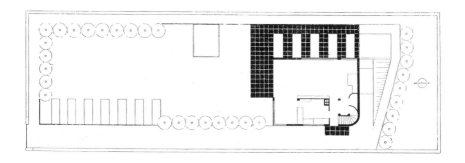

Figure 4.3 (a, b) Jean Canneel-Claes's own Modernist house and garden near Brussels, plan and terrace with rectangular beds with tulips. Also see Figure 2.11.
(Source: Tunnard, *Gardens in the Modern Landscape* (1938), pp. 64–5)

In Germany the recognition of the position of landscape architect was enviable. Tunnard noted how the German state realised the 'psychological value of landscape planning and has begun to experiment with the object of making the country a factor in the drive to improve the nation's mental and physical health'. He considered it 'a wholly estimable ideal for the individual even if its obvious primary aim may be only part of a less commendable militarisation programme'.[15] This was of course part of the Nazi Blut und Boden – Blood and Soil – philosophy which was neither acknowledged by Tunnard, nor elaborated on, although the various elements were explained as separate issues.[16] The maintaining of the connection with the soil, the drive towards the use of native plants were all part of this, which was phrased by Tunnard slightly awkwardly as follows:

> German designers have based their principles on a theory of natural œcological development – the essential land, the verdant sculptured surface of the earth must be preserved in a form acceptable to lovers of wild life. The right to sun and green fields must be made a realisable thing for the public, who are encouraged to use the countryside as a vast playground. Thus one feature of the landscape artist's work has become the maintenance of the country round about the principle (sic) cities and towns, a practice which is carried out by planting native material 'in a manner naturalised to the trees and woods'.

The creation of the highway system in Germany – the *Reichsautobahnen* – was used as one of the greatest Nazi propaganda programmes, being widely published both nationally and internationally. The German Pavilion at the Paris International Exposition exhibited a wooden model, which illustrated well how a new road was 'welded' into the landscape. Landscape policies were evidently well explained and Tunnard noted the differences in the approach taken with the new English trunk roads, which were normally lined with ornamental trees. In German examples the 'planting is instead made compatible with both countryside and road, now swelling over the brow of the hill and running close to the carriageway, now receding to allow wide views over a plane level, now evergreen, now deciduous, according to the exigencies of the site.' Whilst Tunnard took care to introduce the key designers of most countries, he was unable to explain the background to these German schemes and thus omitted reference to Dr Fritz Todt, the general inspector of the German motorway system, and Alwin Seifert, his landscape architect assistant, who devised the landscape approach.

In his conclusions Tunnard noted that because German and Italian policies in design were being influenced by social theories, they were more eager to move forward than any other countries, warning that it is 'probable that they will evolve as rigid a set of rules as any that have come out of France, partly because of restriction in material (both countries favour the use of native plants) and partly because of an ethical rather than a liberal attitude towards design'. Sweden, Austria and Switzerland, though, were described as countries 'in which experiment in design is reaping rich rewards'. Here landscape designers were free 'to accept or reject the theories of other countries' and they are 'surer of evolving a fluid and lively technique for the very reason that they are casting their nets wide and far'.

Association Internationale des Architectes de Jardins Modernistes (AIAJM)

The Paris meeting had been a useful catalyst for ideas being developed in 'many branches of landscape design' and a free exchange of opinions had benefited all. This led to 'the discovery of a similarity of thought among garden architects on the question of contemporary garden planning'. At or soon after the meeting Tunnard and Canneel-Claes wrote the initial version of a manifesto which contained a number of clauses distilling the concerns and ambitions of Modernist landscape design.[17] Canneel-Claes saw the manifesto as a document around which an *Association Internationale des Architectes de Jardins Modernistes* (AIAJM) could be formed and had it printed in both English and French.

Divided into 'objects' and 'resolutions' the manifesto is here quoted in full:[18]

OBJECTS.
1   To study and encourage the spread of the rationally-planned garden in accordance with the physical and mental needs of contemporary life in its individual and collective aspects.
2   To study and develop the relations between the art of gardens, architecture and town and country planning.
3   To establish a direct collaboration between landscape architects, architects and town-planners.
4   To study the relations between the evolution of garden art and that of the other arts, under contemporary conditions, as well as the part played by scientific materials and methods in these evolutions.
5   To defend in all countries the cause of modern landscape architecture and the professional interests of members in countries where defence is not organised or is insufficient.

RESOLUTIONS.
1   We regard garden art not merely as a form of decoration but as a branch of architecture inseparable from the problems of housing and town and country planning, which must submit itself to the demands of society and fulfil with efficiency an active role in the physical and mental development of the individual and of the community.
2   We consider that the basic principle of rational garden planning is embodied in the slogan 'The function determines the form'. This conception does not exclude aesthetic considerations, but acknowledges the necessity for qualities such as harmony, balance and rhythm in the work of art.
3   We regard the servile imitation of natural phenomena as incompatible with artistic creation, but preach the respect of nature and stress the

    desirability in certain circumstances of the intrusion of natural features into a garden plan.

4   We consider that the character of the site and existing features are fundamental factors governing the design, and that only by submission to these factors can harmony within the garden and its surroundings be achieved.

5   We believe that the simplicity of structure and concision in the means of expression will permit the attainment of the serenity necessary for the perfect comprehension of the garden as a work of art.

6   We stress the value of the plan as an aid to clear statement and the value of simplicity of thought in structure and detail as a source of serene and orderly planning.

7   Finally we believe in the probity of the creative art ... the reliance of the designer on his own knowledge and experience and not on the academic symbolism of the styles or outworn systems of aesthetics, to create by experiment and invention new forms which are significant of the age from which they spring.

By early 1938 Canneel-Claes and Tunnard seem to have diverged. Tunnard plunged into work with MARS, becoming more interested in landscape at a planning scale, while also being busy in writing his articles for *Architectural Review*. Canneel-Claes, on the other hand, wished to promote his AIAJM, probably intending to build an international forum for landscape architects in the same way that CIAM had done for architects.

With the second International Congress of Garden Architects looming in Germany in 1938, Tunnard, who the year before thought it 'pleasant ... to know that the work of the Congress will be continued by the invitation of the German delegation, at Essen next year',[19] now declined to attend on the grounds that the German 'State Chamber of Formative Arts ... had been responsible for the death of all rational art in that country'. He also refused to allow his ILA exhibition material to be sent.[20] Canneel-Claes, though, went ahead with a new version of the manifesto, with a revised French text and with the addition of a German translation.[21]

The English version was a straight translation of the French and differed in intent from that which Tunnard had supplied. It introduced the word 'urbanism' instead of 'town and country planning'. It also deleted the fifth resolution which emphasised simplicity of structure and concision in the means of expression, re-placing this by splitting the fourth in two, providing an emphasis on 'geometry as the foundation of garden design', noting that '[h]owever, it should not dominate the composition but rather be modified by the demands of function and the condi-tions of the site. We consider asymmetry to be the most suitable type of geometry.' This was in contrast with Tunnard's view, who had just identified his three new approaches, i.e. functional, empathic and artistic. The new version furthermore maintained that 'the design cannot be dissociated from the whole and must re-spond to the site'. This shows a much lesser emphasis in which the 'character of the site and existing features are fundamental factors', etc. Maybe Tunnard never saw the new manifesto, because he quoted only from the earlier version.[22] Some tension may even have developed between the two men, for although Tunnard reproduced Canneel-Claes's designs in *Gardens in the Modern Landscape*, his name was surprisingly absent in the list of acknowledgements.[23]

Canneel-Claes's project for the AIAJM foundered, and ultimately his work did not attract much attention outside Belgium. His limited foreign influence was actually derived through Tunnard's book, and through Peter Shepheard's, which illustrated similar designs.[24] Tunnard included a plan and photographs of the architect's own garden in Brussels, and both authors showed the maquette made in late 1937 or early 1938 for the Heeremans garden in Liedekerke. Shepheard added two later gardens.

The functional technique

Tunnard took from his architectural colleagues the importance of new materials and science, 'the garden of the future … must necessarily be influenced by new materials and their methods of application – for example, by plant hybridization, and the amelioration of soil and weather conditions'.[25] He was also converted to the philosophy of 'fitness for purpose'. He took Le Corbusier's dictum on the styles being a lie, and Adolf Loos's rejection of ornament, fully to heart.[26] Apart from the quotes from these architects, the main sources for Tunnard's 'functional technique' were the delegates he met in Paris in 1937, and what he learned from the *Exposition Internationale*. The Modernist pedigree of Tunnard's thoughts and suggestions can indeed be fairly easily traced.

The principles to which Canneel-Claes worked were emphasised. Gardens 'must be humanized in accordance with the needs of the twentieth century; they can be made pleasant to live in as well as to look at'. The functional design[27]

> embodies rather a spirit of rationalism and through an aesthetic and practical ordering of its units provides a friendly and hospitable milieu for rest and recreation. It is, in effect, the social conception of the garden.

The Swedish delegates had made clear that their designs were not just for private gardens, but also for communal areas:[28]

> In the Scandinavian countries there are signs that the new garden is already establishing itself … There, the functionalism of garden schemes for workers' dwellings and blocks of flats is directly the result of a whittling down – evidence of the need for the creation of the maximum recreative area in the minimum space.

Tunnard observed that, as in other 'democratic countries', 'the concern of every garden maker [is] with the problem of the small garden and the efforts that are being made to create economical and rational gardens for those who in other countries are unable for lack of professional advice to have aesthetically satisfying surroundings'.[29]

Despite his positive assessment of the Swedes he criticised them for their 'romantic conception of Nature', as he considered that 'nature worship … has proved dangerously stultifying to a free development of garden design'. He had expanded on this theme in his historical chapters in which the fine ideals of the early landscape garden degenerated into meretriciousness at the hands of Lancelot Brown and Humphry Repton.[30] Their work marked

> the passing of rationalism – 'the pleasure of being able to understand, the easy sense of simple orderliness, a smooth balance in ideas as in forms' – and the advent of a quickening sentimental feeling for the past, for exoticism and for the macabre.

He despised the romantic escapism of the cottage garden and the Arts and Crafts movement, lamenting that 'garden designing has for so long been regarded as a craft'.[31] He mocked the 'second stone age, with its plethora of flagged paths and dry walls … the garden has been killed … stone dead'. He also displayed antipathy to the garden city. In support of his view, he found writings by a philosopher of aesthetics, Benedetto Croce (1886–1952), who ridiculed the notion that 'art imitates nature' held by Brown and Repton.

Le Corbusier was also criticised for his conception of a natural landscape treatment. He proposed villas in the countryside raised on *pilotis* with grazing animals reaching to the house, and with roof gardens providing for outdoor living, so that the occupants' 'lives will be set within a Virgilian dream'. Tunnard's argument was provoked by the Villa Savoye in Poissy, which he characterised as 'romantic' in conception, but which might have been with more justice described as naïve. Other contemporary landscape architects besides Tunnard criticised Le Corbusier's design for this villa, despite it finding great favour amongst architects, as it provided simple solutions to complicated problems.[32]

Tunnard's *Gardens in the Modern Landscape* may have been an attempt to interpret European Modernism, but it provided only a partial and limited view of contemporary landscape. His understanding of functionalism was derived principally from architectural sources, as standard references to Adolf Loos, Frank Lloyd Wright and Le Corbusier reveal. He also had a limited knowledge of the debates and issues of the early Modernist landscape architects on the Continent. His review of modern garden design was far from comprehensive and showed a bias to English sources. If he had extended it to central European literature he might have broadened his scope and become a more accurate interpreter of contemporary issues in landscape design for an English-speaking public.

Tunnard was a late arrival in the European context. Leberecht Migge's seminal *Gartenkultur des 20. Jahrhunderts* ('Garden Culture of the Twentieth Century') (1913) had been one of the first Modernist treatises. He had been the main force behind the self-sufficiency movement following the First World War and he had worked with well-known architects such as Bruno Taut, Ernst May and Adolf Loos. Another landscape architect, Heinrich Wiepking-Jürgensmann who had worked with Modernist architects Otto Bartning and Erich Mendelsohn, had started working for the Nazi regime. Tunnard could hardly have omitted Migge's work had he known about it. Other contemporary Modern landscape architects missed by Tunnard include those of the Bornim Circle, particularly Hermann Mattern and Herta Hammerbacher, and had one of their designs been known to and analysed by Tunnard, this would have provided an interesting case study. The work of these landscape architects would have provided a wider context to Modernism and extended Tunnard's limited definition of it.

His design approach, emphasising the artistic process, received a certain amount of criticism, for example from J.T.P. Bijhouwer, one of the main contemporary Dutch landscape architects, who was sceptical about the Modernist credentials of Tunnard's designs. Bijhouwer asserted that they were unsatisfactory in that, despite Tunnard's intention to provide a functionalist approach, none of the examples used were convincing in this respect.[33] This can be confirmed in the lack of detailed analysis in exploring how designs worked both functionally and aesthetically.

Tunnard was almost alone amongst landscape architects working in England before the war who drew inspiration from Modernism. Whilst his approach to design might be criticised from a European perspective, it was his assertion of Modernist values for communal living that assured its postwar value. From that reason Tunnard's book became a classic in Modernism.

The Empathic Approach

Ever since the appearance of Josiah Conder's *Landscape Gardening in Japan* (1893), published texts had been obsessed by the classification of the various stylistic periods, classical landscape features and an attempt to explain the symbolism. In this context Jiro Harada's *The Gardens of Japan* (1928), published by The Studio as a companion volume to Percy Cane's *Modern Gardens, British and Foreign* (1926–7) was a typical example of this genre that would have been known to Tunnard. When Tunnard proclaimed Oriental influence as 'the second source of inspiration for the modern garden', though, he did this from an innovative perspective.[34]

In addition to having seen Japanese gardens on the west coast of America as a teenager, Tunnard's interest in Japanese gardens may well have been sparked by his work with Cane, and by Cane's *Garden Design of To-Day* (1934). This book contained a separate chapter on Japanese gardens as one of a series of thematic garden types that served as a basis for inspiration in laying out gardens, and this was a fairly traditional response to the subject.[35] While Cane acknowledged a range of scales and styles (i.e. formal and informal), as well as symbolism in the design, the placing of rocks and its hills, he concludes that 'A Japanese garden, correct in all the details of this symbolism, would not probably afford in other countries a measure of enjoyment commensurate with the trouble and expense

Figure 4.4 Percy Cane's book provided a traditional response in that it contained a
chapter on Japanese gardens as one of a series of thematic gardens.
(Source: Cane, *Garden Design of To-Day* (1934), p. 137)

involved in making it.' Instead he saw the aim as being to 'catch the spirit of
Japanese design, and to use it in the making of certain parts of English gardens'
which 'would result in something unusual and beautiful'.[36] The various illustrations
provide examples of water gardens with Japanese acers and stepping stones, dwarf
spreading pines, arched bridges and stone lanterns, all capturing something of the
exotic.

Cane emphasised that only plants 'which are beautiful in their habit' should be
used. In garden planning terms, 'there is, in the placing of rocks, trees and shrubs
in a Japanese garden, a quality of beauty which … is unequalled', and 'balance and
proportion … really constitute the essence of a Japanese garden'. These thoughts
must have struck Tunnard as important. He borrowed Arthur Lindsay Sadler's *The
Art of Flower Arrangement of Japan* (1933) from the Lindley Library, probably to
try to understand placement and balance.[37]

In his very first published article, in *Landscape and Garden* in 1935, Tunnard
spoke authoritatively about Japanese garden art. He explained how symbolism
determined a set of fixed points that formed the framework for the design of the
garden, marked by stones known by traditional names. The garden was built on
'this skeleton' and a balance and proper relationship of the separate parts obtained
by a 'mastery of detail and freedom of vision'. In this he referred to paths, wooden
and stone bridges, stepping stones, irregular paving, rest arbours and many pat-
terned screen fences as examples. He considered that 'it is impossible for the

Westerner … to be successful in recreating Japanese gardens as such'.[38] However, some lessons could be drawn from Japanese art and garden art. Slowly knowledge of the grouping and arrangement of plants, placement of rocks in relation to water and 'other subtleties evoking in the onlooker sensory and intellectual pleasures such as lavish display of colour could never arouse' was being gained in English gardens.

Another important pointer towards the Japanese garden was Raymond McGrath's book, *Twentieth-Century Houses* (1934). This described the modern Japanese approach to architecture, using as an example a Modernist private house, Kiti Kawa, of 1928–30 with its 'view of the delicate white top of Fuji' and designed by Horiguchi Sutemi (1895–1984). McGrath noted that instead of a traditional Japanese garden 'there is one more in harmony with such a new house as this', suggesting it was 'pleasingly designed with waterways and stretches of grass'. McGrath published a plan and three photographs.[39]

Not only did Tunnard borrow the illustrations of Kiti Kawa, but parts of Tunnard's text were cribbed from McGrath as well. The latter had written: 'The Japanese architect comes at the beautiful by way of the necessary – by the cutting out of all waste. Quiet space is made by putting away the noise of ornament.'[40] In another passage, McGrath wrote

> Japan has had for a long time a wise and delicate taste in the art of building. In the last ten years it has been seen that the great architects of the present-day – Wright in America, Corbusier in France, Oud in Holland and Miës in Germany – are at work in a way in which, almost for the first time in the history of art, East and West come together.

Tunnard repeated that 'the Japanese come at the beautiful by way of the necessary', that 'it may be noted that here a debt to Japan is acknowledged by such architects as Wright, Mies and Corbusier', and that:

> The absence of superfluous ornament and the elimination of garish colour has a special appeal to the modern mind of all countries. In this respect it seems as if to-day for the first time the arts of the East and West are beginning to draw together.

The linking of house and garden was a particular skill which the West could learn from the Japanese. Recent technical developments permitting wide openings had expanded the possibilities for integrating house and garden in the West. McGrath observed:

> The [Japanese] house is open on the south side so that in summer it may be kept cold by the winds which come from that direction. The screens and paper windows will all take down so that, but for curtains of thin wood, the house may be kept completely open. In winter the wind comes from the north and on that side the only openings are very small.

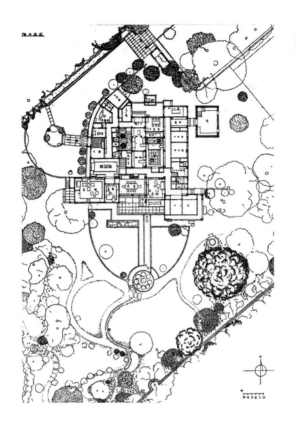

Figure 4.5 (a-c) Plan and photographs of Kita Kawa, Tokyo, a house and garden designed by Horigichi Sutemi in 1928–30 and (d) of House Sakio Tsurumi, Tokyo, designed by Yamada Mamoru in 1931 were provided to Tunnard by McGrath, who had included some of these in this *Twentieth Century Houses* (1934). (Source: Tunnard, *Gardens in the Modern Landscape* (1938), p. 91)

The relation of house to garden is most important. One is open to the other. The rain and wind are not shut out. The rain has to be seen falling on the leaves. The wind has to be in hearing when it goes about in the branches.

Tunnard adapted this to:[41]

Here England and Japan have a talent in common. Each country has made a speciality of the placing of the house in the garden, and each has managed to strike a happy relationship, though even here we are learning from the older civilization. … [Japan] differs from its English counterpart in being almost one with Nature. In warm weather the house becomes part of the garden, the sliding paper screens which keep out the cold blasts and snow of winter being easily removable so that the whole side of a room may be thrown open to let in the cool Summer winds. In this way the owner allows his house and garden to merge so that he may satisfy the longing found in all his countrymen to see the rain falling on the leaves and hear the wind sighing in the branches of the pine trees.

Melding Cane and McGrath resulted in his text on traditional Japanese detailing sitting oddly with Modernist pronouncements and the photographs of Kiti Kawa.[42] In his review of the Chelsea Flower Show gardens of 1936 Tunnard's interest still seemed focused on the Japanese garden there, and he analysed it in terms of traditional Japanese elements.[43] Whilst Tunnard was concerned about a Modern aesthetic, this had not yet been fully explored and it was not clear to him at this point how Japanese principles might be applied.

Six months after his article was published, *Landscape and Garden* printed one on 'Chinese Gardens', and a piece by the London based landscape architect Harvey Bennett. This expanded on the subject of balance, introducing 'hidden balance':[44]

I realized that there were two sorts of Balance. In one case objects of the same size obviously balanced each other. In the other, a large object was balanced by another much smaller but of greater density; the equipoise being not much apparent as intellectually understood.

Asymmetry, or the design of hidden Balance, is founded not upon the opposition of equal masses but on the capacity of the eye to recognise that a large quantity of one substance is equal to comparatively small amount of another … It is this half hidden quality that constitutes asymmetrical design and which by its lack of obviousness makes it sympathetic to nature … some form of art other than symmetry is therefore necessary where man's work comes into contact with that of nature. Hidden Balance supplies this need. It is, as it were, a mediator between the controlled and uncontrolled, bringing order into chaos so gently that the mind is unaware of the transition. The eye, leaving the geometrical conceptions of man, can wander on unimpeded yet soothed and guided, till it becomes lost in the universal.

Figure 4.6 The rounded hills in the background of this Japanese garden at Chelsea were particularly admired by Tunnard, who thought of them as 'so typical of Japanese landscape'.
(Source: *L&G* (Summer 1936), p. 91)

In landscape design, symmetrical, or obvious, balance was 'prone to dullness and a sterile severity', and was 'only appropriate where man completely dominates nature'. Meanwhile 'all good landscape paintings' were examples of asymmetrical, or hidden, balance. This was indeed helpful.

In his desire to move beyond superficial interpretations of the Japanese garden Tunnard realised that he had to increase his knowledge of Japanese culture. At the Lindley Library Tunnard borrowed Lorraine E. Kuck's *One Hundred Kyoto Gardens* (1935), the latter introducing the term 'Zen garden' and thereby implied philosophical aspects with a distinct concept of nature.[45] He also valued his contact with Bernard Leach (1887–1979) which would have been in 1938 or shortly before.[46] Leach, a potter who referred to himself as 'a courier between East and West', was partly raised in Japan and studied pottery there, and had returned to England in 1920 together with Hamada Shoji, a Japanese potter, to set up a pottery at St Ives. From 1925 he was also one of the circle of artists associated with Dartington Hall. Tunnard may have known Leach through the artists' circle at St Ives or through Willi Soukop, Leach's friend, who lived at Dartington.[47] Just possibly Christopher met Leach through his younger brother, Peter, who had joined Michael Chekhov's Theatre Studio founded at Dartington in 1936 at the invitation of Mrs Dorothy Elmhirst.

The essay of 1938 on 'Asymmetrical Garden Planning: The Oriental Aesthetic', reprinted in *Gardens in the Modern Landscape*, showed that Tunnard was by then finding the relevance of Japanese principles to a Western approach to Modern garden design. He was dismissive of Western gardens purporting to be Japanese, noting that since the 1880s 'we have seen enough of the trappings of Japanese art to sicken us of it for ever'. Observing that general perception of the Japanese garden has 'seized upon the least important aspect of Japanese art for the exercise of their zeal', namely 'ubiquitous stone lanterns, torii, shrines and summer-houses', he noted that 'the excessive use of ornament is an idea repugnant to the Japanese'. Tunnard observed about Japanese gardens that the 'original garden art of that country has never been understood by European garden makers'.[48] Nevertheless[49]

> When the sentimental, superficial approach to this Oriental art through its merely decorative aspects has been abandoned by the Western mind it will be discovered that the underlying principles may very well serve as part of the basis for a modern technique.

In this essay he identified the Zen-inspired 'oriental aesthetic' as quite different from that of Western art. The unity of all people and with nature provided a different starting point for art, and was the foundation of virtuosity in Japanese landscape art. This included 'The appreciation of form and texture which combine to create unity between architecture and its surroundings', the 'Japanese grasp of rhythm and accent in plant arrangement' and the 'marshalling of detail into significant and relevant patterns'. By absorbing the oriental aesthetic he suggested that 'we shall help to rid ourselves of individualism in art and gain identity with art and life'.[50] This conclusion must have been given additional force by its congruency to the Socialist imperative:

> In all spheres of modern art creation is increasingly demanding identification with the social problem, and garden art, though at present sadly retrograde in this respect, must soon embrace the communal idea or cease to function as an integral part of modern life.

Differing attitudes of Man's relationship with Nature were contrasted. Tunnard suggested that in the West Man and Nature are considered in antithesis, while in the East 'his identity is not separate from Nature and his fellow beings, but is at one with her and them'.[51] Tunnard proposed that the concept of 'empathy' underlay the Japanese approach to design. This was a widening of McGrath's definition of 'empathy' which he had seen in the context of Vitruvius and the Renaissance principles of proportion in design:[52]

> [T]he relation of the parts of a good building will be based on the relation between the parts of the beautifully formed body of a man. This 'empathy' as it is named – this putting of ourselves into the forms of things and giving them

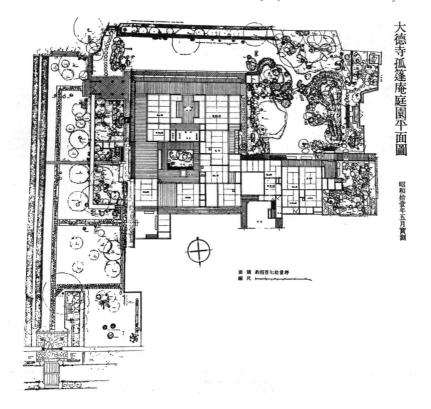

大德寺孤篷庵庭園平面圖

昭和拾壹年五月實測

面積 約四百七拾壹坪
縮尺

Figure 4.7 The Daitoku temple served as an example to demonstrate the close
relationship between house and garden.
(Source: Tunnard, *Gardens in the Modern Landscape* (1938), p. 85)

feelings which are in fact ours – is at the back of the theory that building-forms
are best when they take the body as their example.

Tunnard wrote that the aim of modern garden design was to re-establish humanity's
'empathic' vision, expressing an affinity for, and intimacy with, nature. The
'empathic technique' was posited as an abstract, universal, ahistorical concept that
might serve the full range of design disciplines. Tunnard suggested that

> until the European has learned to cultivate the empathic attitude and
> has discovered that apart from the symbolism of the East and behind it is
> an aesthetic antithetical and complementary to his asymmetrical classic
> conception of composition, the universality of art can never become an
> accomplished fact.

He proposed that nature should be seen not as a refuge from life, but as a sustainer
of it.[53] It was to invigorate life and provide a stimulus to body and mind. This

also had aesthetic implications; Tunnard saw symmetrical gardens, i.e. those planned on the axial system, as expressing the Western desire for control over nature. He therefore advocated asymmetrical garden planning.[54] However, he did not suggest that nature should be 'copied or sentimentalized', nor should she be 'overridden'.

> The banishment of antagonistic, masterful attitude towards Nature, of excessive symmetry, a recognition of the value of tactile qualities in plant material, a grasp of rhythm and accent, contribute to the supple and fluid adaptation of the site, which is the landscape architect's chief arbiter of design.

This principle was highlighted by illustrations; one depicting the traditional Japanese tea house at Bagshot Park seen through a wisteria-clad Japanese arbour, which was contrasted with one of a little summerhouse proposed for the garden at Gaulby. Drawn by Gordon Cullen, it showed a simple open-fronted timber pavilion set on posts over an irregularly shaped pond, which is traversed by informal stepping stones. 'Water, stones and planting are linked intelligibly to the small pavilion' the caption proclaimed. To Tunnard it illustrated how rather than 'borrowing the superficial style' this 'adopted an aesthetic principle from the Japanese instead'.[55]

Tunnard came to prefer the term 'occult balance' to Bennett's 'hidden balance'. The occult suggests something being hidden or shut off from view, but which he defined in a rather elaborate, almost mystical, manner as 'essentially a relative quality depending on the interplay of background and foreground, height and depth, motion and rest, but as such it can be reduced to a science and obtains through all composition in art and nature'.[56] He possibly got the idea for the term 'occult' from one of the reviews of Finella, a house in Cambridge designed for Mansfield D. Forbes by Raymond McGrath. This proposed items being 'lit occulty from above', i.e. 'hidden' from above.[57] Tunnard may have used the term 'occult' in order to emphasise the mystery and secretiveness of hidden balance which he suggested was an inbuilt response of primitive peoples. For example, a flower placed on one side of a face might serve to accentuate the symmetrical balance of the face. In Japanese gardens he noted that this 'form of balance often requires the steadying influence of a frame or boundary', observing that this served to control 'a force of opposing movements'. He illustrated this with a plan of the Daitoku temple, Kyoto.[58]

The idea of asymmetrical balance was in itself nothing new. It had been one of the underlying principles of the picturesque. In the 1920s it had been one of the debates within modern architecture. The Modernist Dutch architect Theo van Doesburg, for example, promoted '*a balanced relationship of unequal parts*' instead of symmetry in 1924.[59] The universal application of asymmetry was reflected in the AIAJM manifesto of 1938 issued by Jean Canneel-Claes. It stated that: 'We consider asymmetry to be the most suitable type of geometry.'[60] Tunnard suggested that landscape designers had not paid much attention to it, but that it might provide potential in respect of his search 'for a new technique for the contemporary garden, for a garden designed to be a complement of contemporary architecture, which embodies to a large extent the principle of asymmetrical balance'. He was not dogmatic about this: 'It must not be imagined, however, that "occult" balance and asymmetrical compositions in general are being advocated here as having any special merit above the more usual kinds of order and arrangements', but 'it would be neglecting a wide field for experiment … when a form directly in sympathy with modern aesthetic needs is asking to be employed.'[61]

Paradoxically, in formulating a 'new' functionalist approach to domestic design that rescued the garden for Modernism, Tunnard argued also for 'functionalism's expressive handmaiden, the empathic', or the asymmetric.[62] In other words, Tunnard was reinstating the style that, at the time, could not speak its name – the picturesque. It is interesting to note how skilfully he preserved many of the original precepts of picturesque theory whilst using a new vocabulary in the Modernist language – the integration of pictorial art and sculpture in landscape design, the artifice of naturalism, and formal principles such as continuity, harmony, subtlety, mystery and asymmetry – and then attributed those same principles to Asian art and landscape. References made to both Japanese and picturesque values thus seem to have helped advance the project of abstracting and universalising the functional and spatial integration of landscape with architecture.

The Artistic Approach

The garden as a work of art

The garden was not merely a place to display works of art, but a whole work of art in itself: 'We do not aim at the creation of beauty, as in the past, but at creating the work of art.'[63]

The public had been pandered to by 'nurserymen, horticultural journalists and contractors'. However 'A garden is a work of art. It is also a number of other things, such as a place for rest and recreation. And for the pursuit of horticulture, but to be a garden in the true sense of the term it must first be an aesthetic composition.'[64] Tunnard predicted that 'the tendency of the future will probably be away from "natural gardening" towards an architectural style, that is, away from unplanning towards conscious and balanced arrangement'.[65] For such reasons it was paramount that design should be by a designer, and not left to the horticulturalist; a position that he shared with the Institute of Landscape Architects which excluded designers 'in trade', working for nurseries, from its ranks.

Tunnard cited trends in painting, music, and architecture towards the recognition of pure form, line or colour as the determinants of aesthetic pleasure, rather than figurative representation or detail.[66] He particularly cited painting and sculpture as important sister arts:[67]

> It would be pleasant to think that when the landscape artist is allowed to return to the garden he will bring with him the inspiration, if not the active

co-operation, of the graphic and plastic artists, who will be instrumental in forming his own taste as well as that of the age.

He thought that the painter could share insights about the interrelation of forms, plane and colour values. The sculptor knew about texture, masses, and the experimental technique. The garden designer worked with the site and the materials of nature:

> Much as the sculptor derives inspiration from the form and quality of the material he uses, the garden designer can consider the site and its features … The true garden artist learns to co-operate with Nature, and, while not becoming a slave to her demands, is content to let her express his meaning in the simplest yet most convincing manner. Only thus can there be perfect harmony within the work and between it and its surroundings.

Tunnard had been particularly impressed by Paul Nash's *objets trouvées*, illustrating a piece called 'object' in *Gardens in the Modern Landscape*, and trying his own hand at Carl Koch's house in Cambridge, MA. In Tunnard's papers there is a Christmas card sent by Nash in 1938 before Tunnard's departure. It is a landscape into which a frame had been inserted in an anomalous position as if to frame a distant or borrowed view. In his note to Tunnard Nash refers to his inclusion of 'object' in *Gardens in the Modern Landscape*, which had been given to him for Christmas.

Nash was also fascinated by the prehistoric, and the mysterious stone monuments and earth banks of Wiltshire. Tunnard too was inspired by the remains of Neolithic human habitation of England, and reproduced Nash's 1937 painting 'The landscape of the megaliths' in 1955.[68] The image of the megaliths in the landscape dovetailed with the increasing feeling of the appropriateness of the surreal as an aesthetic that could express the changes within the British landscape. John Piper, whom Tunnard thanked for photographs in *Gardens in the Modern Landscape*, was an associate editor and photographer for the Shell guides to the shires, whose chief editor was John Betjeman. His photographs, especially of churches and ancient and religious objects, seemed to capture the quirky nostalgic qualities of the English landscape. Piper's surrealist paintings are from this period.

Tunnard's emphasis upon art and his preference for abstract forms was not to every garden critic's taste. Bijhouwer thought that Tunnard had gone out of his way to avoid any stylistic references, resulting in a pre-occupation with aesthetics and furnishings, rather than the way the landscape was structured and the spatial quality of the design.[69] Bradford Williams, Fellow of the American Society of Landscape Architects (FASLA), expressed doubts about whether the claims for art and design were justified:[70]

> The history part is good. So are the theories in their expression as ideas; but their illustration as completed work, even by as competent drawings and as admirable photographs as the book shows, with rare exception fails to satisfy. It is perhaps not unfair to suspect that the technique of the new design has

not yet been mastered generally … While as a landscape architect he is keenly aware of the need for his profession in the solving of many varied problems of present-day living, after examining his philosophy and method of attack one is tempted to ask whether Mr Tunnard's views are those of a born and bred landscape architect adapting the principles of design to his work, or a skilled designer who happens to be working in the field and the materials of landscape architecture. Nevertheless if you would know more of the new landscape ('the garden without boundaries') which is to supplant the 'present antisocial private garden system,' you would do well to read this entertaining well-written book.

New forms expressive of our own time

Examples of whole gardens designed as collaborative works of art were scarce. Even so, the architects' liking for mature landscape gardens in which to set their buildings, rather than the Arts and Crafts approach, had been apparent for some time, and Tunnard's prediction of the 'garden without boundaries' was perhaps fairly safe:[71]

> A style for our own time is being formed. I believe that it will not be very different from the humanised landscape tradition of the eighteenth century, but that it will, nevertheless, be based on broader conceptions of nature and of art.

He was vague on the source of the new forms, merely saying 'that inspiration can be drawn from the underlying principles of contemporary life and art'.[72] More radical was that Tunnard envisioned the reining-in and coordination of individualistic landscape designs and a return to the 'unity' of the English landscape garden.

With respect to small gardens, he was personally in favour of the 'open centre' approach, whereby the lawn was opened up from the windows of the house. He quoted Shenstone:

> I think a plain space near the eye gives it a kind of liberty it loves … and the picture, whether you chuse the grand or the beautiful, should be held up at its proper distance.[73]

Others were thinking the same, though also being vague on further guidance. Thomas Adams and Peter Youngman rejected axiality and symmetry and thought that 'The garden of the future will need to be more free and flowing in its pattern, with less emphasis on its plan, groupings and on the relationship of these to the architecture of the house.'[74] Tunnard recommended that any borders, flower gardening and walks should be kept to the sides of the garden. 'Simplicity' would be necessary, and he echoed Pevsner:[75] 'if there is not to be a period of horticultural *Art Nouveau* such as occurred in the field of architecture and decoration before the present forms evolved'.

Tunnard could point to some more definite ideas when it came to individual elements of gardens. At the time garden ornament was dominated by historic forms:[76]

> Most garden ornament of today is, in fact, something in the nature of a gesture to the past; sundials, well heads, lead tanks, Italian stone benches, millstones, antique statuary are anachronisms.

His instinct was to let the necessities of site planning and function determine surfaces and garden furniture: 'discard … mere surface trimming in favour of structural decorative methods'. There were enough examples around for him to say with confidence:

> That which takes their place should be modern in spirit and design. Seats, gates and vases of simplicity and usefulness and sculpture by artists who create essays in forms … are already proving their excellence.

One page in the book was devoted to photographs of 'Modern interpretations of traditional forms'.[77] A mural, a drinking fountain, and modern topiary and treillage were shown, though these were merely old ideas in a modern idiom.

More convincing were examples which he included in his final section on 'Garden Decoration'.[78] A garden house in Stuttgart by Otto Valentien was fully glazed 'to obtain less rigid forms of enclosure'.[79] The example given for a conservatory was the entrance hall to a block of flats in Zurich by A. and E. Roth and Marcel Breuer,[80] perhaps not an ideal example, though he did not seem to be aware of that in the Tugendhat Villa in Brno by Mies van der Rohe, and the conservatory at St Ann's Hill was illustrated elsewhere.

Tubular metal gates specified by Maxwell Fry for a house at Hampstead demonstrated 'elegance derived from a proper use of modern technique'.[81] A steel recliner seat designed for mass production by Christopher Nicholson, brother of the painter Ben, was similar to those bought by Chermayeff for his terrace at Bentley Wood.

Tunnard showed off his 'granolithic' paving in the conservatory courtyard at St Ann's Hill which was incised every two feet in order to conceal cracking, and recommended honesty in laying square mass-produced paving stones. The commissioning and placing of sculpture was given much space. It should be abstract, arousing curiosity, to 'force the onlooker's attention to some aspect of formal unity in the world around us'. Because the appeal of sculpture was in part its subtle detail, it 'is best placed in relation to plain undecorated surfaces such as walls, level lawns or water', he thought. On the other hand, where a piece was wanted to be seen at a distance at a focal point some simple abstract form was preferred.[82] His illustrations included Willi Soukop's fountain at St Ann's Hill and a 'stabile' by Alexander Calder.

A photograph of a freestanding glass screen was included: it was from a garden design by Harry Maass, a landscape architect who was particularly interested in technical aspects, and first wrote about and depicted his examples of glass screens

Figure 4.8 The 'flower-window or glass-walled room containing decorative planting' was seen as the modern equivalent of the conservatory, with, as example, an entrance hall to a block of flats in Zürich designed by A. and E. Roth and Marcel Breuer.
(Source: Tunnard, *Gardens in the Modern Landscape* (1938), p. 182)

Figure 4.9 A wire frame covered with ivy in André Véra's garden at St Germain-en-Laye was considered as a modern interpretation of a traditional form.
(Source: Tunnard, *Gardens in the Modern Landscape* (1948), p. 99)

Figure 4.10   Tunnard preferred simple abstract forms, such as this 'stabile' by Alexander
Calder.
(Source: Tunnard, *Gardens in the Modern Landscape* (1948), p. 106)

in the late 1920s.[83] The German Pavilion designed by Mies van der Rohe for the
1929 Barcelona International Exposition was described as a 'garden house' and
was used to illustrate the innovative use of a new material, i.e. 'black glass walls'.[84]
In fact these black walls consisted of polished stone slabs, and the pavilion's innovation was in relating a building to its environment and the gradual progression
from the inside to the outside, with a particular emphasis on the area in between.
Tunnard's research might have been improved on these matters if he had been
more rigorous. A seminal publication by Arthur Korn entitled *Glas im Bau und als
Gebrauchsgegenstand* ('Glass in architecture and as a commodity'), was published
in 1929. This might have been known to Tunnard as he knew Korn.[85] McGrath
had also written a book on glass.[86]

Tunnard continued his quest for the principles and forms of modern landscape
design through his article on 'Modern Gardens for Modern Houses', discussed
above. His old friend Frank Clark was also passionately keen to see how modern
principles and forms could be developed for modern gardens, and continued to
ponder this question into the 1950s.[87] At this time, though, Tunnard was more
interested in three-dimensional form, and had come to see that many of his earlier
design principles for gardens were illusory.

Figure 4.11 This freestanding glass screen by Harry Maass was commended for providing shelter to tender plants whilst not excluding light.
(Source: Tunnard, *Gardens in the Modern Landscape* (1938), 105)

Figure 4.12 The German Pavilion designed by Mies van der Rohe for the 1929 Barcelona International Exhibition was described by Tunnard as a 'garden house'.
(Source: Tunnard, *Gardens in the Modern Landscape* (1948), p. 105)

The Planter's Eye

During his time with Percy Cane, Tunnard had become a knowledgeable plantsman. He acknowledged the contribution of William Robinson and Gertude Jekyll in the popularisation of the hardy plant: they were 'pioneers in the art of adapting living material to the site'. The carefully grouped colours of the Jekyll style of planting had been a perfect adjunct to an early Lutyens house in the vernacular style. However, to Tunnard, this was 'a very good reason for its being unsuitable for a modern house, but as yet in this country no alternative to the "colour garden" has been devised'.[88] It was this alternative that Tunnard sought, aided by Clark with his understanding of modern art.

His writing on planting thus showed a transition from traditional to modern. When, as a 25 year old, Tunnard wrote his first article on plants and planting design it could have been written by any attentive ex-student of the Royal Horticultural Society's garden at Wisley who had then gone into a design office. The ease with which he discussed plants and their ecology in this and other early articles suggests that Percy Cane had seen his skills as being in planting plans and specifications. The article, on 'Interplanting', concerned new planting within existing schemes, and was a confident synthesis of his own and others' experience.[89] Tunnard gave suggestions for well-tried combinations that 'harmonise in form and colour or prolong the period of bloom'. The suggestion that these combinations were 'already well-known' and 'had been tried and found successful' indicated that he was building on contemporary practice.

Nevertheless Tunnard was already constructing a critique of Jekyll's narrow focus on colour gardens, which, whilst they gave wonderful effects, worked independently of the garden's architectural framework. He was coming to appreciate the primacy of the garden architect's concern for form and line in garden layout. Colour had an important place, not for its own sake, but in reinforcing and enlivening the overall design. Two recently published books made these points. The first was Richard Sudell's *Landscape Gardening* (1933) which observed about the use of colour:[90]

> Line and form come first, as a matter of course, when a garden plan is being outlined on paper. But without a sense of colour values, the effects of good line and form can easily be destroyed.

'Colour value' was seen, for example, as the 'ability to differentiate between neutral shades such as blues and greys and warmer colours such as reds and oranges, and between the relative value of thick heavy conifers as compared with, say, Silver Birches'.

The second book was Percy Cane's *Garden Design of To-Day* (1934), on which Tunnard may have assisted. Cane's observation that 'The Japanese have long known that beauty of form is art of a higher degree than a mere display of colour' referred to the form of plants, but reinforced the general point of primacy of form over colour.[91]

Tunnard developed Cane's thoughts: 'the chief criticism which a Japanese has to make of our European gardens is against what seems to him the barbaric massing of colour'.[92] As if to assert the redundancy of Jekyll's work he remarked that: 'until recently we have regarded the grouping of colours as one of the most sublime of human arts'. Clark's knowledge of art may have helped too, as contemporary abstract art concerned pure patterns of form, line and colour. He may also have emphasised economy of expression. Several of the Impressionist painters had collected Japanese prints, and Tunnard had heard of James McNeill Whistler's study of them: 'we have learned a good deal by way of Whistler who found economy of line and colour in the Japanese print'. Tunnard concluded: 'Now … the trend in all art is slowly moving towards acceptance of form, line and economy of material as being of the first importance.'

Tunnard's and Clark's joint attempt to align planting design with the trends in other arts was contained in a section entitled 'The Planter's Eye' in *Gardens in the Modern Landscape*.[93] Tunnard considered that 'it is possible to put forward aesthetic theories which will hold good for the planter's art', and indeed 'the author once took the trouble to collect material for such a theory'. However 'aesthetic harmony cannot be felt and analyzed simultaneously'. Rather than try to capture rules, Tunnard advocated that 'the solution of problems of colour out of doors will be made by employment of an empathic approach', by which he meant a reliance on the designer being able to read his and others' associations and feelings stimulated by plant arrangement and colour, and a new tradition born of experience. 'To plant well is … to evolve a tradition of experiment which will stand superior to the traditions of past ages.' He argued for education of landscape designers to appreciate 'formal relationships, whether they be of texture and outline as modern Scandinavian and Swiss designers find them, or of mood and feeling as developed by the eighteenth-century romantics in the grotto and the wilderness'.

His conviction that the colour garden was not that new tradition was restated and reinforced. He acknowledged that Jekyll did

> accomplish a careful and accurate estimate of colour effects through observation and experiment. Hers was not the eye to overlook gradations of tone in plant foliage, for instance, or the intensification of tonal value in flowers of pure colours when placed in close proximity to white.

Her systematic colour classification was certainly an advance. However she disregarded the problem of colour changing with light:

> When gardeners followed the Impressionists by allowing the existence of a natural colour system … they failed to recognise the Impressionists' chief discovery that the earth was lit from the sky; in other words that light was the main factor and the key to the whole situation.

Tunnard asserted that 'tonal values in themselves have never been able to carry us very far', and that 'the colour garden per se is valueless as a contribution either to aesthetics or to the English scene'. A recent book by Adrian Stokes (1902–1972), *Colour and Form* (1937), was taken as corroborating this:

> Systems of colour harmonies are interesting, but no more so than common chords played upon the piano ... isolated from form, sensation of colour does not lead to a pure art of colours, or anything that can be called an art.

Somehow the landscape designer needed to get away from the usual practice of considering colour planning as an end in itself, and begin to think of how colour could be employed in the planning of the garden as a whole. Tunnard advocated the use of 'structural colour', which he saw as weaving 'the thread of colour pattern through the material of a garden plan so that it strengthens and enlivens'.

He had some ideas on how this might be achieved, but first he needed to dissect the problems in doing so. First there were the greens in the English landscape, 'varied but not balancing tones'. For reasons cited by Goethe and Stokes, Tunnard thought that they were 'not an ideal colour for a landscape background'. Second, there was the quality of light in England, which seemed to 'drain the life from colour'. Hence 'colour gradations in borders and walks often fail of their effect for the reasons given above – namely, the devitalizing power of illumination and the limiting influence of green'.

What was needed was to 'set colour free in order to allow it to play a satisfactory part'. The problem of the quality of English light draining colour could be counteracted by 'the use of chiaroscuro and plant illuminants'. He saw variegated plants as one form of 'illuminants' that 'tend to spread and absorb the light and their surroundings', and these could be incorporated in the backgrounds which is necessary 'in introducing massed colour effects out of doors for physiological or emotional stimulation'.

The problems with the greens of the English landscape could be somewhat negated if attention was drawn to form rather then colour, he thought. The logic underlying effective 'structural colour' was thus:

1   The green landscapes of England demand a formal emphasis – i.e., their aesthetic appreciation can safely be allowed to remain an appreciation of outline, contours and drawn lines, coupled with a visual emphasis of tones rather than hues.

2   Colour can under certain conditions revivify these tones and renew the structural life of landscape (a) through concentration of purely physiological colour in architectural surroundings which nourish it and lessen devitalizing power of light in a heavy northern atmosphere, (b) through employment of the methods of chiaroscuro (light coming out of darkness) or of illuminative backgrounds in the open garden or larger landscape compositions.

This theoretical approach was rather limited in application. It was primarily for aesthetic effect, and ignored seasonal colour and, more seriously in the context of a Modernist approach, there was no reference to the functional purposes of vegetation. Tunnard's own planting, particularly at Gaulby and Bentley Wood, showed that he chose to vary its character with increasing distance from the house. Form and strong colour were emphasised close to in beds, giving greater detail near the viewer, whilst further away sweeps of grass usually planted with thousands of bulbs led to less formal planting. In many ways this was quite traditional, and his selection of plants was quite contemporary, with a similar range to that recommended by Sudell, for example. The only scheme which he held up as in any way representing his theories was a section of the garden at Gaulby.[94] The plans showed how he would have provided screening of the drive from the garden and given the impression of perspective along a walk through varying colour. However, Tunnard himself noted that the 'planting requirements … necessitated a conventional mixed planting' of trees, shrubs and herbaceous. Perhaps further schemes might have allowed him to explore the application of his ideas on structural colour, but in 1938 he could not cite any. Perhaps aware of how unconvincing the Gaulby plans were, he replaced them with a section on 'Architects' Plants' in the second edition of *Gardens in the Modern Landscape*.

'Architects' Plants' had initially appeared in instalments in *AR* in 1939, and Tunnard's descriptions were accompanied by sketches by Gordon Cullen. It was not the intention to suggest a method of planting, simply to point out 'structural material … which in various ways can be employed to contribute to the shape or atmosphere of certain familiar settings'.[95] Cane's earlier use of the word 'atmosphere' suggests that probably 'character' would be used instead today.[96] Tunnard looked at the following situations: hardy plants for exotic effect, room plants, variegated evergreens, conifers, plants with grey foliage, woody plants for sandy soil, shrubs for the roof garden, and shrubs for garden decoration in winter. They actually represented a range of plants that was first popular in the 1860s as foliage plants, particularly in subtropical bedding.[97] The emphasis was firmly on foliage colour, shape and texture of the plants as a whole, instead of the conventional emphasis on flower colour.

Frank Clark afterwards provided his own statement on striking indoor plants in 1952, accompanied by further sketches by Gordon Cullen.[98] Tunnard's term 'architects' plants' was perhaps based on the '*formes architecturales*' described by the Swiss alpinist, Henri Correvon (1854–1939), and seems in turn to have been the forerunner of the postwar term 'architectural plants', being those with big, bold or spiky leaves whose sculptural qualities are not reliant on flowers and which often provide a long season of interest.

Space arrangements

By the time that the second edition of *Gardens in the Modern Landscape* was issued in 1948, Tunnard had had much time to reconsider his earlier views. He claimed that his 'personal approach to landscape gardening has not changed', though that referred only to the professionalism in carrying out schemes, not to the theory underlying the design.

Conifers

Figure 4.13 (a–d) Tunnard's descriptions of 'architects' plants' were accompanied with
sketches by Gordon Cullen.
(Tunnard, *Gardens in the Modern Landscape* (1948), pp. 122–5)

In 1947 Lewis Mumford took issue with the creed of functionalism and how it
produced 'a sterile and abstract modernism', preferring 'that native and humane
form of modernism which one might call the Bay Region style, a free yet unobtru-
sive expression of the terrain, the climate, and the way of life' of the Californian
coast.[99] Tunnard was amongst those that agreed with the basic sentiment. Contrary
to the propaganda of the 1930s which asserted that the new architecture was a
rejection of the styles, he saw that it had become formulaic, and had set into a
recognisable style. He criticised architects who were adopting Modernism 'without
regard to its origins and philosophy'.[100] These people 'do not investigate enough;
they have discarded the older styles without bothering to find out what they rep-
resent'. He quoted the architect Matthew Nowicki in saying: 'sometime ago our
design became a style … A style as pronounced, as defined, more limited perhaps,
and as legitimate for our time as the style of Renaissance had been in its days.'[101]
And he made the then surprising claim, which did become true, though slower
then he envisaged, that:[102]

> In the next twenty years we shall see a revolution in architectural taste and
> form which will be of tremendous significance to city planning … which
> will, in fact, go hand in hand with the new urbanism. The distinguishing
> features of the new architecture will be an emphasis on scale and proportion,
> on ensemble, on ornament, on humanism.

Tunnard no longer believed in many of the underpinnings of his earlier landscape theory. The rejection of style had been illusory, the cavalier assumption that beauty sprang from good functional design had been replaced by a recognition that beauty had to be a designer's concern, and the abolition of private space had been too simplistic and authoritarian. As it happened, the same year of the first publication of *Gardens in the Modern Landscape*, Harvard had granted a year-long visiting lectureship to the Swiss architectural historian, friend of Gropius and CIAM member, Sigfried Giedion. His lectures were published three years later as *Space, Time and Architecture* (1941). In this, Giedion sought an explanation for the way that Modernist architecture had unfolded. Part of the answer was that the aspirations of every age except the nineteenth century were eloquently expressed in the handling of space. The revolution in twentieth-century architecture was because architects once more were beginning to appreciate that buildings were more effectively designed and analysed in terms of the contained space rather than the enclosing solid.

Mies van der Rohe's design for the German pavilion at the Barcelona exhibition of 1929 became much admired and cited as an example of how space within a building could be treated fluidly, abolishing the assumption that rooms automatically had four walls. Both Garrett Eckbo and James Rose transferred this thought to garden planning whilst still students at the GSD.[103] However 'space' is a word with several meanings, and these early essays in fluid space were two-dimensional garden planning, experiments in form only, just as Eckbo's interest in Pierre-Émile Legrain's saw-tooth path edge was,[104] and also the various imitations of Burle Marx's designs by others.

Also, Giedion's ideas concerned volumes, and they were first unequivocally applied to garden design in an article by Joseph Hudnut in 1940.[105] Rejecting 'that very provocative principle which is called *functionalism*' as the essential basis of landscape design, he posited a 'new aesthetic' in both house and garden, 'most clearly exhibited in the *new quality of space* and in the new command of space'. Space was 'a new material of expression whose range and resourcefulness we have until now scarcely guessed at'. In every age the garden had been shaped in characteristic ways to reflect the needs and aspirations of society, just as the interiors of buildings had been. Gardens, he noted, were built of space formed by terraces, walls and foliage. The great garden designers had 'looked into the heart of their time and made it visible'. This gave some hints to the landscape designer:

> So varied, powerful and unhackneyed a medium cannot be forever neglected by the landscape architect. The time will surely come when he will wish to awaken and intensify by his art a consciousness of a garden space at one with that of the house: of the house which is, or should be, only a sequestered part of his garden.

Hudnut wanted architects to recognise that simply designing houses for the modern man was not enough. They should be designing to give people, people that he called 'post-modern', the freedom to express themselves through inner experience, and bringing beauty into their homes. At the same time the architect's technique should embrace the 'shapes, proportions and relationships of buildings, and … the shapes, proportions and relationships of the spaces between and around buildings'.[106] Tunnard's growing awareness of civic design, in which the organisation of spatial volume is fundamental, must have convinced him that Giedion and Hudnut had hit upon an important truth, and a new basis for a technique of landscape design. He even had Hudnut's essay reprinted in the second edition of *Gardens in the Modern Landscape*.[107]

That year he was asked to give a paper to a conference on 'Aesthetic Evaluation' at Ann Arbor held under the auspices of the College of Architecture and Design at the University of Michigan. He took the opportunity to précis his tentative new thoughts on landscape design. The importance of spatial design and new materials had been important innovations of the twentieth century, but

> this is not proving to be sufficient; we now need a positive drive toward the creation of beauty, not as a by-product, but as an integral part of our design.

It was the imagination that could convert a satisfactory spatial arrangement into a place of beauty. Tunnard reminded his audience of Alexander Pope's advice to find inspiration from the site: the 'genius of the place'. He mentioned the use of water, a topic that continued to fascinate him.[108] He also mentioned that designers needed imagination as to what not to do, for example over-enthusiastic planting.

Having said that, the 'new use of space and materials' was the medium for the imagination. In other words the composition had to be of 'trees and plants, sticks and stones, light and shadow, and space'. Explaining that 'formerly, much of the work was done with an eye to picturesque effect', by which he was indicating the Beaux-Arts approach, he wrote that that was[109]

> not always for the best space-organisation for use. These set pieces … are now giving way to space arrangements for specific purposes. This new approach should not sacrifice beauty, but should create beauty through well planned and executed designs. The landscape architect is learning … to rely on mass, line, and form for pleasing effects in the landscape.

He stressed the parallel with the spatial design of interiors, yet landscape had its own colour range, and far greater possibilities for axes and extensive horizontal areas:

> landscape is something more than a setting for buildings. It has aesthetic rules which apply to it alone. Among these are the rule of color … the rule of distances … also the rule of planes.

Many of Tunnard's ideas were shared by Garrett Eckbo. At the time of *Landscape for Living* (1950) Eckbo was still stressing functionalism but was also fully embracing the potential of volumetric space in the hands of the designer to:[110]

give the richest, most plastic and satisfying form to the space which is being organised; the other is to concentrate always on that space as an arena, volume background and shelter for human life and activity.

Tunnard had virtually finished designing himself, so he never tested his ideas concerning imagination and beauty in the landscape sphere, and he did not pursue the question of space in landscape design after 1948. So it was Eckbo's book that introduced the landscape architect to what he called 'spatial design'. In this way the handling of space did become a general concern amongst landscape architects in the second half of the twentieth century, though without reference to Tunnard's theoretical musings. The latter's hesitant attempt at a new design theory was sufficiently formed to show that he had abandoned his 1930s' functionalist doctrine, and was already groping for another way, but it was a dead end for him in the context of landscape design. On the other hand, his ideas on space and imagination were not wasted, as they were to have a strong influence on his new thinking on civic design.

Notes

1 Gabo (1936), p. 846.
2 Tunnard, *Gardens in the Modern Landscape* (1938), p. 95.
3 Ibid., p. 5.
4 The landscape garden became a topic of intense interest for the next forty years at the hands of Frank Clark, Nikolaus Pevsner, Rudolf Wittkower, John Dixon Hunt and others.
5 Tunnard, *Gardens in the Modern Landscape* (1938), p. 10.
6 Hussey, 'Bentley, near Halland, Sussex', p. 370; see also Hussey, 'Carrygate, Leicestershire', p. 268.
7 Tunnard, *Gardens in the Modern Landscape* (1938), pp. 67–8.
8 Colvin (Autumn 1937), 142–4.
9 Tunnard (Summer 1937), 'Landscape Design at the Paris International Congress', pp. 78–83; also Tunnard (April 1938), 'The Functional Aspect of Garden Planning', pp. 195–8.
10 Voets (November 1987), p. 40.
11 Woudstra (1995), 'Danish Landscape Design in the Modern Era (1920–1970)'.
12 Tunnard (Summer 1937), 'Landscape Design at the Paris International Congress', p. 81.
13 Tunnard (April 1938), 'The Functional Aspect of Garden Planning', plan and photograph of Langangen 218, Stockholm, with caption of a 'simple' design by Hermelin on p. 196.
14 Tunnard, *Gardens in the Modern Landscape* (1938), p. 78.
15 Tunnard (Summer 1937), 'Landscape Design at the Paris International Congress', 82.
16 For *Blut und Boden* philosophy see Bramwell (1985), pp. 40–5.
17 Joint authorship was claimed by Tunnard in the Foreword of *Gardens in the Modern Landscape* (1948), pp. 5–6.
18 Canneel-Claes, *Association Internationale des Architectes de Jardins Modernistes* (AIAJM) in Box 6 archive papers, LI Archive. Canneel-Claes gave himself as the secretary.
19 Tunnard (Summer 1937), 'Landscape Design at the Paris International Congress', 78.

20 Tunnard to Loftus Hare, 7 May 1938; LI library; reproduced in Imbert (Spring 2007), 'Landscape Architects of the World, Unite!', p. 12.
21 Imbert (2007), 'The AIAJM: A Manifesto for Landscape Modernity', pp. 223–4.
22 Tunnard quoted one of the 'objects' and one of the 'resolutions'. See *Gardens in the Modern Landscape* (1938), p. 106, and *Gardens in the Modern Landscape* (1948), p. 6.
23 Tunnard, *Gardens in the Modern Landscape* (1938), pp. 64–5 and 80.
24 Shepheard, 26–33.
25 Tunnard, *Gardens in the Modern Landscape* (1938), pp. 72–3.
26 Ibid., p. 62.
27 Ibid., p. 81 and 106.
28 Ibid., p. 68.
29 Tunnard (Summer 1937), 'Landscape Design at the Paris International Congress', p. 81.
30 Tunnard, *Gardens in the Modern Landscape* (1938), p. 9, 21, 33, 40 and 60.
31 Ibid., pp. 94–5.
32 Woudstra (2000), 'The Corbusian Landscape: Arcadia or No man's Land?'.
33 Bijhouwer (1954), p. 119.
34 Deming (Spring 1996), 'Christopher Tunnard, Modern Landscape Architecture and the "Empathic" View of Japan'.
35 Cane, *Garden Design of To-Day*, (1934), Chap. XIII, pp. 135–48.
36 Ibid., pp. 135–6.
37 Tunnard's borrowings from the RHS Lindley Library included 'Sadler, Art of Flower Arrangement in Japan' (19 March 1935).
38 Tunnard (Summer 1935), 'The Influence of Japan on the English Garden', pp. 49–50.
39 McGrath (1934), pp. 189–90; plan and three photographs opposite p. 200.
40 Ibid., pp. 186–7.
41 Tunnard (Summer 1935), 'The Influence of Japan on the English Garden', p. 51.
42 Ibid., pp. 49–53.
43 Tunnard (Summer 1936), 'Garden Design at Chelsea Show, 1936', p. 91.
44 Bennett (1935), pp. 132–3.
45 Tunnard's borrowings from the RHS Lindley Library included 'Kuck, *One Hundred Kyoto gdns*' (17 February 1938).
46 Tunnard, *Gardens in the Modern Landscape* (1938), p. 6.
47 Cortazzi, Sir Hugh, book review of Bernard Leach; Life and Work (Yale University Press, 2003), *The Japan Society Reviews*. Available online at http://www.japansociety.org.uk/05leach.html, accessed 27 June 2008.
48 Tunnard, *Gardens in the Modern Landscape* (1938), p. 88.
49 Ibid., p. 91.
50 Tunnard (May 1938), 'Asymmetrical Garden Planning: The Oriental Aesthetic', p. 248.
51 Ibid., p. 245.
52 McGrath (1934), p. 35.
53 Tunnard, *Gardens in the Modern Landscape* (1938), p. 107.
54 Ibid., p. 84.
55 Ibid., p. 93, caption.
56 Ibid., pp. 84–6.
57 Frost (1929), p. 270; thanks to Alan Powers for this suggestion.
58 Tunnard, *Gardens in the Modern Landscape* (1938), p. 85.
59 Van Doesburg (1970), pp. 78–80.
60 Canneel-Claes [1938].
61 Tunnard, *Gardens in the Modern Landscape* (1938), 85.
62 Neckar (1993), p. 146.
63 Tunnard, *Gardens in the Modern Landscape* (1938), p. 94.

64 Ibid., p. 9.
65 Ibid., p. 17.
66 Ibid., p. 74.
67 Ibid., p. 95.
68 Tunnard (May–June 1956), 'The Conscious Stone', Fig. 1.
69 Bijhouwer (1954), p. 119.
70 Williams (April 1939), p. 145.
71 Tunnard, *Gardens in the Modern Landscape* (1938), p. 5.
72 Ibid., p. 125.
73 Tunnard, *Gardens in the Modern Landscape* (1938), p. 67, citing from A. R. Humphrey, *William Shenstone* (1937), Cambridge University Press (page not given).
74 Adams and Youngman (1939), pp. 14–15.
75 Pevsner belittled Art Nouveau as a transitional style between Arts and Crafts and Modernism.
76 Tunnard, *Gardens in the Modern Landscape* (1938), p. 97.
77 Ibid., p. 100.
78 Ibid., pp. 168–82.
79 Ibid., p. 172; a 'green corner' of Valentien was illustrated on p. 115.
80 Ibid., p. 182.
81 Ibid., p. 174.
82 Ibid., pp. 98–102.
83 Maass (1929), p. 197; also Maass (1932), 'Glasschutz im Garten', pp. 162–3.
84 Tunnard, *Gardens in the Modern Landscape* (1938), p. 105.
85 McGrath (1967).
86 McGrath and Frost (1937).
87 Clark (March–April 1934), 'The Principles of Landscape Design'.
88 Tunnard, *Gardens in the Modern Landscape* (1938), p. 59.
89 Tunnard (Autumn 1935), 'Interplanting', pp. 110–12.
90 Sudell (1933), p. 193.
91 Cane, *Garden Design of To-Day* (1934), pp. 138–9 and 142.
92 Tunnard (Summer 1935), 'The Influence of Japan on the English Garden', pp. 50–1.
93 Tunnard, *Gardens in the Modern Landscape* (1938), 108–24.
94 Ibid., pp. 118–22, 'Planting Plans for a Section of a Garden near Leicester'
95 Ibid., p. 118.
96 Cane, *Modern Gardens: British and Foreign* (1926–7), p. 4
97 Elliott (1986), pp. 152–4.
98 Jones and Clark (1952).
99 Lewis Mumford, 'Skyline', in *New Yorker* (11 October 1947), p. 106 and 109.
100 Tunnard, *Gardens in the Modern Landscape* (1948), p. 6.
101 Tunnard (May–June 1954), 'The Conscious Stone', p. 24.
102 Tunnard, *The City of Man* (1953), p. 234.
103 Walker and Simo (1994), p. 127; Treib and Imbert (1997), Fig. 17.
104 Treib and Imbert (1997), cf. Figs 13 and 26.
105 Hudnut (May 1940), 'Space and the Modern Garden'.
106 Pearlman (2007), p. 172.
107 Tunnard, *Gardens in the Modern Landscape* (1948), 175–8.
108 Tunnard (September 1939), 'The Adventure of Water'; (April 1949) 'Art and Landscape Design'; *The City of Man* (1953), Chapter 11.
109 Tunnard (April 1949), 'Art and Landscape Design', pp. 105–11.
110 Eckbo (1950), p. 6.

5 Landscape design

Landscape designs in England

An analysis of Tunnard's garden designs reveals the various influences that helped to shape them. Within a brief period of four or five years he matured from layouts in the Arts and Crafts style of Percy Cane's office, as shown in his design for Salcott, Burwood and Ravenhead, to ones that reveal the search for Modernism. Initially this was sought in the English landscape garden, and this was made manifest in his approach to St Ann's Hill and his scheme for a weekend house in Cobham. But almost immediately, as a result of attending the Paris congress, he experimented with cubist forms in his designs for Walton-on-Thames and Gaulby. By the time of the publication of *Gardens in the Modern Landscape* in 1938 a range of contemporary Modernist influences from home and abroad in architecture, landscape and garden design, and art can be discerned.

His initial designs appear to have derived from personal contact with wealthy patrons, particularly Gerald Schlesinger. Soon, however, his best contacts were architects, foremost amongst whom was Raymond McGrath. Tunnard's work and his writings enabled him to extend his circle of Modernist architectural contacts, including Serge Chermayeff, Wells Coates and Oliver Hill.

For all his enthusiasm and later influence in the theory and design of Modernist landscape, Tunnard was no great draughtsman. His training as a horticulturalist had evidently not adequately equipped him in this respect. His early practice drawings in 1936 showed unsophisticated draughtsmanship and inexpert use of stencils. From that time he increasingly relied upon Frank Clark who appears to have drawn most of his plans and whose sketches of the 'All-Europe house' and the 'Small Garden' in 1939 were very polished.[1] Another ploy later used by Tunnard was to make models of his schemes.

St Ann's Hill, Chertsey

Tunnard may well have already been familiar with St Ann's Hill, a pronounced knoll in an otherwise flat landscape, through one of Percy Cane's designs for a 36-acre public park given to the town of Chertsey by Sir William Berry that made full use of the extraordinary views north over the Surrey landscape.[2] St Ann's

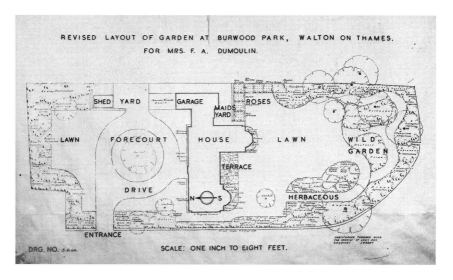

Figure 5.1 Design for a garden at Burwood Park, Walton on Thames, for Mrs F.A. Dumoulin, c. 1936.
(Source: Clark Papers)

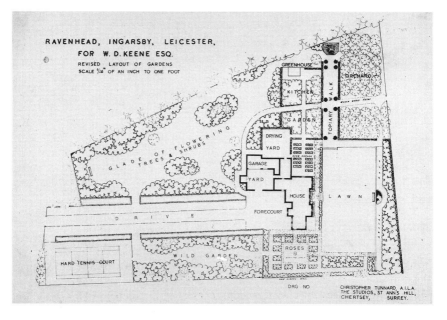

Figure 5.2 Design for a garden at Ravenshead, Ingarsby, Leicester for W.D. Keene, c. 1936.
(Source: Clark Papers)

Figure 5.3 Eighteenth-century pavilion in the gardens of St Ann's Hill.
(Source: English Heritage)

Hill House was across the road, on the hilltop, but looking south. This property had been the *cottage ornée* retreat of the politician Charles James Fox in the late eighteenth century, and a two-storey grotto, the small Temple of Friendship of 1792, and some mature cedars remained from that time. The estate was 25 acres in size, consisting of lawns surrounded by mature trees, beyond which were a kitchen garden, elaborated by bedding and herbaceous borders, and a woodland alongside.

Gerald Schlesinger, the client, accepted McGrath's circular design for the house, perhaps in order to take advantage of the wide views south. McGrath himself likened the unusual form to 'a cheese, with a slice cut for the sunlight to enter the whole house'. He also recalled that 'the modern garden was done by Christopher Tunnard'.[3] However, the dilapidated St Ann's house and its 25 acres of landscape garden was a major challenge in 1936 for the very recently qualified landscape architect used to working in the Arts and Crafts idiom. He was very conscious that no design tradition existed that could be a suitable match to McGrath's Modernist design. This was a magnificent opportunity for an ambitious designer like himself, but where to start?

In response Tunnard sunk himself into the development of a methodology for the reanimation of the grounds. By subscribing to the eighteenth-century notion of 'landscape into garden' he saw the new landscape as 'the garden without boundaries', which meant that he referred to his treatment, which respected the evolution of the landscape, as 'remodelling'.[4] Thus seeing the modern garden as being 'in a landscape garden setting',[5] or, 'in the remains of an eighteenth-century landscape' he summarised the changes as follows:[6]

> The formal and kitchen garden remain; also the careful planting in clumps; but unnecessary paths have been removed and the whole scene simplified. The house has been rebuilt in reinforced concrete and around it formal modern garden elements … link the modern house to the scene, but still fit aptly in the park-like setting.

In the service yard between the new house and the old stables was a stepping-stone path, as he would have seen in photographs of work on the Continent, a device to provide a path without interrupting the flow of the grass.

The three-storey building was round, sliced out on the south side in a terraced manner, in order to create balconies at each floor. The circular form of the building was prompted by the desire to retain vistas to two existing large Lebanon cedars, with one being framed by the windows of hall, study and dressing room, and the other by the study, living room, dining room and pools in the formal garden. The circular shape also enabled the sun to reach the garden door in the morning as well as the afternoon, on a July day. This arrangement additionally meant that on approaching the entrance through a courtyard from the north-west side, the perception would be that of a complete circular building, with the view unfolding only on entering the living room through the entrance hall. The sliced-out area in front of the living room meant that the views were guided by the sectional walls. The latter additionally ensured privacy and some shelter when on the terrace outside.

Towards the west a winter garden, *cum* conservatory, in a walled space provided a sheltered area. Designed as a small symmetrical formal garden, with a rectangular and circular pond, and a number of planted beds, it was aligned on one of the cedars. The north wall of this garden was a legacy from the service courtyard while the screen wall with large openings to the south framed the landscape views.

To the east a swimming pool was planned. The overall shape was curved in order to fit round a rhododendron clump. A fountain was commissioned from Willi Soukop who met Schlesinger and McGrath after the house was completed, but before it was occupied.[7] It was decided that he would create a sculpture for the north end of the swimming pool. His idea was of a running stream up through the middle, spewing out of the top. He ordered a five-foot high block of Hopton stone

Figure 5.4 Old garden wall at St Ann's Hill prior to being plastered and painted as enclosure to the 'architectural garden'.
(Source: English Heritage)

Figure 5.5 Architectural garden at St Ann's Hill with Willi Soukop sculpture in front of plastered wall and large cedar tree.
(Source: Tunnard, *Gardens in the Modern Landscape* (1938), p. 180)

with a vertical hole drilled through it to be delivered to his studio at Dartington. The larger hole sideways through the bottle-shaped block was to show the water shooting up through it.

However, once it arrived Tunnard moved the sculpture into the centre of the round pool in the conservatory garden instead, replacing a globe-like feature that had been placed there initially.[8] Tunnard presented Soukop's piece as an abstract sculpture, suggesting that the 'breaks in the outline ... echo the sawn limbs on the trunk of the cedar in the background'.[9] This had never been intended by Soukop, who was surprised to see this published, as he had meant 'nothing really' by these breaks.[10]

There was no new planting in the landscape garden. Existing vegetation had been maintained throughout. Even the old wisteria against the former Regency house had been carefully preserved and re-attached to the new house. New planting therefore was restricted to the formal garden associated with the conservatory, which displayed a whole array of what Tunnard referred to as 'architects' plants', which he understood to be 'useful structural material' not 'chosen especially for their interest in flower'.[11] The selection included grey foliage plants, a Phoenix palm tree and cypresses, while there were concrete containers with flowering plants. On the roof terraces there were similar concrete containers, while indoors there were 'room plants' arranged on low tables or on the floor.[12]

Figure 5.6 The architectural garden at St Ann's Hill. This was the only formal garden area adjacent to the house. The conservatory to the left was devoted to the culture of tender plants.
(Source: Tunnard, *Gardens in the Modern Landscape* (1938), p. 134)

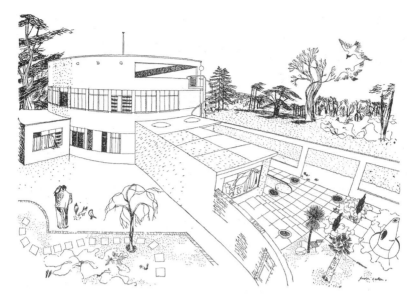

Figure 5.7 St Ann's Hill house and garden, taken from the position of the existing stable
block. Sketch by Gordon Cullen.
(Source: Tunnard, *Gardens in the Modern Landscape* (1938), p 74)

Figure 5.8 The newly completed St Ann's Hill house according to designs by Raymond
McGrath, with stairs up to swimming pool to right; large drifts of daffodils in
foreground.
(Source: English Heritage)

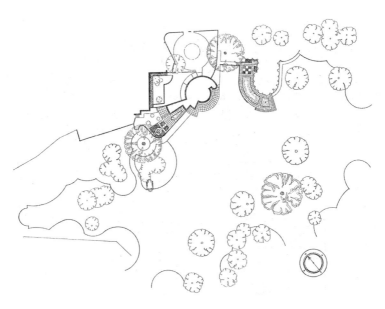

Figure 5.9 Tunnard's plan demonstrated his concept of the modern house set in a landscape garden. It indicated the new house, architectural garden, old stable block and swimming pool.
(Source: Tunnard, *Gardens in the Modern Landscape* (1938), p. 136)fi

Figure 5.10 Aerial view of the newly built St Ann's Hill in its setting.
(Source: Tunnard, *Gardens in the Modern Landscape* (1938), p. 132)

Figure 5.11 The new St Ann's Hill was built on the position of the dilapidated eighteenth-century country house, to right, and in front of the old stable block.
(Source: English Heritage)

Figure 5.12 The swimming pool at St Ann's Hill during construction.
(Source: English Heritage)

Figure 5.13 The swimming pool at St Ann's Hill seen from the roof terrace.
(Source: Tunnard, *Gardens in the Modern Landscape* (1938), p. 135)

Figure 5.14 Table and chairs on ground floor terrace at St Ann's Hill.
(Source: English Heritage)

Weekend house at Cobham

The association with McGrath led to further work, including a project for a weekend house at Cobham. The timber house was little more than a two-storey cabin with a veranda and balcony, and the whole was 'frankly planned as a playground for low-cost upkeep'.[13] A lawn spread down from the house to a combined swimming pond and boating lake, with a diving board and beach for sunbathing. There was also an island. The stepping-stone motif at St Ann's Hill was seen again linking house and pool. Existing plants were to be kept: 'All original trees remain on the site and new planting consists of flowering shrubs and waterside plants.' The design was a classic, if miniature, rendering of the English landscape garden with modern elements.

Walton-on-Thames and Gaulby

Tunnard's encounters with Canneel-Claes and Hermelin had provided him with some motifs of the modern continental style. The positioning of useful elements on the margins of a central lawn, the setting of paving slabs in grass like stepping stones to avoid dividing the lawn into areas, and the repetitive beds for flowers and

Figure 5.15 A weekend house at Cobham, designed by McGrath, was little more than a two-storey cabin. Landscape by Tunnard; sketch by Gordon Cullen.
(Source: Tunnard, *Gardens in the Modern Landscape* (1938), p. 72)

herbs, were all seen in Tunnard's designs. These now took the foreground, with the English landscape garden look of St Ann's Hill in the middle distance.

Tunnard used his design for a one-acre garden at Walton-on-Thames to illustrate his theories and practice of Modernist garden making. The house was placed in the north-west corner of the site 'in order that access from the road shall not spoil the privacy of the garden and to give it a south-east aspect with the principal rooms overlooking the garden'. Access to house and service quarters was from the north where there was also a kitchen garden, separated from the pleasure garden by a hedge. To south of the house was a wide terrace, with low planting enabling views across, and a swimming pool to the far west side sheltered by dense planting of flowering shrubs. Tunnard emphasised the importance of retaining the open effect of the centre of the site, locating a series of independent 'gardens' along the perimeter of the site. A stepping-stone path ran between the square blocks of tulips and roses that flanked the lawn. It then led into a grass walk between a square of cypress trees, followed by a more informal walk between flowering shrubs around the rest of the lawn. An existing mound was planted with rhododendrons, while tree planting along the southern boundary was strengthened, making it possible to incorporate a winding walk that completed a circumferential walk. In its design this garden betrayed the many motifs referred to by Tunnard: the landscape garden with respect to its informal arrangement and views; the Swedish garden for the

Figure 5.16 A garden at Walton-on-Thames showing the influence of Canneel-Claes in the arrangement of geometric flowerbeds. Landscape by Tunnard; sketch by Gordon Cullen.
(Source: Tunnard, *Gardens in the Modern Landscape* (1938), p. 73)

type of features it contained, and the gardens of Canneel-Claes for their geometric designs. Tunnard made a model of his scheme, and photographs and text illustrated its intended sequencing.[14]

The proposals for a house at Gaulby, Leicestershire, were for a similar-sized site to that at Walton-on-Thames, but its elevated situation on the southern edge of the tiny village in rural countryside, about eight miles east of Leicester, provided a different context.[15] The site was a slightly irregular-shaped plot already containing two labourers' cottages. The house, designed by McGrath for Charles R. Keene, a Leicester businessman and city councillor, had an extensive gestation period with initial design commencing in July 1936, but it appears that Tunnard did not get involved till almost a year later. A sketch by McGrath of the view 'looking S.W. to King's Norton church from the site of the house' suggests that he had already selected the house position at the western corner to obtain the most expansive views over the surrounding landscape.[16] Just enough room was left for some garden space in the foreground. This resulted in the main garden lying to the east of the house. Christopher Hussey thought that the 'landscape aspect' could not have been in more sensitive hands than McGrath's, referring to McGrath's general layout for the site.[17]

Tunnard became involved after this decision on the house's position had been determined. His earliest plan appears to have been drawn in about May 1937.[18] The garden area south-west of the house was to be shaped into a huge bastion with a ha-ha, and was labelled 'look out'. To the south-east of the house there was to be a hedged garden set out in an array of square beds like those at Walton-on-Thames. From these two garden areas a formal path ran to the southernmost corner of the site where 'space for shelter' was indicated. McGrath designed this shelter, illustrated by Gordon Cullen for the March 1938 issue of *Architectural Review*.[19] There was to be a circumferential walk, the section beyond the shelter running between flowering shrubs densely planted along the boundary and in island beds. One gap only along the south-east boundary was at the point where there was a large existing tree. This arrangement left the lawn as undivided as possible. The circumferential walk was completed by a more complex planting arrangement close to the house which was the subject of a study entitled 'Planting plans for a section of a garden near Leicester' embedded into *Gardens in the Modern Landscape*.[20]

Hence the planting scheme had three themes. A 'more sophisticated' section near the house with an 'obviously geometric layout' had highly ornamental plants in the beds. The section of the circumferential walk north-east of the house was to have prominent autumn leaf colour, but the main theme was

> perspective colour gradation in the long walk … Tonal progression of foliage colour has been arranged … to include bright golden variegation at the end of the walk nearest the house. This tones through green to glaucous purple in the centre of the walk and finishes with grey at the farthest end.

This arrangement would have been rather garish, though may have assured an

1

It is assumed that the site is fairly flat, but has a slight rise forming a mound near the south-east corner. The road runs along the north side. There are a few existing trees, mostly along the south boundary and on the mound. The house has been placed on the north-west corner, in order that access from the road shall not spoil the privacy of the garden and to give it a south-east aspect with the principal rooms overlooking the garden.

2

The house is planned with an open shape to take advantage of the diagonal views. A small entrance forecourt occupies the space between it and the road. The remainder of this (the north) side of the site, with access to the service quarters, is set aside as the kitchen garden, which is separated from the pleasure garden by a hedge that serves also to keep out noises from the road.

3

In front of the house a wide paved terrace is provided, on to which the main living-rooms would open. It is separated from the rest of the garden by some formal planting which, however, is kept low so as not to interrupt the views. Extending beyond the terrace, and linked with it by more paving, is a pool. The pool is protected on two sides from the prevailing south-west winds by a fairly dense plantation of flowering shrubs.

4

The lay-out of the immediate surroundings of the house having been decided upon, the designer turns his attention to the main portion of the garden. A scheme such as is commonly carried out by garden owners would be to extend from the terrace a straight path on the axis of the façade of the house, terminating in a formal arrangement of, perhaps, rose-garden and sundial. The disadvantages of this, however, are that the open effect of the site is lost by breaking up the centre, the new axis created finishes at no strong point and the portion of the garden seen directly from the house would be that most liable to untidiness.

5

Abandoning this scheme, the designer adopts a less formal plan which comprises, in effect, a series of independent gardens, each with its own character, arranged round the perimeter of the site, the centre being left free. First is the formal rose-garden that the owner required, divided into small geometrical beds to facilitate cultivation and the constant cutting that roses need. Next is a grove of cypress trees, as a foil to the rose-garden.

6

As we get further from the house the planting in this series of gardens becomes less formal. After the cypress trees, in the north-east corner of the site, is an herbaceous garden, mixed with flowering shrubs. The mound near the south-east corner is treated as an essay in scenic landscaping, as it is the most prominent object in the view from the house. It is planted principally with rhododendrons.

7

The southern boundary of the site, farthest from the house, is planted with additional deciduous trees, through which a winding walk is planned. Finally the south-west corner contains a specialized garden such as a heather-garden or a bog-garden (if land-drainage allows). The end of this brings us back to the pool and terrace. The centre of the site is planted as a lawn for walking and recreation, from which (as well as from the terrace of the house) the series of gardens round the edge provide a great variety of views.

Figure 5.17 (a, b) Tunnard used the garden at Walton-on-Thames as a theoretical example of a 'typical garden problem' associated with the country acre. (Source: AR, 85 (1939), p. 36)

Figure 5.18 A sketch by Raymond McGrath of the view from Gaulby 'looking S.W. to King's Norton church from the site of the house' suggests that he had selected the house position at the western corner to obtain the best views over the surrounding landscape. (Source: AR, 90 (1941), p. 132)

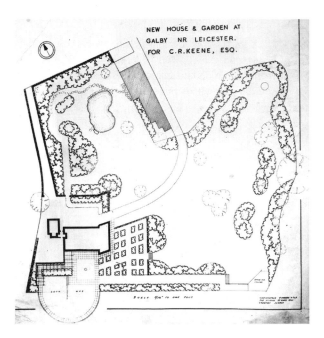

Figure 5.19 The initial proposal for Gaulby by Tunnard in 1937 suggested a bastion-type arrangement in front of the proposed house with a walk along the edge of the grounds to a shelter in the southernmost corner; to the south-east of the house is an array of square beds like those at Walton-on-Thames. (Source: Clark Papers)

Figure 5.20 The shelter proposed by Tunnard in the southern corner, drawn by Gordon Cullen. (Source: *AR*, 83 (1938), p.132)

optical illusion of lengthening the perspective. The plants selected consisted of a range of ornamental plants, some of which with coloured or variegated foliage including: *Cupressus macrocarpa* 'Lutea', *Acer platanoides* 'Schwedleri', *Berberis vulgaris* 'Atropurpurea', *Sambucus nigra* 'Aurea', and *Ligustrum ovalifolium* 'Aureum'. These were fronted with a range of common perennials including; *Iris*, *Geum*, *Monarda didyma*, *Penstemon*, *Malva moschata* 'Alba', *Santolina incana* and *Anemone japonica* 'Alba'.

Third, planting further from the house and where the garden backed onto nearby pinewoods was of a more 'rugged nature'. There bold masses of plants were proposed in order 'to gain a broad and spacious character, rather than intimacy, which has been achieved in the parts of the garden nearest the house'.

The house scheme underwent several redesigns.[21] McGrath's application was refused by the Rural District Council on account of the windows not conforming to accepted specifications.[22] A new design of July 1937 specified traditional materials 'to fit in with the scenery', namely recycled 'bricks from Beaudesert Manor in Yorkshire' (actually Staffordshire) on the ground floor and English elm weatherboarding above. In rather more of a Modernist idiom, the house was elongated and cranked, giving more enclosure to the 'look out'.[23] The projection of this area was to be less pronounced and the array of square beds was to move to its western edge. Where the array of beds had been suggested a circular 'winter garden' was indicated. The shelter, circumferential walk and 'rugged' planting scheme from Clark's drawing remained.

About the start of 1938 Tunnard acquired photographs of the cubist-inspired garden of Villa Noailles at Hyères in France by the architect Gabriel Guevrekian.[24] The original was a triangular garden narrowing to a point where a piece by the

PLAN 1

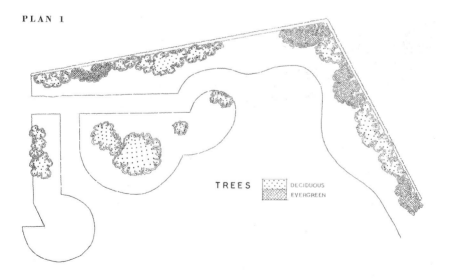

TREES   DECIDUOUS   EVERGREEN

PLAN 2

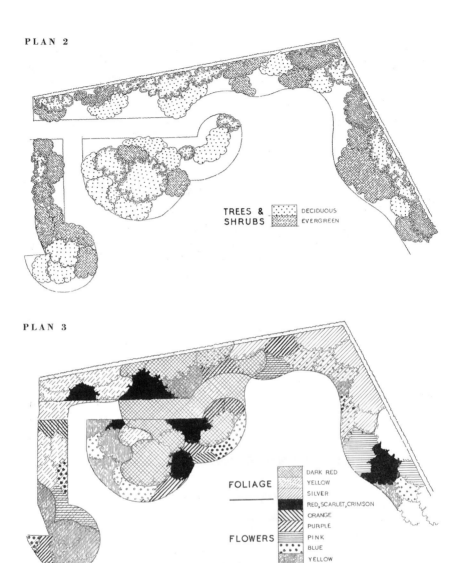

TREES &
SHRUBS
DECIDUOUS
EVERGREEN

PLAN 3

FOLIAGE

FLOWERS

DARK RED
YELLOW
SILVER
RED, SCARLET, CRIMSON
ORANGE
PURPLE
PINK
BLUE
YELLOW
WHITE

PLAN 4

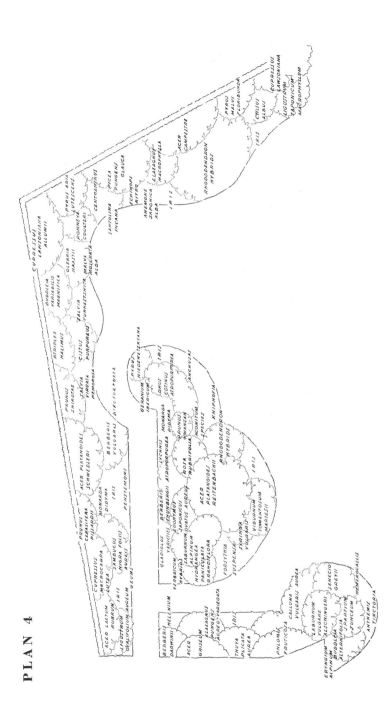

Figure 5.21 (a–d) A series of planting plans for an area along the entrance drive at Gaulby emphasises the aesthetic criteria for plant selection for the various layers: trees, trees and shrubs, flowers.
(Source: Tunnard, Gardens in the Modern Landscape (1938), pp. 119–22)

Figure 5.22 Gabriel Guevrekian's design for a garden at Hyères.
(Source: Tunnard, *Gardens in the Modern Landscape* (1938), p. 70)

cubist sculptor Jacques Lipschitz was placed. The floor of the garden had slightly raised rectangular planters giving a distinctive chequerboard effect. By February 1938 at the latest the south-eastern hedged garden at Gaulby was back but had been revised to a chequerboard pattern clearly inspired by Guevrekian's design at Hyères.[25] It was to be 'planted with alpines and dwarf shrubs set in flat beds between alternate squares of grass and paving'. A low wall in local stone supported this formal garden above the sloping path along the south-west boundary, and where this garden ended, six winding steps led up to the central lawn.[26] The 'look-out' was given a large circular plunge pool.[27] One minor change that took place more or less when Cullen's sketch was being published in March was the circular pool being replaced by a rectangular one with paving around. This was shown on a plan from Christopher Tunnard's practice.[28]

Further changes to the design took place during the detailed design stage which began in the ensuing months.[29] They included shrinking the house.[30] Clark drew a new landscape plan.[31] The essentials remained, but the pool had been replaced by a lawn and boundary planting with a stepping-stone path down to a little outlook house at the best viewpoint. The chequerboard pattern in the hedged garden was

Figure 5.23 A further design for the gardens, required after a redesign of the house, proposed an enclosed garden in a distinctive chequerboard inspired by Gabriel Guevrekian's design at Hyères, France. Sketch by Gordon Cullen.
(Source: Tunnard, *Gardens in the Modern Landscape* (1938), p. 75)

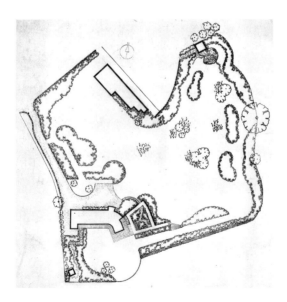

Figure 5.24 The final proposal for Gaulby from Tunnard's practice in 1938. Drawing by Frank Clark.
(Source: Clark Papers)

abandoned for an informal arrangement where Keene's 'alpines and dwarf shrubs' could still be planted, and the shelter was cut out. New, however, was to be a small pavilion – actually built – raised on stilts at the eastern corner of the site. This was to overlook a small pool which was to have been traversed by stepping stones in Japanese style.[32] Calculations for Tunnard's and Clark's planting design were prepared in September 1938 – 'area of borders – forecourt bedding bed; shrub borders surrounding alpine garden; shrub borders on boundary; hedges; turf for edging, forecourt & turf paths in alpine garden'.[33]

This was the scheme as built, except that some raised beds were added to the 'look-out' area.[34] Construction did not start before 1939 and the house probably remained unfinished when war broke out.[35] It was probably completed in 1940 for it to be named 'Carrygate' and photographed in 1941 with some reasonably well-established planting. Tunnard was credited with the 'major portion of the garden'. On the other hand there is no record of plant orders made by Tunnard's practice and it is now uncertain how much of the planting design was implemented. Nevertheless, he had explored on paper, at least, references to the English landscape garden, functionalism, cubism, and oriental garden design. Hussey, after noting Tunnard's 'broad naturalistic plantations of flowering shrubs … to provide interest and colour', remarked that 'the whole garden design is interesting as a reversion to picturesque composition in relation to modern architecture, in place of the extreme formality usually found'.[36]

Figure 5.25   Instead of a pavilion on the edge of the site, one was proposed at the lowest point in the garden overhanging a pond, 'which adopts an aesthetic principle from the Japanese instead of merely borrowing superficial style'. Sketch by Gordon Cullen.
(Source: Tunnard, *Gardens in the Modern Landscape* (1938), p. 93)

Figure 5.26 North front of Gaulby as modified in its final scheme.
(Source: *AR*, 90 (1941), p. 133)

Figure 5.27 View to south from the living room at Gaulby, with rectangular pool in foreground.
(Source: *AR*, 90 (1941), p. 134)

Figure 5.28 Set of three garden views of Gaulby showing Japanese-inspired pavilion and informal planting beds.
(Source: AR, 90 (1941), p. 132)

Bentley Wood, Halland

On McGrath's recommendation, Tunnard became involved at Bentley Wood, the house designed for himself by the architect Serge Chermayeff. He had acquired an exquisite site on high ground overlooking the South Downs. It included an outgrown chestnut and hazel coppice at the upper end, pastureland with neglected hedges further down, and a sand quarry on the eastern boundary. In order to exploit the views, Chermayeff would have to place the house at the high corner of the wood, and to thin out enough trees to create vistas. There was an added inconvenience of a public footpath running very close to this position: the Chermayeffs, who liked to sunbathe nude, were understandably concerned for their privacy.

The project became one of the *causes célèbres* of Modernist architecture in the mid-1930s. Chermayeff's initial idea appears to have been for a six-bay timber house facing south, with an approach from the north-north-west past a long garden wall towards a courtyard that was screened by a service building placed perpendicular to the house.[37] To the east side the courtyard was enclosed by a wall; that at the level of the house and south of it was replaced by a timber frame, mirroring that of the house. To the south of house was a wide terrace, with the area south of the long garden wall including a border and a series of square beds and a small square plunge pool. This garden area appears to have been raised to the south where it was confined by a ha-ha wall, protruding west to a rounded ending.

Chermayeff had submitted his plans to the Uckfield Rural District Council, which rejected them in 1935 on the grounds that the design was 'unsuitable in the particular position chosen'.[38] Chermayeff appealed to the Minister of Health. There was an inquiry after which the inspector reported that the architect 'had tackled with rare seriousness the problem of modern architecture's relationship with its landscape setting'. Hence Chermayeff got his permission in spring 1937.[39]

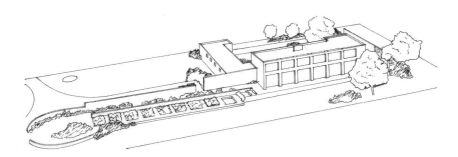

Figure 5.29 Model of the 1935 scheme for Bentley Wood, by Serge Chermayeff for himself, was rejected by the District Council, but was later given permission by the inspector. A sketch by Laurence Pattacini.
(Source: AR (1937), p. 293)

At some point the layout had changed. The position of the drive was altered to the shortest solution, arriving from the east, resulting in the garden wall being repositioned in that direction. Chermayeff 'started clearing the corner of the wood nearest the projected site of the house leaving pleasant groups of trees in open glades'.[40] Tunnard subsequently pondered the two ways of bringing 'a close relationship between house and garden', one referred to as the 'formal method' involving 'the use of hedges, regular curves and lines and architectural planning'. The other was the 'natural method' meaning 'irregular, atmospheric planting'. Chermayeff had selected 'the method predominantly emotional in its appeal; but, with the eye of his profession, he declared in favour of atmospheric showing an architectural character; a free yet controlled scheme, related but in contrast to the formality of the building'. Tunnard conceded that it 'was a subjective and essentially pictorial approach which we eventually made'.

Tunnard wrote that he and Chermayeff then planned much more extensive clearances to show off the more shapely oaks and birches and to reveal sheltered glades running into the wood. He cited William Mason's eighteenth-century dictum of 'three well-mark'd distances' in affirming the desirability of visual gradation with respect to foreground, middle distance and horizon. The long-distance views were achieved by selective clearance of existing woodland but it also required a well-detailed foreground, and a defined middle distance that relied on broad masses.

The area to be cleared would have 'irregular but carefully planned boundaries', whilst informal planting along the edges of the woodland included rounded and columnar evergreens. This would create a 'chain of planting' from the house to the furthest corner, with links including 'bright variegated' plants planted in the

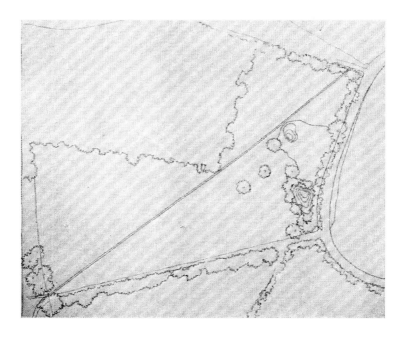

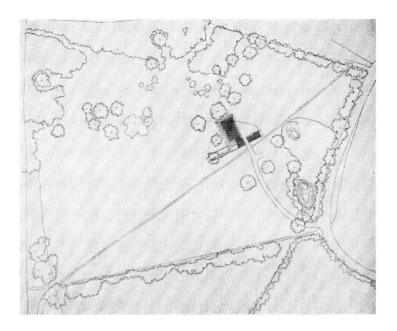

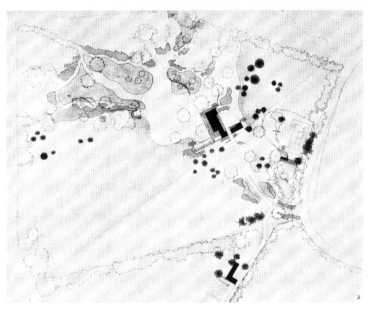

Figure 5.30 (a–c) Three plans indicated the decision-making process with respect to the position of the building. A public footpath crossed the site east of the house. The final drawing indicated how long views were created by opening up the woodland, the extent of the work, and selected new planting (highlighted as dark points).
(Source: *AR*, 85 (1939), p. 62)

middle distance, and other links of red and purple foliage and one of grey foliage. This planting palette was similar to that used at Gaulby, but the selection of plants was much more extensive, ranging from rhododendrons, conifers, lilacs, cotoneasters, magnolias, cherries, and plants with purple or copper foliage; beech, berberis, smoke tree, hazel, etc.[41] He suggested that in the end this planting should emerge from its surroundings as a 'tree line', while the existing planting was otherwise respected.[42]

As to the cleared area, 'after the whole had been grubbed and drained' it was seeded down to grass. Drainage pipes emptied into a shallow ditch that became a planted dell with moisture-loving plants such as primulas, water grasses, astilbes and irises. Drier banks were planted with 'colonies of scillas, bluebells, primroses and foxgloves' that connect with the natural vegetation of 'bluebells, primroses and foxgloves in the wood below'. Also in the dell was a stepping-stone path, leading into the wood where large drifts of daffodils were naturalised under the oaks and birch trees.

Tunnard was involved enough by June 1937 to calculate the seed for 40,000 square feet of lawn, presumably the cleared area.[43] Calculations for the extensive

Figure 5.31 Sketch by Gordon Cullen showing Bentley Wood in its context.
(Source: Tunnard, *Gardens in the Modern Landscape* (1938), p. 76)

Figure 5.32 Bentley Wood from the south showing cleared and restored areas with new grass sward and stepping-stone path through one of the valleys. (Source: AR, 85 (1939), p. 65)

Figure 5.33 Higher ground near the house was dominated by birch trees that were left after the area was selectively cleared and sown with grass. (Source: Shepheard (1953), p. 82)

grassed areas were made in July and the seed ordered in September, while 6,500 daffodils, 1,000 snowdrops and 2,000 chionodoxa ordered at the same time were planted in these areas before the grass was sown. Clark worked on this job in order to get the ground preparation, tree and herbaceous planting and the setting of daffodil bulbs underway during the winter of 1937/8. When the daffodils flowered the next spring the house was still under construction.

A kitchen garden and orchard were located away from the house, at the site where a gardener's cottage was proposed, screened with a line of gorse. This kitchen garden was to contain vegetables and herbs, with Jerusalem artichokes delegated to a separate bed, but including: potatoes, onions, Brussels sprouts, broccoli, leeks, tomatoes, cos lettuce, as well as sage, parsley, mint, chives, and thyme.[44] Proposed tennis courts and pavilion were to be located in the sand quarry and planted with heathers and prostrate brooms.

Chermayeff recollected that he and Henry Moore saw the terrace under the eastern wing wall as an opportunity to manipulate perspective and to juxtapose disparate elements, biomorphic and geometric, representative and abstract, by means of the open frame at the end through which the view was seen under the canopy of a mature tree. This surreal quality was heightened by the thinning of the woods and the planting of daffodils with the deepest yellows closest to the viewer.[45] Chermayeff placed a reclining figure by Moore at the end of the terrace as the foreground to the views southwards;[46] he had commissioned the Hornton stone recumbent figure for £300 and paid a deposit of £50 in 1938.

Chermayeff wanted Tunnard to help with the planting on the terraces by the house.[47] The latter referred to that under the eastern wing wall as a 'garden', and proposed to stock it with a range of tender plants and a traditional 'mingled flower border' with mostly low-growing species of shrubby character selected for wind resistance that provided interest throughout the year. His plant section sought to provide interest all year round, rather than having been planted for special colour effect, and included *Camellia, Berberidopsis corallina, Choisya, Azara microphylla* and *Feijoa*. There was also a border for scented bedding plants, a pool for waterlilies and a small rectilinear lawn. In the autumn that year tree ivy was planted by the Moore sculpture at the end of the terrace in order to link it with the landscape beyond.

The terrace immediately outside the living room was given a narrow border of low plants selected to provide a year-round colourful effect. This planting included: *Juniperus squamata* 'Meyeri', *Veronica cupressoides, Saxifraga megasaeflora, Penstemon heterophyllus, Muehlenbeckia complexa* and *Yucca gloriosa*, with *Sedum monstrosum, Equisetum scirpioides, Sedum acre*, and *Polygonum baldschuanicum* in the paving cracks. A wisteria was planted against the house, an obvious reference to that in the same position at St Ann's Hill. Further climbers were added to the house the following autumn: two Russian vines to cover the front, a pear espalier and two cordon pears on the west wall, a Japanese quince on the north wall, escallonias on the terrace wall, and vines and clematis on the pergola. The garage was to be planted with more Russian vines and Virginia creeper.[48] These two terraces were the only areas of true garden, and for them Tunnard provided planting plans.[49]

Figure 5.34 Sculpture by Henry Moore was placed at the end of the terrace.
(Source: *AR*, 85 (1939), p. 66)

Figure 5.35 Garden terrace of Bentley Wood, with sculpture by Henry Moore.
(Source: Tunnard, *Gardens in the Modern Landscape* (1948), p. 68)

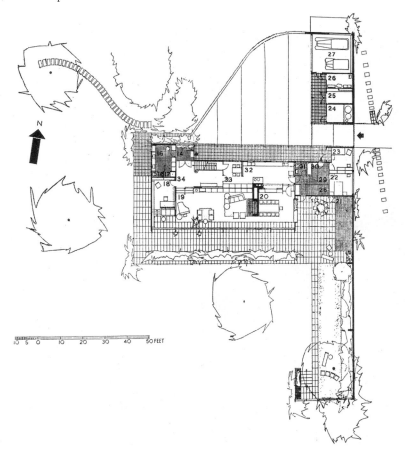

Figure 5.36 Ground-floor plan and terraces at Bentley Wood.
         (Source: Shepheard (1953), p. 84)

Tunnard noted that the main lessons emerging from this project for him were
to meet an architect who believed in planting as part of architecture, and that the
use of local materials was not necessary, but that it is important to utilise natural
features on the site. This is what he believed made 'architecture a part of the
countryside'.[50] Ideas about the countryside coming 'right up to the house', with the
use of the terrace wall in a Bauhaus manner in order to incorporate the landscape
within the realm of the house, the views through a timber frame, the paving being
carried through from the inside of the house onto the terrace, the use of pergolas
to link the house with the service building, and use of trelliswork on the balcony
in order to encourage climbing plants to link house with landscape, all seem to
have derived from Chermayeff.[51]

Yet the respective roles of the two men have been variously interpreted. Jim
Richards, who went to stay at Halland on occasions before Chermayeff sold it in

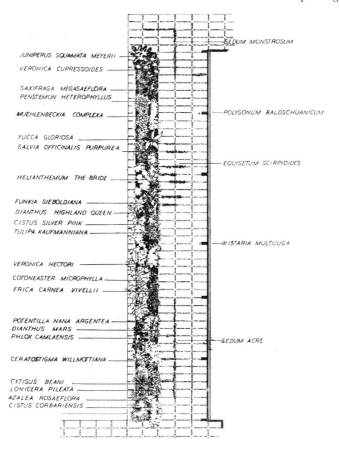

Figure 5.37 Planting plan of the terrace border at Bentley Wood immediately in front of the living-room. Drawing by Christopher Tunnard.
(Source: *L&G* (Spring 1939), p. 27)

August 1939, remembered they did not discuss the garden much, but recollected that the further areas consisted of a little earthmoving and areas mown close in various shapes. He thought that Tunnard collaborated with Chermayeff in the design of the terrace leading to the Moore sculpture.[52] Tunnard's involvement was not acknowledged in the two *Country Life* articles by Christopher Hussey, even though the landscape was discussed.[53] Sir Geoffrey Jellicoe said that when he accidentally met Chermayeff in the Museum of Modern Art in New York after the war, he was told that he had very little help from Tunnard.[54] Chermayeff told another that Tunnard was particularly retained for advice on 'plant material and advice on plant arrangement exclusively to form my own specific landscape plans'.[55] Even at the end of his life Chermayeff was keen to limit Tunnard's contribution:[56]

Figure 5.38 Bentley Wood by night, emphasising the intimate inside-outside relationship. (Source: *AR*, 85 (1939), p. 66)

> I called in Tunnard at the suggestion of my friend Raymond McGrath to help me in identifying plants by their proper names for the terrace of our New House. All the other Landscaping was completed by me before the House itself was finished. Tunnard did not in any way assist.

However, Chermayeff's remembrance was not entirely accurate and illustrates the problems of attribution in cases where landscapes are created in close collaboration between client and designer. Tunnard's own practice notes reveal that he was involved over the clearances already by June 1937 (only a few weeks after planning permission was obtained), made calculations and ordered the grass seed, wild flower seed and great quantities of bulbs for the cleared areas, and specified and ordered vast numbers of trees, shrubs, bog plants, and other material for the terraces, kitchen garden and wider landscape.[57] Frank Clark attended to supervise. Letters between Chermayeff and Tunnard show that at one time they worked together very closely; in August 1938 Chermayeff was flatteringly wishing that 'our respected collaborator & good friend Coney Tunnard would fix his own day next week to a) discuss & b) to stay i.e. first guest in new house'.

Chermayeff's desire to limit the credit to Tunnard may have stemmed from Tunnard's article in *L&G* entitled 'Planning a Modern Garden: An Experience in Collaboration' which gave the impression that theirs was a collaboration of equals. This may well have irritated Chermayeff who was, as client and architect, the dominant side of the relationship and, at this perilous time in his career, would be unwilling to share the credit elsewhere. Apparently there was no sign of the formerly good relations when both were in America.

Claremont, Esher

In *AR* in March 1935 there were two articles extolling the virtues of apartment blocks in parkland as the modern democratic equivalent of the country house. One was by Walter Gropius and Maxwell Fry who had been commissioned by Isokon to design some such blocks at St Leonard's Hill near Windsor.[58] The assumption was that the country house itself was doomed, but that the park and estate attached continued to have aesthetic value for modern society. The alternative to unrestrained suburban sprawl covering the parkland, of which there were many examples to be seen, was, then, to replace the old house with a population – including servants – of 40 people with 'concentrated development' capable to accommodating 500 people who would collectively keep the amenity of the parkland.

These ideas were very similar to the basic philosophy of Le Corbusier's project for '*La Ville Radieuse*', also published in 1935. That provoked intense interest amongst architects and urbanists as it provided an image of how the city of the future might appear. With tall blocks providing the floorspace required in a city, the ground could be devoted to communications and greenspace – 'a vertical garden city', Le Corbusier claimed.

William Arthur Eden, in the third of his lengthy articles in *AR* about the English countryside, looked at 'The Re-birth of the Tradition'; that is, the tradition of improving the countryside as required for contemporary use. Eden's example was, somewhat cheekily, Blenheim Palace.[59] He noted that 'every day great estates are being broken up and broken into by the speculative builder'. He showed montages of how Blenheim could look if the speculative builder took it over, and another of Blenheim 'developed on another principle'; that is, a block of flats housing 120 families.

Tunnard was expanding his knowledge of garden history in 1936 and it was to be expected that he would visit the famous landscape gardens of Surrey: Claremont, Esher, Oatlands, and Painshill. He was dismayed that the first two had been sold to developers in the 1920s and were being divided up. The golf course at Oatlands was not an entirely happy solution, he thought, but had been made 'without detracting in any great measure from the original character of the estate'.[60] He feared for Painshill, and suggested that the landscape garden might be saved if the house was redeveloped as a hotel or as a block of flats.

No doubt his enthusiasm for the landscape garden was not just aesthetic, as a suitable setting for modern architecture as at Joldwynds and St Ann's Hill, but also because a vision of the communal gardens surrounding Le Corbusier's and Gropius's apartment blocks needed crystallising. Maxwell Fry and W.A. Eden had assumed that, in the English context at least, it would be parkland which would thereby be saved. Tunnard undertook his own exercise to see how differently Claremont could have been developed.[61]

Having derided the conventional 'butcher method' of dividing up the land into lots, Tunnard then introduced his 'suggested re-development' of six ten-storey

THE   BUTCHER   METHOD

Developed by five distinct firms of builders, the extent of whose operations to date is shown in the plan above, the Claremont Estate was inevitably cut up into small enclosures, a process which will no doubt continue until there is nothing left to cut up.   Thus, despite all the developers can do to retain the amenities (and they have tried hard), the real amenity, represented by the free landscape of Kent and Brown, is destroyed.

THE   NEW   INCLOSURE
[WHITE REPRESENTS OPEN SPACE. BLACK, INCLOSURE]

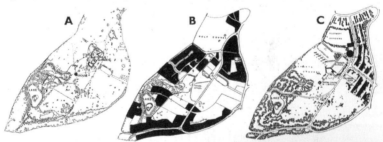

In place of the old landlord's inclosure there is taking place all over the countryside a new and more concentrated form of inclosure which in parcelling the landscape into minute private properties is acting more seriously against the interests of the community than did the old. Estates such as Claremont, A, are becoming permanently sterilized as built-over areas, B, while with a rational planning of the whole area, and the concentration of dwellings in certain parts of it, more people might be housed yet and virtually the whole estate might be left open for the benefit of the residents and public, C.

Figure 5.39 Tunnard's hypothetical project for Claremont was a response to its division into building lots. Tunnard would have wished for a more concentrated approach to dwelling, leaving the majority of the estate as a public amenity. (Source: Tunnard, *Gardens in the Modern Landscape* (1938), p. 149)

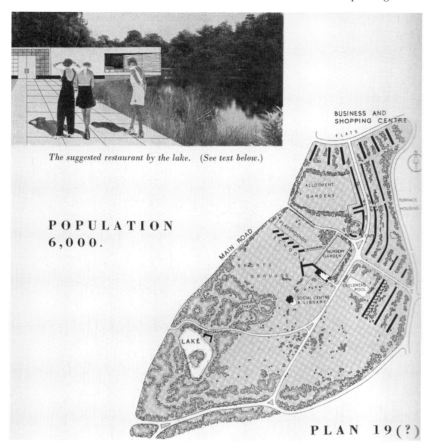

The suggested restaurant by the lake. (*See text below.*)

POPULATION 6,000.

PLAN 19(?)

Figure 5.40 Instead of detached houses Tunnard for Claremont proposed parallel blocks of flats and terraced housing with communal grounds set in parkland. (Source: Tunnard, *Gardens in the Modern Landscape* (1938), p. 152)

blocks of flats on the land closest to the town of Esher, to which was attached an area of allotment gardens, terraced housing, schools and playing fields on the way to the most valuable part of the landscape garden. Apart from a restaurant on the lake, this was left open for the recreation of the 6,000 inhabitants. There was a wealth of historical information on Claremont, and Clark drew plans for how the landscape would have been in 1816, another depicting how it actually was in 1938, and a third on how it could have been if Tunnard's suggestions had been followed. Gordon Cullen provided some photomontages.

Figure 5.41 Photomontage of the Claremont scheme by Gordon Cullen.
(Source: Tunnard, *Gardens in the Modern Landscape* (1938), p. 151)

Hill House, Hampstead

Gerald Schlesinger commissioned a further house, said to have been for his estranged wife and their daughter, in 1938. He commissioned Oliver Hill to design the house, and he built a red-brick house 'in the style of Mies van der Rohe' with accommodation for one lady with boudoir and balcony attached, a child in the night nursery, two maids and a guest room.[62]

The plot of land that Schlesinger had acquired was at 87 Redington Road, a steep road and an even steeper plot, on Telegraph Hill in Hampstead, though facing south. Hill placed the house on the slightly flatter top of the site, giving space for terracing round the house, but at the cost of a lengthy uphill path from the

Figure 5.42 Located at the top of Telegraph Hill, Hampstead, Hill House was designed by the architect Oliver Hill, with Tunnard responsible for the planting. (Source: AR, 85 (1939), p. 187)

garage by the road to the 'entrance portico'. A wall on the north side of this path separated off an area labelled as a 'kitchen garden' and reached from the kitchen at the eastern end of the house.

Hill had designed a loggia, terraces and paved walks around the house, with associated steps and retaining walls, no doubt so that the view could be enjoyed whilst sitting out. The rest of the garden was designed by Christopher Tunnard.[63] A terrace stretched south to a circle of paving. To its west the ground could be left as a lawn 'at natural levels', and further west to the boundary was a heath garden and a small area for roses. To its east curved terraces were approximated to the lie of the land, giving three grass walks one above another, and in between flowering shrubs covered the banks.

The house was dubbed 'Hill House', no doubt as a pun on Hill's name that suited the sloping site. Tunnard's practice made calculations for walls, borders and lawns. Red 'Noelite' stone was ordered from August 1938, and the first plant order was in October.[64] Amongst other plants, privet, hypericum, irises and lupins were specified. It is impossible now to assess the scheme further, as the garden was largely built over in the 1970s.

Block of apartments, 10 Palace Gate, Kensington

Tunnard must have been given an opportunity to assist on a block of flats at 10, Palace Gate, Kensington, through its architect Wells Coates (1895–1958), one of

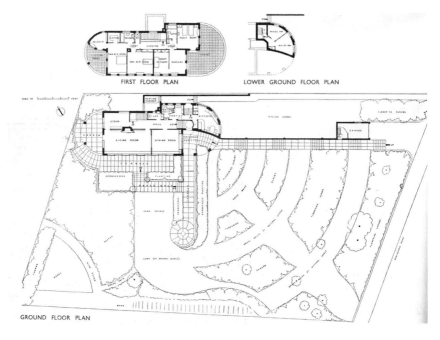

FIRST FLOOR PLAN

LOWER GROUND FLOOR PLAN

GROUND FLOOR PLAN

Figure 5.43 The landscape proposals for Hill House provided bands of shrubs to the
south, providing level grass walks in between, while heather was planted to
north of the house to link with the Heath.
(Source: AR, 85 (1939), p. 188)

Figure 5.44 (a–c) A block of apartments in Palace Gate, Kensington, by the architect Wells Coates redefined apartment living, with luxury flats with double height spaces, large balconies and sliding glass walls. Sketches by Gordon Cullen.
(Source: *AR*, 85 (1939), pp. 183–4)

the pioneers of the Modern Movement in England. Nearly the whole basement of the building was given over to garaging, and two ramps, one on either side of the entrance, provided access to it. Tunnard was probably commissioned quite late on in this project, when he was given responsibility for the 'ground between the ramps and the building and the triangular corner at the north-west' which he planted with shrubs and turf. He also probably initiated proposals for the east side of the building, where the remainder of the site was 'laid out as a terrace garden, sub-divided for the private use of the ground floor flats whose living rooms open on to it'.[65] Tunnard's ledger included calculations for soil replacement, planting, paving and water-worn cobbles.[66]

Emboldened by this connection with Coates, Tunnard proposed a landscape scheme for an earlier block of flats designed by him, the Lawn Road flats in Hampstead.[67] These had been built in 1933/4 for Isokon, a furniture company, and were famous both for being described as an ocean liner by Agatha Christie, a resident, and as the home of several émigrés, including Walter and Ise Gropius, Marcel Breuer and Lazslo Moholy-Nagy. Tunnard was writing to the owner, Jack Pritchard, in February 1939, and by the time of the ILA exhibition in June was showing a 'plan of garden for restaurant, Lawn Road Flats'.[68] At the same exhibition he provided a photograph of 'Entrance Planting at Highpoint II', so it is possible that he worked with Berthold Lubetkin (1901–1990) on finishing that project.

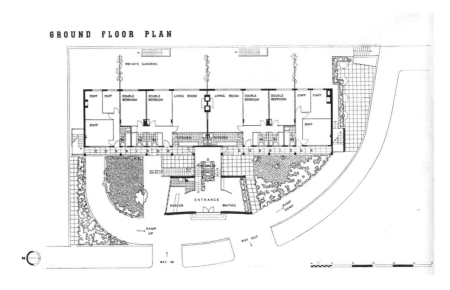

Figure 5.45 Tunnard provided the landscape design for a block of flats in Palace Gate, London consisting of planting on left-over triangular areas alongside the slopes down to the basement garaging.
(Source: *AR*, 85 (1939), p. 176)

Landscape designs in America

Tunnard had spoken about modern gardens in the USA in a lecture to the ILA in 1947.[69] The passage in question was expanded and illustrated as an extra chapter, 'Modern American Gardens', in the second edition of *Gardens in the Modern Landscape*.[70] Many of the examples were ones to which Tunnard had contributed. The captions carefully noted which architect had designed the houses, from which it appears that several architects connected with Harvard and Walter Gropius sought Tunnard out once he was in America, perhaps hoping that the collaborations with Raymond McGrath and Serge Chermayeff could be replicated across the Atlantic.

One of them was Carl Koch (1913–1999), who had studied architecture at Harvard, and was an ardent admirer of Gropius. He had worked both for Sven Markelius in Sweden and for Gropius, but in the early 1940s, when he collaborated with Tunnard, he was in private practice.[71] One project was for the layout of a development of small houses on a steeply sloping hillside at Belmont, MA,

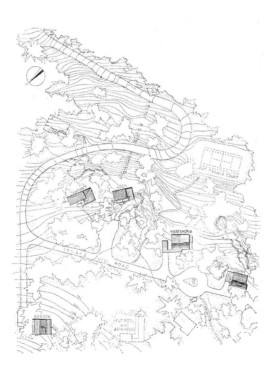

Figure 5.46 Tunnard's association with architects helped to provide him with further opportunities; here a small housing development at Snake Hill Road, Belmont, MA, by Koch and Tunnard, showing positioning of houses, including Koch's own country house, and new approach road on steeply sloping site. It included proposed communal facilities.
(Source: Tunnard, *Gardens in the Modern Landscape* (1948), p. 173)

a small version of the sort of exercise that Tunnard was tutoring his students in. They also collaborated on the design of a Defense Housing Project in Stamford, CT, in 1941.[72] Koch's own small town garden in Cambridge had already featured as one of the examples in Margaret Olthof Goldsmith's *Designs for Outdoor Living* (1941),[73] and Tunnard, who was mentioned too in this book,[74] suggested improvements that were implemented and featured in the second edition of Tunnard's *Gardens*. Tunnard altered the orthogonal layout to one at a diagonal, suggesting that it had been 'made to appear larger by diagonal emphasis', on the basis that diagonals give the longest vistas possible. Another reason for the diagonal may, though, have been his preference for 'balance on a diagonal axis' over symmetrical design.[75] Local stone was used in the perimeter wall, and to make a raised bed. On this bed and elsewhere Tunnard placed tree roots, in the manner of *objets trouvées*, and mentioned that this was 'after meeting Paul Nash in England'.

G. Holmes Perkins (1904–2003) was a native of Cambridge, MA, who had likewise studied architecture at Harvard.[76] He built himself a Modernist residence in Brookline, MA, in 1938, and involved Tunnard at two private residences in the same state. The Monks' residence was in wooded country at Lincoln, where the layout was, again, on the diagonal, paths were of the stepping-stone variety, and there was a low retaining wall of local stone broken by a flight of steps, much like that at Gaulby. The other, at Winchester, stood at the top of a mainly open slope down to a lake. The landscape garden treatment was appropriate here, and a stepping-stone path, starting at the broad garden terrace, swung around the perimeter of the lawn on its way down to the landing stage.

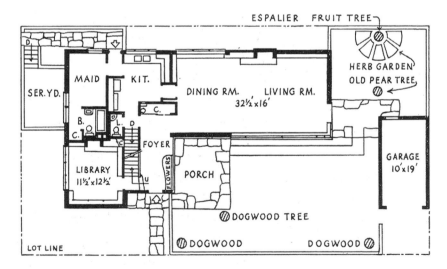

Figure 5.47 The original layout for the architect Carl Koch's own house at Cambridge, MA, was orthogonal, relating to the house.
(Source: Goldsmith (1941), p. 136)

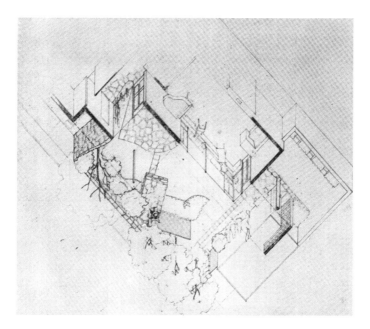

Figure 5.48 Tunnard revised the layout of Carl Koch's garden by introducing a diagonal
emphasis in order to make it appear larger.
(Source: Tunnard, *Gardens in the Modern Landscape* (1948), p. 168)

Figure 5.49 Carl Koch's garden with '"*objet trouvé*" of surrealist invention' installed by
Tunnard inspired 'after meeting Paul Nash in England'.
(Source: Tunnard, *Gardens in the Modern Landscape* (1948), p. 168)

Figure 5.50 Paul Nash's *'objet'* was noted as conveying an 'equal significance to that of a
sculptured form'.
(Source: Tunnard, *Gardens in the Modern Landscape* (1938), p. 95)

Towards the latter part of World War II, the centre of Tunnard's circle of
acquaintances shifted to the vicinity of Yale. One commission that was modest
enough, but which brought him closer to the art world in America, was another
terrace supported with local stone at the home of James Thrall Soby (1906–1979)
in Farmington, CT. Soby's family had been successful in manufacturing and in a
tobacco business, enabling him to indulge his artistic passions as an author, critic,
connoisseur, collector and patron of the arts. In 1936 he acquired and modern-
ised the Greek Revival house. One of his many painter and sculptor friends was
Alexander Calder who supplied and installed a well-head mobile in the garden
in 1938. Soby was also great friends with Henry-Russell Hitchcock, the architect
and architectural historian, who designed a gallery addition to the house for Soby's
modern paintings. Soby curated numerous exhibitions for the Museum of Modern
Art (MOMA) in New York over the years, and in 1940 started his formal association with that institution by joining its Acquisitions and Photography committees.
He was made a trustee in 1942 and played a prominent role in MOMA's affairs
till the 1960s.

The connection to Soby may well have been how Tunnard came to produce
a garden plan for MOMA, though Joseph Hudnut had connections there too.[77]
Its collection had been rehoused in 1939 on West 53 Street in an International

Figure 5.51 The Koch garden in various seasons.
(Source: Tunnard, *Gardens in the Modern Landscape* (1948), p. 169)

Figure 5.52 (a, b) Project for a sculpture garden at the Museum of Modern Art by
Tunnard, with plan on a diagonal and exhibits including Standing Youth by
Wilhelm Lehmbruck (1913).
(Source: Tunnard, *Gardens in the Modern Landscape* (1948), p. 174)

Style building designed by Philip L. Goodwin (1885–1958) and Edward Durell Stone (1902–1978). The first garden, designed by its curator of architecture, John McAndrew (1904–1978), had been a hurried affair. It had two colours of pebbles and sculpture was positioned within spaces defined by wooden screens. The few trees were augmented by potted plants. The museum asked Goodwin in 1942 to provide a design for a restaurant addition and a new garden layout to include an outdoor dining area. His idea was a grid of plane trees with tables and chairs scattered underneath and with the sculpture placed around the perimeter of the grid.

Tunnard prepared his landscape design in 1946, and he later showed a photograph of a model in the second edition of *Gardens in the Modern Landscape*.[78] He claimed that the garden would have been 'completely redesigned to harmonize with the proposed structural alterations'. Once more using a diagonal arrangement in this small space, and stone walls around raised grass panels and planting beds, there was much in common with Koch's even smaller town garden. Whereas in Cambridge Tunnard had placed twisted tree roots to effect, at MOMA he could have had the chance of a real sculpture garden. However, Tunnard's proposals were overlooked, and at length, in 1953, Philip Johnson, with landscape architect James Fanning, were retained to design the new Sculpture Garden.

The MOMA garden marked a move towards designs in the public sphere, particularly those with sculpture or memorial. This appears to have been deliberate, as he became less interested in maintaining some presence in the landscape design world than in testing his ideas on urbanism and on art in the public sphere. Tunnard used a model for the MOMA garden, and when drawings were required he generally used others, often young architects with far greater graphics ability than himself, to illustrate his ideas.

In 1947 Tunnard was a member of the team that submitted a scheme for the Jefferson National Expansion Memorial Competition on the St. Louis waterfront.[79] Three young New York architects came together with him. William N. Breger (b. 1923) had been a student of Walter Gropius at Harvard, and had worked for him. Caleb Hornbostel (1905–1991) had worked for Edward Durell Stone in 1936–1938 on drawings for the Museum of Modern Art, and George Sherman Lewis (1916–1993) worked for the architectural firm of Skidmore, Owings & Merrill and then briefly for Marcel Breuer. The Breger, Horncastle and Lewis partnership appears to have been for the Jefferson National Expansion Memorial Competition only. Winning third prize was no mean achievement as there were hundreds of entries.[80] The central feature was a pair of immensely tall marble shafts, the opening 'orientated to the western horizon' and 'the form of the monument suggests a funnel, through which the surge of western migration passed'. Perhaps reflecting Tunnard's emerging views on art in the city, 'the wing walls at the base of the monument are treated with sculptural reliefs in panels … A figure suggestive of Jefferson the man stands at the approach to the site'. The layout was of open parkland surrounded by trees – 'the tree forms and masses were studied on a scale model' – amongst which were set museums, a theatre and an area for reconstructed buildings.

In the same year Tunnard was a member of the Connecticut State Site Selection

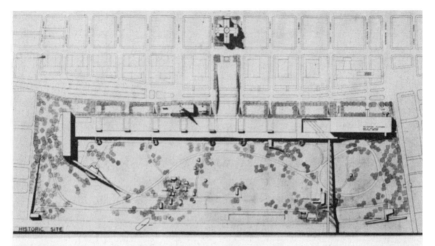

FIRST STAGE A single great idea in the form of a terrace carried through with conviction made this a Jury choice.

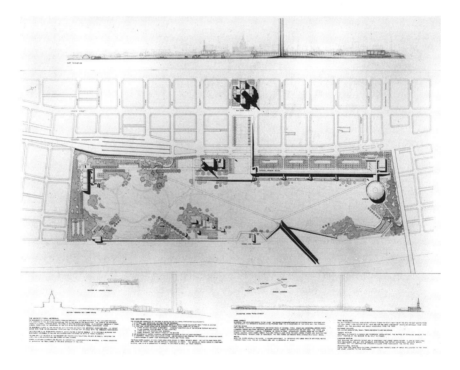

Figure 5.53 (a, b) Tunnard's team won third prize in the competition for the Jefferson National Expansion Memorial, which was won by Eleil Saarinen and his team. The competition went through two phases: initial submission (top) and final submission (bottom).
(Source: *Architectural Record* 103 (1948), p. 98)

Figure 5.54 Sketch of project for Jefferson Memorial by team involving Tunnard that
won third place.
(Source: *Progressive Architecture*, 29 (1948), p. 62)

Committee for the United Nations.[81] Two years later he produced his own proposal
for gardens at the United Nations Headquarters in New York.[82] George Sherman
Lewis may have been a help here, as in 1948 he had joined the United Nations
Planning Office where he contributed to the design of the secretariat building. In
Tunnard's view 'the site is so completely dominated by the building masses that
any formal or axial treatment … could not succeed in appearing anything but
arbitrary', so he proposed that the geometry should be 'softened by the weaving
of the tree pattern, which, with its irregular bays and openings, provides a setting for sculpture not always immediately seen'. A sketch also suggested several
fountains.[83] It would have been a public space, apart from an enclosed delegate's
garden situated between the General Assembly and Secretariat buildings. Here
there would be 'several quiet spaces and a good deal more colour in the way of
flowers, mosaic pavements and mural paintings on the walls', and Tunnard hoped
for 'a number of sculptures which it is hoped the United Nations will commission
from the world's great artists'.

Such projects appealed to his instincts for site planning and civic art, but in
1949 he was drawn back into designing a smaller garden, probably as a favour,
or possibly to try out current ideas in garden design. Tunnard sent photographs

Figure 5.55 Tunnard's project for the garden surrounding of the United Nations
Headquarters in New York.
(Source: *AR* 106 (1949), p. 336)

of a design to Peter Shepheard to be included in *Modern Gardens* (1953).[84] The
property was the summer residence of George Henry Warren, Jr, and his wife
Katherine in Newport, RI.[85] George, Sr, had been a notable collector of furniture,
and Katherine was a founder member of MOMA's Committee on the Museum
Collections, chaired by James Thrall Soby. This was probably how a gilt bronze
abstract sculpture, Jean Arp's 'Chimerical Font', came to be set in a rectangular
pool at the end of the central lawn. Soby was very interested in Arp's work, who
visited his house in Farmington sometime when he was in the United States in
1949 and 1950. 'Chimerical Font' had been made in 1947,[86] and it seems likely
that it was shipped over from Europe for the Warrens two years later.

This was another design with a diagonal axis. To the sides of the central lawn
fountains were set in small basins, perhaps a subconscious link to the theme of the
sculpture, and these were embraced by small hedged semicircles, reminiscent of
Tunnard's idea for the sculpture garden at Walton-on-Thames. This time, though,
there was no stepping-stone path, and no local stone walling. Instead, the hedged
semicircles were set amongst planting beds in organic shapes. The obvious inspiration was the designs of Roberto Burle Marx. From 1943 – when MOMA held an
exhibition on 'Brazil Builds', with the catalogue by Philip L. Goodwin – and for the
rest of the 1940s, professional periodicals in North America and Europe (including
the *Architectural Review*) reported on Brazilian architecture, ensuring that Marx's
work came to notice. In particular, Marx's roof gardens in Rio de Janeiro were
much admired for their swirling organic forms, so novel to those tired of European
modernist austerity. His forms were redrawn by Sylvia Crowe,[87] and adapted by
Geoffrey Jellicoe for a roof garden at Harvey's in Guildford, Surrey.

Figure 5.56 Perhaps inspired by the work of Roberto Burle Marx in 1949, Tunnard
created sinuous patterns in this private garden for George Henry Warren Jr.'s
summer residence at Newport, RI.
(Source: Shepheard (1953), p. 80)

Tunnard's adoption of similar forms in Newport symbolised his disenchantment
with the pre-war Modernism he had once promoted so earnestly. Like many in
England, he felt that Modernism had become formulaic, observing that: 'the modern movement has drifted into many curious forms and mannerisms'.[88] He took a
keen interest in Nikolaus Pevsner's new advocacy of the picturesque, and the rise
of neo-Palladianism promoted by Rudolf Wittkower. Frank Clark, now an expert
on the landscape garden, and with several publications, proclaimed in his *English
Landscape Garden* (1948), that 'the English had invented a new environment …
The irregular informal landscape … was the enemy of the monumental, of geometry, of regularity and the formal'.[89] Tunnard agreed, speculating that 'Sharawadgi'
– the picturesque beauty of the irregular – about which he, Clark and Pevsner had
been writing, 'might well have a present-day application'.[90]

Another indicator of his new interests was the design for the garden of Shaw
Mansion, the premises and museum of the New London County Historical Society
in New London, CT. The society had acquired the modest and much altered garden attached to a mid-eighteenth-century house in 1907. It most notable feature
was a summerhouse of 1792 on a rocky knoll. Tunnard's design, this time drawn by
himself, concentrated upon making useful level spaces by hedges, retaining walls,
paths and steps.[91] Immediately behind the house he devised or adapted flower beds
laid out in the eighteenth-century manner. The scheme was awarded a Bronze

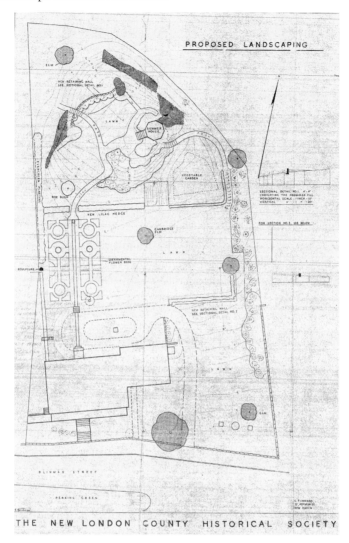

Figure 5.57 The proposals for the Shaw Mansion, New London, CT, was an historicist
   scheme.
   (Source: New London County Historical Society)

Medal by the Federated Garden Clubs of Connecticut for the Outstanding Civic
Project of 1949.[92] Although perhaps not too much should be read into modest
changes for an historical society, their general tenor, and the historicist garden area
in particular, show a surprising indifference to the ideals of Modernism.

During a visit to England in the summer of 1947 Tunnard had met up with Clark
again.[93] Tunnard may have been 'struck all over again by the quality of its greatest
works of landscape architecture',[94] but it became apparent how his interests had

Figure 5.58 The summer house in the rear of the garden of Shaw Mansion.
(Source: New London County Historical Society)

diverged from those of his old friend. Clark was loyal to their former joint venture in examining history for hints of how the Zeitgeist of an age generated its forms, and retained his special passion for the landscape garden. During World War II, Clark had undertaken extensive reading in the British Library as his shiftwork for the Light Rescue Service (i.e. of people in bombed houses) permitted. He was lionised by Wittkower and Pevsner for his insights into romanticism and the picturesque. After the war Clark worked briefly for the London County Council and then from the academic year 1946/7 took on the two-days-per-week teaching on the Reading landscape diploma course which Geoffrey Jellicoe had provided before the war. During his time at Reading, Clark continued the search for ideas and forms that were appropriate to landscape design in the twentieth century.[95]

Tunnard's new fervour for the primacy of the 'socio-economic process of town planning' was to the chagrin of Clark who was to be appointed in 1949 as consultant landscape architect for the Festival of Britain 1951. In this position he was responsible for the most exciting landscape architectural work in Britain since the war. Tunnard, though, disapproved of the Festival, seeing it as a piece of mere frivolity, not addressing the social needs of the time.[96]

Nevertheless Tunnard evidently remained willing to contribute to further museum and art centre projects. Stone asked his advice when designing the Fine

Arts Centre at the University of Arkansas, opened 1951. In 1952 he was landscape architect to the sculpture garden, whilst Louis Kahn (1901–1974) was architect, of the new Yale Art Gallery.[97] His scope there was severely curtailed, though, by mature elm trees casting their canopy over much of the garden. Tunnard's landscape architectural commissions were by that time becoming scarce. He had no design office to support him, and anyway he found teaching and writing absorbing most of his interest and time. Indeed, his deepening convictions in community planning were leading him to disengage from design altogether.

Notes

1 Tunnard credited Clark with the following: the thumbnail plans to accompany Gordon Cullen's sketches (*AR* 83: 198); the Minimum Garden and the base plan of Claremont (*AR* 84: 115); and the sketches of the All-Europe House (*Journal of the RIBA* 86: 815). Most of Tunnard's practice's other plans have similar styles of draughtsmanship to these.
2 Cane (1930), 'Public Parks'.
3 Hanson (July 1977), 'Rhapsody in Black Glass', p. 64.
4 Tunnard (March 1938), 'The Garden in the Modern Landscape', *AR*, 83 (1938), p. 127.
5 Ibid., p. 131.
6 Ibid., p. 130; also *Gardens in the Modern Landscape* (1938), p. 132.
7 Interview, David Jacques with Willi Soukop, 24 February 1989.
8 See photograph in *AR*, 83 (1938), p. 132.
9 Tunnard, *Gardens in the Modern Landscape* (1938), p. 180; *L&G* (Spring 1939), p. 39.
10 Interview, David Jacques with Willy Soukop, 24 February 1989.
11 Tunnard (March 1939), 'Architects' Plants', p. 147.
12 Anon. (Spring 1937), 'Garden Work by Christopher Tunnard', showed photographs of the roof garden and the pool courtyard. *AR* (September 1937), pp. 117–22, also carried photographs of St Ann's Hill.
13 Tunnard, *Gardens in the Modern Landscape* (1938), p. 72.
14 Tunnard (February 1939), 'The Country Acre'.
15 Kitson (September 1990), 'A Country House near Leicester'.
16 Anon. (November 1941), 'House at Galby (sic), Leicestershire'.
17 Hussey (7 August 1942), 'Carrygate, Leicestershire', p. 268.
18 Christopher Tunnard AILA, photograph of initial garden plan for Norton Gorse; Clark Papers, 758/69. The draughtsmanship appears to have been Clark's.
19 Tunnard (March 1938), 'The Garden in the Modern Landscape', *AR*, 83 (1938), p. 132.
20 Tunnard, *Gardens in the Modern Landscape* (1938), pp. 118–22.
21 Kitson (September 1990), 'A Country House near Leicester', examined the sequence of drawings for Gaulby generated by McGrath's practice.
22 *AR*, 90 (November 1941), pp. 132–4.
23 RIBA Drawings Collection, McGrath Collection, drawing 173/16; illustrated in Brown (1989), Plate 157.
24 Tunnard (April 1938), 'The Functional Aspect of Garden Planning', p. 195.
25 Tunnard, *Gardens in the Modern Landscape* (1938), p. 70.
26 Tunnard (March 1938), 'The Garden in the Modern Landscape', *AR*, 83 (1938), sketch by Gordon Cullen.
27 Tunnard, *Gardens in the Modern Landscape* (1938), p. 75, inset plan.
28 Kitson (September 1990), 'A Country House near Leicester', p. 24; source not given.

29 Raymond McGrath, plans for the services, May and October 1938, in the possession of Mr and Mrs Townsend, the owners of the property as at 1989.

30 Anon. (November 1941), 'House at Galby (sic), Leicestershire'.

31 Christopher Tunnard AILA, photograph of revised garden plan for Norton Gorse; Clark Papers, 758/69.

32 Tunnard, *Gardens in the Modern Landscape* (1938), p. 93, sketch by Gordon Cullen.

33 Christopher Tunnard AILA, 'journal'; Clark Papers, 758/69.

34 Anon. (November 1941), 'House at Galby (sic), Leicestershire'.

35 Information from Mrs Townsend.

36 Hussey (7 August 1942), 'Carrygate, Leicestershire', p. 268.

37 AJ (18 February 1937), p. 293, shows the 1935 design illustrated as a model; see also Powers (2001), pp. 119–41.

38 Tunnard (attributed) (February 1939), 'Modern Architecture in the Sussex Landscape', pp. 61–2.

39 Professor Charles Reilly, note in *The Builder* (April 1937), p. 136.

40 Tunnard (Summer 1939), 'Planning a Modern Garden', pp. 23–7.

41 'Selection of trees and shrubs for Bentley Wood, Sussex', n.d., Clark Papers, MS/758/69.

42 Tunnard (attributed) (February 1939), 'Modern Architecture in the Sussex Landscape', includes a section on 'Site planning', p. 62; also Tunnard (Summer 1939), 'Planning a modern garden: an experience in collaboration'.

43 Christopher Tunnard AILA, 'journal'; Clark Papers, 758/69.

44 Tunnard in a letter to Serge Chermayeff, dated 19 February 1938. Clark Papers, MS/758/69.

45 Interview, Lance Neckar with Serge Chermayeff, October 1988.

46 Powers (2001), pp. 128–9.

47 Christopher Tunnard AILA, 'plant orders' folder; Clark Papers, 758/69.

48 'Bentley: Notes on the work to be carried out in the Autumn, 1938'. Clark Papers, MS/758/69.

49 Tunnard (Summer 1939), 'Planning a Modern Garden', p. 27; depicts planting plan of terrace border.

50 Ibid.

51 Tunnard (attributed) (February 1939), 'Modern Architecture in a Sussex Landscape', p. 62; this is also confirmed in a letter in the Avery Library, Chermayeff to Geoffrey Jellicoe (19 April 1957); quoted in Powers (2001), p. 135.

52 Interview, David Jacques and Sir James Richards, 27 July 1989.

53 Hussey (26 October 1940):, 'A Modern Country House', pp. 368–71, 390–3.

54 Interview, David Jacques with Sir Geoffrey Jellicoe, 19 September 1989.

55 Powers (2001), pp. 133–5.

56 Serge Chermayeff to David Jacques, 29 September 1990; David Jacques Papers.

57 Frank Clark Collection, MS/758/69; plant orders folder.

58 Gropius and Fry (1935), 'Cry Stop to Havoc'; the scheme foundered through lack of finance.

59 Eden (1935), 'The English Tradition in the Countryside III', p. 195.

60 Tunnard (October 1937), 'Landscape into Garden: Reason, Romanticism and the Verdant Age', p. 150.

61 Tunnard, *Gardens in the Modern Landscape* (1938), pp. 142–53.

62 Anon. (April 1939), 'House at Hampstead', pp. 187–9.

63 Elrington, *et al.* (1989).

64 Christopher Tunnard AILA, 'plant orders'; Clark Papers, 758/69.

65 Anon. (1939), 'Flats in Palace Gate, Kensington', pp. 173–84.

66 Christopher Tunnard AILA, 'journal'; Clark Papers, MS/758/69.

67 University of East Anglia, Pritchard Papers, PP/16/3/3/46; cited in Pearlman (2007), p. 98.

68 LI Archives, Box 6; Christopher Tunnard (ed.), 'Garden and Landscape' (printed catalogue of ILA exhibition held in June 1939), p. 11.
69 LI Archives, Box 6; Christopher Tunnard, 'Town and Country Landscape, U.S.A.' (text of lecture to the ILA, 1 July 1947).
70 Tunnard, *Gardens in the Modern Landscape* (1948), pp. 168–77.
71 When back in civilian life after World War II, Koch returned to Cambridge, MA, and became a champion of low-cost housing. During the 1950s he gained a reputation for his 'Techbuilt' prefabricated houses with wooden frames and panels.
72 Tunnard Papers, Box 15, folder 235, biography.
73 Goldsmith (1941), p. 61 and 133–41
74 Ibid., p. 196 [St Ann's Hill]; pp. 323–4 [unidentified English pond].
75 Tunnard, *Gardens in the Modern Landscape* (1938), p. 84.
76 Perkins went on to great heights in education. He was appointed the Charles Dyer Norton Professor of Regional Planning at Harvard 1945–50, and became Dean of the School of Fine Arts at the University of Pennsylvania 1950–71.
77 Pearlman (2007), p. 45.
78 Tunnard, *Gardens in the Modern Landscape* (1948), p. 174: The photograph by Louis Checkman also appeared in *Landscape Architecture*, XXXIX (April 1949), opposite p. 105; although Tunnard's caption in the latter publication stated that the model was 'commissioned by the Museum in 1946', there are no records of the design in the MOMA archives, and it was probably thus the outcome of a private or academic exercise.
79 National Park Service, Jefferson National Expansion Memorial Association Records, JNEM Drawings D-104-232 through D-104-235.
80 'Competition: Jefferson National Expansion Memorial', *Progressive Architecture*, 29 (May 1948), pp. 51–73.
81 Tunnard Papers, Box 15, folder 235.
82 Anon. (1949), 'Project UN HQ, NY, entrance to 47th Str', p. 336.
83 The sketch was by Charles Prentice Thompson, a young architect who also helped Tunnard with illustrations for *The City of Man*.
84 Shepheard (1953), pp. 80–1.
85 Paul Miller of the Preservation Society of Newport County to David Jacques, 11 September 2008; Katherine Warren was the society's founder, and from her death the house became its headquarters offices, until sale of the property in 1993 to a private owner.
86 Soby (1958), p. 85.
87 Crowe (1958), p. 76.
88 Tunnard, *Gardens in the Modern Landscape* (1948), p. 7.
89 Clark (1948), p. 36.
90 Tunnard, *Gardens in the Modern Landscape* (1948), p. 7.
91 C. Tunnard, 'Proposed Landscaping' (1949?) (blueprint held by the New London County Historical Society); a positive print from the blueprint was marked up by Tunnard as a planting plan and has subsequently been framed.
92 Tunnard Papers, Box 15, folder 235.
93 Interview, David Jacques with Marjorie Clark, 30 June 1989.
94 Tunnard (April 1949), 'Art and Landscape Design'.
95 Clark (March–April 1954), 'The Principles of Landscape Design'.
96 Telephone conversation between David Jacques and Laurie Fricker, 3 January 1990.
97 University of Pennsylvania, Architectural Archives, Louis I. Kahn Collection, Yale Art Gallery 1951–3.

6   Civic art and design

The era following World War II in which Tunnard taught at Yale began with vigour and excitement in the planning field as new federal programmes sprang to life in a national effort to meet the housing needs of the veterans, the pent-up civilian housing demand as well as the challenges of the new suburbanisation and of the decay of the older cities. The federal government launched a new Veterans' Administration and stepped up Federal Housing Administration mortgages, and later a rash of programmes like planning assistance to states and cities, urban renewal, model cities, park acquisition funds, and the massive interstate highway programme.

This surging effort to improve the quality of life for the urban and rapidly growing suburban population attracted professionals, some involved in earlier New Deal programmes, as well as academic experts, young public administration graduates, and many eager to be aboard this new bandwagon. Although an idealism permeated the early days of these programmes, a pragmatic 'can-do' attitude in the late 1950s and early 1960s propelled many of those involved in both the federal agencies and in cities and towns. Planners in this era were becoming 'statistic and survey-dominated,' as they tried to influence the political decisions shaping the course of these postwar developments.

Cities aggressively competed for federal dollars. Richard C. Lee, mayor of Tunnard's own city, New Haven, emerged as one of the most successful competitors, luring not only more federal dollars per citizen than any other mayor, but also attracting a bright and enthusiastic staff. The hope was to eliminate slums and renew the aging inner city with new and sanitary buildings, so it could compete with the increasingly popular and fast-growing suburbs. Major swathes of New Haven were razed for new housing, commerce, and highways, making parts of its downtown look like postwar Dresden while other sections were treated more gingerly for rehabilitation.

The humanistic and visual concerns that Tunnard advocated were rarely on these planners' agendas. He quickly understood the dangers of the technocratic approach in dehumanising the city and in isolating people and neighbourhoods from the life of the city. In re-evaluating his personal agenda he cleaved to some pre-war principles and practices, such as historical analysis and collaborative working, or reinforced them. His belief in the crucial creative contribution of

"*The patron saint of planners*"

Figure 6.1 The emperor Nero, 'the patron saint of planners' had an 'impetuous but very
thorough method of slum clearance'. Drawing by Tunnard.
(Source: *Architectural Record*, 94 (Oct. 1943), p. 47)

the designer was transferred from gardens to cities. He radically reassessed other
ideas, like functionalism and the social aspects of design. Eventually he spoke to
the technocrats in their own terms, arguing for intangible values to be weighed
alongside economics.

History and continuity

One of Tunnard's characteristic modes of thought, throughout his career, was his
use of history in order to organise his thoughts about landscapes and cities. Even
in *Gardens in the Modern Landscape*, his most iconoclastic book, nearly half of the
book was devoted to historical themes. About 90 per cent of *American Skyline* was
devoted to historical research and analysis. Such an approach, he found, had great
explanatory power. It also permitted the perspective required in order to look into
the future: 'with the reservoir of the past to draw upon', he wrote in the latter
book, 'the future can be given some direction'.[1]

The humanised landscape

Modernist architectural colleagues from Continental Europe tended to believe
in minds untrammelled by using historical analysis, as exemplified by Walter
Gropius. On the other hand, English writers on towns and landscapes continued

to use it to good effect. Thomas Sharp (1901–1978), an English town planner, explored the evolution of town, village and countryside in his polemical *Town and Countryside* (1932), followed by *English Panorama* (1936). He was passionate about maintaining the distinction between town and country, and attacked the garden city suburb's 'romanticism'. Despite purporting to be rural in spirit, such places were to him unnecessary urban sprawl, a 'popular edition of Bournemouth'.[2] He brought the phrases 'humanised landscape' and 'cultural landscape' into use amongst his peers.

Just as important for Tunnard was William Arthur Eden, an architect running the Civic Design course at the University of Liverpool. He agreed well with Sharp's version of the landscape's history and its humanisation when he wrote 'The English Tradition in the Countryside' for *AR* in 1935. In order to illustrate Eden's explanation of the evolution of the landscape, *AR* asked an artist, Robert Austin (1895–1973), to prepare 15 images of the same imaginary scene. One series depicted an eighteenth-century country house, nineteenth-century mining and subsequent descent into graceless urbanisation.[3] Another showed how the landscape might have been altered by a major highway.[4]

Surprisingly, perhaps, in his own book intended to herald the Modernist approach to landscape architecture, Tunnard included sections on garden history including lengthy historical accounts of Painshill in Surrey and Redleaf in Kent.[5] He used the series of four plans published by John Claudius Loudon in *Country Residences* (1806) to characterise unaltered countryside, and formal, landscape and picturesque treatments of the same. He also had a series of plans of St Ann's Hill at seven stages of its development – from a tract of the Windsor Forest with successive houses till the early twentieth century – published in *Gardens in the Modern Landscape*.[6]

He did not elaborate on the purposes of these latter drawings, but they were clearly intended by him or the artist to analyse the changes to the garden at various points in its history. These drawings not only showed a considerable awareness of the history of garden making, but also that Tunnard considered the new landscape to be merely the latest manifestation in a continuum of history subjected to various fashions, rather than the clean-slate approach so fashionable with many Modernist architects.

Tunnard's belief that contemporary design should reflect the needs and aspirations of the time was not because he had faith in the mysterious workings of the Zeitgeist. Instead it was an empirical approach to improvement: an understanding of how social, economic and artistic forces have shaped the environment at different points in the past trains the mind for comprehending the probably confusing and uncertain connections of one's own time: 'This book sets out to sketch that picture [of what a garden should be] by outlining the trends of the past and relating them to some possible contemporary methods of garden and landscape design.'[7] In the second edition he set out his 'approach to landscape gardening and planning'. The first requirement was 'an eighteenth century understanding of the "genius of the place"'.[8] In *The City of Man*, this was rephrased as 'a thorough understanding of the site'.

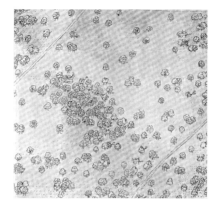

a 17th Century.

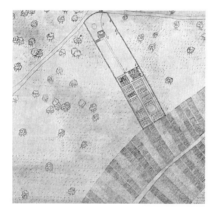

b 1700: Pre-landscape.

c 1725: Transitional period.

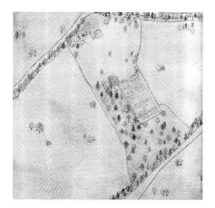

d 1760: Early landscape period.

e 1810: Late landscape period.

f 1850: Victorian period.

g 1910.

Figure 6.2 (a–g) A series of drawings by Letitia Hicks-Beach for Tunnard to illustrate a
partly imagined history of the development of the grounds at St Ann's Hill
from the seventeenth to the twentieth centuries.
(Source: Tunnard, *Gardens in the Modern Landscape* (1938), pp. 129–32)

Cities as culture

It could not have escaped Tunnard's notice that Lewis Mumford's *The Culture of
Cities* (1938) was constructed around an historical survey of the life of cities. At
Harvard he was offered a choice between Gropius's emphasis upon the inspirational
in design, or Joseph Hudnut's trust in a liberal arts education, including history, as
the appropriate grounding for study in architecture. Tunnard lent his conviction
to the latter, and was to declare that he preferred 'accumulated knowledge rather
than intuitiveness'.[9] Whereas both Hudnut and Gropius wished to overturn the
Beaux-Arts tradition, this did not, to Hudnut, mean that humanistic traditions in
architecture and civic design were redundant. He felt that Gropius's approach was
in danger of forgetting ordinary human needs in making design itself the aim.[10]
Hudnut's misgivings of mainstream Modernism at the time 'did anticipate in a
number of ways the post-modernist critique that came several decades later',[11] and
Tunnard was an early ally. In bemoaning the takeover of Civic Design by social
scientists and engineers, he wished that cities could once more be designed by
architects and artists to be places where people lived:[12]

> Why are we lacking in what Joseph Hudnut has called the 'homely ordinance'
> of architecture in our city streets – an architecture which has the power to
> give them life and to create an atmosphere of urban charm?

Hudnut had been a friend of Fiske Kimball, a well known architectural historian,
in the 1920s and had been appointed Professor of the History of Architecture at

Columbia University in 1926.[13] Tunnard must have been impressed by Hudnut's depth of understanding, and as he pursued his studies on cities he came to rely increasingly on historical analysis and on the elimination of prejudice about buildings of the past.

In speaking to the conference at MOMA in 1948 he argued:[14]

> We have to look at the buildings of the past we have been taught not to look at. We have got to look at the buildings that have received the approbation of critics and the buildings which people like, and reconcile public taste and good architectural performance.

The Guggenheim Fellowship for 1950 helped with travel costs so that he could pursue his study of American cities. He assembled a vast quantity of factual historical information on the land and its development, Utopian ideas for ideal towns, industrial towns and the suburbs. In *The City of Man*, even in his chapters detailing his proposals for 'a recovery of beauty in the city' he rolled out further swathes of historical facts. His collaboration with Henry Hope Reed was not simply Reed supplying the history.

Tunnard's subsequent books abundantly confirmed his belief in the power of historical understanding, but the crowning triumph of the method was *American Skyline*, co-authored with Reed. This was a small book, with line drawings only,[15] and the title was perhaps confusing, even if it sounded interesting. It really only applied to the latter part of the Introduction which explained the American skyline in terms of 'Temples of Commerce', 'Temples to God', and 'Temples of Government'. The book has unjustly, if understandably, been given less attention than it deserves.

It was purely about the American tradition in cities, which was divided into eight eras, starting with 'the Colonial Pattern 1607–1776', and coming up to date with 'The Regional City 1933–'. At the time Americans and foreigners alike were wont to state that American towns and cities were hopelessly haphazard. However, Tunnard examined each era's building activity, identifying and describing the forces at work. He found that, far from being accidental, every construction project of every city was susceptible to analysis and explanation, and had been formed by planning on the part of some agency or individual. This led to an important conclusion that the apparent confusion and lack of beauty in American cities was primarily because the agencies of planning were not coordinated, a message that had considerable relevance at the time he was writing.

Understanding the dynamics of cities thus assisted in visualising the future in the planning sphere as well as in landscape: 'One of the purposes of this book is to encourage a knowledge of these forces so that we will be better able to create a city which reflects our national aspirations and desires.'[16]

Continuity and preservation

Sharp and Eden had been able to view landscape as the accumulation of human activity through history, a perspective that came to be elemental to the cultural landscapes movement. As Tunnard's own understanding of garden history developed, he appreciated that there was interest in all periods, not simply the landscape garden:[17]

> The author's original rather cursory estimate of the nineteenth century has undergone considerable revision as the result of further investigations, which have proved ... great daring and originality ... Nineteenth-century revivals were ... productive of entirely new forms and expressions.

The longer view of history allowed Tunnard to see cities as palimpsests, with each overlay being part of the story and having interest of its own. He appreciated the past as part of the continuum of human endeavour into the future. The relationship of the old and new became intertwined in much of Tunnard's thinking and writing.

Already in 1939 he was pointing out the importance of historical perspective when the task was to 'reconstruct a neglected period design or adapt an old garden for modern uses':[18]

> In such cases the historical knowledge and consideration for existing site values of the qualified landscape architect provide a vital and necessary background for the creation of new landscape features.

Similarly he was to assert the vital part that the past had to play in the future of cities alongside the new. He stated the purpose of *American Skyline* in this way:[19]

> This is a book about the American townscape – the manmade America of industries, homes, skyscrapers, hotels, highways and parking lots. It describes how this scene was shaped, how it became part of the American heritage, how it affects the lives we lead, and how we may in turn shape it toward the future.

Providing a sense of continuity with the past became a bedrock in his philosophy of civic design. In fact, many came to consider him primarily a preservationist. Tunnard regarded many aspects of American cities as the nation's heritage. The buildings were more than the structures and their decoration, though; they embodied the planning ideals and artistic impulses of earlier generations and provided symbolism and meaning to the present: 'save that which seems worth salvaging, not only in the form of physical salvage, but in the realm of ideas'.[20] If we ignore our visual heritage, Tunnard said in discussing historic preservation, 'we are putting a lower value on man himself and blighting his aspirations for the future'.[21]

In the first half of the twentieth century the American preservation move-ment, dominated by the architectural historian and Colonial Dame, was primarily committed to preserving and protecting individual historic buildings, usually as museums. The National Trust for Historic Preservation, which Tunnard was to support, was founded in 1949 to support preservation of historic neighbourhoods as well as buildings. Tunnard did not sneer, as most architects would have done:[22]

> evidence of this longing for identification with the past is to be found in recent increases in the number of historical studies and in the rediscovery and restoration of historic shrines.

Tunnard and Reed were in the vanguard of a professional interest in the subject. When he advocated historic preservation it was not for its own sake, though, but because familiar scenes in cities could be loved far above rational and often massive construction projects in housing and highways. New attitudes were desirable within the planning profession:[23]

> we will not achieve approbation by those growing numbers of people who are demanding that the city be a positive expression of culture unless we are also willing to cultivate new approaches. One of these must be the inculcation of the sense of tradition which is missing from so many of the planning schemes of today.

Hence

> It would be folly on the part of the city planner to continue the tradition of the 1930's and 40's [sic] when so many planning schemes ignored this demand by sweeping away everything in their path. It does not need much imagination to see that a completely different approach to city planning will be necessary in order to integrate the past with the present while we are planning for the future.

As in so much of his work, Tunnard was leagues ahead of most American preservationists, especially in the 1950s and early 1960s. In 1960, he proposed historic preservation district legislation for Connecticut. He was an early advocate of broadening the types of buildings, spaces, and districts to be considered for preservation. As he commented at a 1967 National Trust for Historic Preservation International Relations Committee meeting, 'only a limited number of buildings are significant enough to be preserved solely for exhibition purposes'.[24] And later that year the Advisory Council on Historic Preservation established the principle 'that historic properties should be considered in relationship to their environment, not as isolated entities'.[25]

In contrast to the early preservationists, who usually required new buildings in historic districts to conform to the district's predominant architecture of the past, Tunnard supported a more ecumenical approach of allowing a mixture of existing styles in such districts. For Tunnard, uniform style districts missed the cultural vitality and diversity of the past and prevented communities from adding to their history. This had occurred in Santa Fe, NM. The popular effort there to continue a dominant architectural style within an historic district had resulted in unfortunate look-alike adobe buildings mixed in with the authentic ones. For him, preservation was a way of retaining those buildings and features, man-made and natural, which had distinctive qualities worth preserving. Sometimes it was architectural quality, sometimes the character of a place and other times it was the beauty of a natural feature like Bartholomew's Cobble on the Housatonic River. It was the total townscape for Tunnard: the total city fabric, the total landscape, the buildings, the groups, the scale, the vistas, the open spaces, and the old and the new.

Tunnard also defended the inclusion of new, high-quality buildings in historic districts, a rare position in the 1950s and early 1960s among architectural historians and preservationists, often preoccupied with the retention of only 'old' buildings. In 1963 while attending a meeting of the Central New York Architectural Historians in Schenectady, NY, Tunnard noted that no new buildings were allowed in the city's famous historic district, The Stockade, which prompted him to comment that 'each building was once contemporary'.[26] The innovative inventory and preservation work in Providence, RI, supported his thesis that all its buildings, not just the historic ones, should be included in its building surveys to assure appropriate and harmonious relationships among the old and new

Figure 6.3 Isometric illustrating the revitalisation of a block on the Hill in Providence, RI, devised by Davis, Cochran and Miller, architects, in association with Tunnard and Harris, planning consultants, 1962.
(Source: Tunnard and Pushkarev, *Man-made America* (1963), p. 437)

buildings. Quoting from the 1959 study, he affirmed that 'Good design should be encouraged so that this era's philosophy of architectural design can take its place among those of its forbears.'[27]

Tunnard's reputation as an articulate advocate of preservation meant that his advice was sought on projects around the world. His archives are jammed with letters to planning and preservation commissions, politicians, university administrators, and newspapers, and with statements in public hearings urging the preservation of buildings and landscapes from demolition, highway incursions, or neglect. But his most vigorous experience with local preservation issues was in New Haven when he served on the City Plan Commission and on the board of the New Haven Preservation Trust. Here he dealt with constant threats to buildings and neighbourhoods by planners, developers, and even nationally known architects like I.M. Pei who was proposing radical changes to the city's old post office and court buildings. While some of the issues were dramatic, most were everyday problems like neon lighting, out-of-scale buildings, billboards, and jarring building materials such as wild coloured vitriolate glass facing. Yet for such problems, which are cumulatively important in creating what a place looks like, Tunnard offered Mayor Lee pragmatic solutions such as specific design regulations and a Civic Design Committee to advise owners, builders and architects.

Balancing this local preservation work were his varied assignments around the globe which gave opportunities for observing new situations – and gaining new insights. He made some remarkably perceptive comments on preservation and urban life in his trips to foreign places. In his notes on his trip to Tokyo in 1960, for example, Tunnard confirmed some of his long-held thoughts on preservation and on retaining the old alongside the new. Here he found 'a modern city in which traditional Japan still thrives' where 'the art of everyday living' was far more interesting than its monuments. The 'scale [is] detailed and intimate – the little shops and the incidents on the street – a family airing their possession on the sidewalk, a young man filling his cigarette lighter from a gas pump, the clean and exquisitely arranged vegetable markets'.[28] The street life, the mix of rich and poor, and the many small family-run shops of these vibrant neighbourhoods struck a chord with Tunnard. This is the Kerouac and Camillus in Tunnard's preservation thinking, exhibiting once again his openness and optimism.

The social landscape

The MARS Group

Several of Tunnard's contemporaries in the late 1930s, including Serge Chermayeff, Wells Coates, Elizabeth Denby, Maxwell Fry, Berthold Lubetkin, Raymond McGrath and Jim Richards, were connected with the Modern Architectural Research (MARS) Group. MARS was the English wing of CIAM, the *Congrès Internationaux d'Architecture Moderne*, founded in June 1928 by a group of 28 architects promoted by Le Corbusier. Initially it had primarily been concerned with the Modern Movement in architecture, and saw 'architecture as a social art'. The second CIAM meeting in 1929 was held in Frankfurt with its main theme being 'minimum existence'. The fourth CIAM meeting in 1933, on 'the functional city', broadened the organisation's scope into urban planning, with Le Corbusier's concepts of tall apartment blocks at widely spaced intervals gaining attention. The chairman at this conference and for many years afterwards was Cor van Eesteren, the Amsterdam city architect.

By 1936, the MARS Group had grown to 58 members, and it felt ready to undertake an exhibition, initially intended to open in the summer of 1937, to show off the benefits of modern architecture to the public. The manifesto proclaimed that, 'Now that the experimental stage is over there are enough examples to show the practical examples of such buildings.' The Hungarian-born Bauhaus emigré László Moholy-Nagy (1895–1946) started off the organisation, but handed over to Misha Black (1910–1977) when he departed Britain for the United States. Tunnard, attracted by the activity afoot, appears to have become associated with the Group in late 1937.[29] The exhibition opened six months late at the New Burlington Galleries in January 1938, but was a great success in the architectural world.[30]

Arthur Korn, a German émigré and a committed socialist, started the Group's Planning Committee in December 1937. He had previously produced a plan for Berlin[31] and took the opportunity to illustrate CIAM ideas at a town-planning scale using London as a case study. Tunnard became involved in this committee soon after its formation. Also included in his group were Arthur Ling, Maxwell Fry, Godfrey Samuel, William Tatton Brown, Aleck Low, Felix Samuely, Elizabeth Denby, Bronik Katz and Robert Shaw.[32] By this time Tunnard had moved to central London and could thus participate freely. He was the only active landscape architect in MARS, and, no doubt to his surprise, found himself 'Chairman of the Open Spaces Committee'.[33]

In keeping with its CIAM philosophy, the Group envisaged a highly radical reshaping of the city for its ten million inhabitants. Tatton Brown had early on considered that London had always been a concentric city, held together by multiple radial communications, and that this should continue to be so. However, Korn and his band prevailed with a plan in the form of a spine reminiscent of Soviet planning ideas of the 1920s. Early on it was decided that a hierarchy of residential areas was required. The residential unit (1,000 people) would be a component of the larger neighbourhood unit (6,000 people), which would be a component of the borough unit (50,000 people), and so on. London would become linear bands of development, with an east-west industrial spine two miles wide, with a central shopping and administration zone, and sixteen mile-wide ribs extending north and south into the surrounding countryside. These ribs would consist of functional neighbourhood units strung along high-speed roads. The wholesale process of reconstruction could allow only a few familiar landmarks and historic buildings to remain. However, the result would be a decentralised city, with areas of protected countryside between the developed areas.

Tunnard was to write that he was amongst those in the Group that 'replanned London by sweeping it all away and projecting a series of *cités linéaires*'.[34] His contribution, with some assistance on statistics from Arthur Ling, then a planner in

Coventry, included calculations for the open-space requirements at these different levels of community.[35] Tunnard postulated 'the requirements of the residential unit of 1,000 inhabitants', and carried out the calculations at the different levels till he had the overall requirements for London. He projected areas for horticulture as well as open space for various recreational uses based on population profiles.

Meanwhile other members were carrying out research with respect to socio-economic and geographic issues relating to Greater London and provided a bold attempt 'to eliminate the losses in efficiency that years of uncontrolled expansion have entailed'. Their proposals adjusted 'the town to its needs', considering the ultimate aim of town planning to be to 'provide the maximum number of amenities for the population'. One important premise of the Group's approach was the abolition of private open space. Calculations of requirements for housing, industry, administration and shopping, showed that almost 70 per cent of the land would become available for leisure as 'an inestimable resource of public health and culture'. The neighbourhood units could then stand within collective open land, reached no further than ten minutes' walk from any dwelling. The greenspace in between the belts of development reached the heart of the city, and were large and long enough to be 'sufficient for long continuous walks, combined with sports grounds'. The plan was adjusted to fit the actual topography, so the open space included the Brent, Colne and Lee valleys.

The pages in *Gardens in the Modern Landscape* that reflected MARS Group thinking had not been published previously in *AR*, which suggests that they were composed during 1938, which indeed coincides with Tunnard's first year as a member of the Town Planning Committee. Most likely this year was one of cross-fertilisation, with Tunnard learning much from Korn, and imbibing his socialistic principles. He argued for the abolition of private space, and for the creation of communal gardens so that 'areas reserved for industry and agriculture can be parted to make way for the flow of the landscape, used for rest and recreation'.[36] In return he converted these ideas into schematic form on paper that provided the template for the subsequent MARS plan.

Korn had been impressed by Cor van Eesteren's General Development Plan for Amsterdam of 1935, and the proposals for housing and parkland were well covered by his article in *AR*.[37] This would have introduced English readers to the Amsterdam Bospark, seen by Van Eesteren as an integral component of the overall plan, providing opportunities for extensive walking, cycling and riding at the edge of the city. In his analysis of the plan for the Bos, Bijhouwer pointed to the complete absence of an axial arrangement, marking a break from Beaux-Arts influences; the absence of serpentine walks, oval-shaped spaces and specimen trees as references to the landscape style; and the eschewal of devices from contemporary German park design such as sharp rectilinear spaces surrounded by woodland, an attempt 'to regain the monumentality of the baroque period without copying the annoying symmetry'. He noted instead the search for 'naturalness' in the disposition of open spaces, informal boundaries, and a coherence of the different parts of the landscape.[38] Tunnard was impressed for similar reasons, illustrating the Bos in *Gardens in the Modern Landscape* as a park design of a radically new form and comparing it in size to Richmond Park.[39] 'In its layout, devoid of traditional clichés', he wrote, 'van Eesteren may be said to have produced the modernist's challenge in this branch of landscape design.'

More generally, though, Tunnard's conception of 'the social landscape' underwent revision and expansion as he faced landscape issues at a city-planning scale. He came to see that design was only a tool in the greater endeavour of ensuring environmental and aesthetic quality across an urban area. A decidedly socialist-sounding article titled 'Modern Architectural Research and Landscape Planning' appeared in *Landscape and Garden* in summer 1938. It was signed 'by a member of the MARS group', who was most probably Tunnard. In this it was claimed that the group 'includes nothing less than an investigation into the whole of the physical framework of civilisation'. The writer declared that in 'discarding the hampering styles and tradition of past ages … many of the conventions which surround [the problems of landscape planning] to-day can be dispensed with in favour of a humanist technique'. Functional design which met the collective needs of society was advocated. The Amsterdam Bos was mentioned as an example of a park 'simply and harmoniously planned to fit the purpose for which it was created'.

Geoffrey Jellicoe obtained Maxwell Fry to give a talk on 'Garden Design in relation to Modern Architecture' to the Architectural Association early in 1939.[40] Fry argued the MARS case for communal gardens, and against individual gardens: 'no gardens of half an acre and under seemed to him to carry the possible seeds of development, the small garden of the suburbs seeming to him the symbol of the dead end of individualism'. Modern architecture's 'whole nature is communal and not individualistic'. Tunnard was there and prominent in the discussion afterwards, speaking about the 'minimal garden'.[41] The ILA President, Thomas Adams, perhaps not totally convinced, summed up by saying 'that the body of opinion at the meeting was that there was a need for the small garden of good design'.

Tunnard's departure for Harvard ended his active participation in the affairs of the MARS Group, though he maintained contact with several of its members. His connection to the MARS Group was maintained at least till 1954, although the last-found mention of him as a member (abroad) was in 1950.

The Communal Garden and the Minimal Garden

This work for the MARS Group provided Tunnard with a fresh stream of thought, on the 'communal garden'. The various theoretical schemes to develop blocks of flats in English parkland may have been partly inspired by the desire to save what was possible of eighteenth-century landscape gardens and parks for aesthetic reasons, but dedicating them as 'communal gardens' was also seen as socially progressive.

Tunnard wrote 'The Case for the Communal Garden' in building up his argument for Claremont.[42] His conviction was that the landscape should be a shared asset, and predicted that the 'garden of tomorrow' will be 'a unit of the broad green landscape itself, controlled for the benefit of all'. In fact, he foresaw a return of the landscape garden in a new guise:[43]

A far greater affinity will probably be apparent between the first landscaped gardens of two hundred years ago and the freely-planned landscapes of tomorrow, which, made possible through the operation of very different economic and social laws, will embrace garden, town and countryside in one unfettered whole.

Through the communal garden citizens could reach schools, shops, and work, whilst connecting to the public footpath system in the countryside beyond the built-up area, so one would discover 'the social fabric in a pattern of verdure'. The amount of open land that he envisaged would mean the abolition of large private gardens which 'permanently sterilized' space that should belong to all, and were thus antisocial. 'Today the suburban plot, tomorrow the garden without limitation.' 'Until a general conception of the garden without boundaries can arise in this county the small garden will remain the English problem.'[44]

The advantages would far outweigh the loss to a few individuals:[45]

> The liberating influence of open spaces and communal gardens flowing through these developed areas, a continuous stream of verdure, would be more satisfying than any of the so-called 'beautification' schemes … and even more valuable than a 'green belt,' since it would start from the doorstep and grow outwards to the open countryside. Such centralization and such an open treatment can become the nucleus of a new landscape, beautiful and satisfying in all its parts …

There were European parallels to the communal garden, particularly in Germany with the Bornim Circle, landscape architects associated with the Karl Foerster perennial nurseries in Bornim in the Nazi era after 1933. Some of the Circle's work was illustrated in *The Studio* annuals *Gardens and Gardening*. Otto Valentien (1897–1987) was loosely associated with this group, and his views were reported in 1939, under the title 'The garden is an emotional release'. This recognised contemporary problems and proposed a new type of garden design not dissimilar to Tunnard's vision. It maintained that: 'Our task is not to lose sight of the wider landscape background in our pre-occupation with designing the individual garden as a dwelling-place and a place of refreshment for soul and body.'

Actual community gardens were illustrated by Tunnard using examples at Neubühl near Zürich (by members of the Swiss Werkbund, 1930–1932),[46] and the Römerstadt development in Frankfurt, designed by the Frankfurt city architect Ernst May, in association with the landscape architect Leberecht Migge. The lengthy block of flats at the latter had no private front gardens and at the rear looked out over, successively, drying grounds, allotment gardens and a protected agricultural zone. Tunnard's interest in this scheme, with its sophisticated network of greenspace and a system of the minimal garden to go alongside the proposals for the minimal house was probably aroused through architectural publications.

As Tunnard noted, the development at Römerstadt included dwellings of two

Figure 6.4 The development at Neubühl, Zürich with 'Family houses and gardens with
simple screen hedges and collective planting' served as a prototype for the
idea of the communal garden.
(Source: Tunnard, *Gardens in the Modern Landscape* (1938), p. 139)

storeys for families with children. He likewise included housing terraces for larger
families in his Claremont scheme. He accepted that such families might appreciate
some outdoor space for recreation and cultivation. He thus developed the idea of a
'minimum garden' as a compromise with the principle of making all outdoor space
communal. With all the functional requirements for seating, play and horticulture,
Tunnard very much saw these gardens as 'an extension of the house: an out-of-door
living room planned by the landscape architect and decorated to a greater or lesser
degree by the owner'.[47] Clark drew up the illustrative plan showing gardens with
cultivation beds edged by square paviours, a detail that harked back to Canneel-
Claes's own minimalist garden.

'Minimum gardens' facing each other at the backs of opposite terraces would
allow for a strip of communal garden in between. The communal gardens would
then fulfil the owner's need for 'space and freedom'. This idea was not exactly
new, as the rear gardens in the nineteenth-century Ladbroke Grove development
backed onto communal gardens, but it gave the concept fresh impetus and was
adopted in certain New Towns in the 1950s. Harlow New Town, for example, was
given 'green wedges', communal landscape extending from the town centre to the
countryside around the town.

Tunnard's promotion of the minimal garden led him towards the houses to which
they would be attached, in particular the work of Elizabeth Denby (1894–1965).
In November 1936 she became the first woman to address a sessional meeting
of the Royal Institute of British Architects. A well-known housing expert, she
was renowned for her writing on the design and furnishing of the working-class
flat and her work on two blocks of model flats designed in conjunction with E.
Maxwell Fry. Her book entitled *Europe Re-housed* investigated trends in housing in

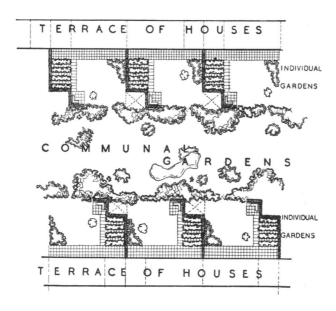

Figure 6.5 Tunnard proposed the 'Minimum Garden', by way of an 'out-of-door living room', backing onto communal gardens which led to parkland and the countryside beyond.
(Source: Tunnard, *Gardens in the Modern Landscape* (1938), p. 155))

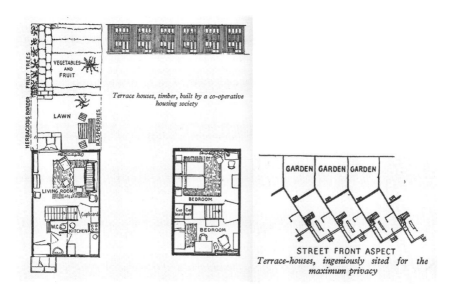

Figure 6.6 (a, b) Two examples of terraced housing by Swedish co-operative societies served as a basis for Tunnard's proposals for the All-Europe House with respect to design and organisation of the garden spaces.
(Source: Denby (1938), pp. 70 and 71)

six different countries. It is likely that as a result of this publication she was asked to produce an exhibit at the Ideal Home Exhibition in 1939.

Tunnard must have seemed like a natural choice to collaborate with Denby in the construction of an All-Europe House that was to combine 'ideas for easy, pleasant, economical living from many different countries … put together in such a way that an Englishwoman would not find them strange'. These ideas included those by Swedish co-operative societies for building in echelon.[48] He provided the garden layout for a typical 'All-Europe House', whilst Clark worked up an eye-level view and polished sketches of how a terrace with its gardens and 'common garden' might look.[49]

The All-Europe House was an example of a terraced house planned for a mixed development with apartments, proposed at a density of 20 per acre. There was no front garden as such, but the front entrance was set back by staggering the houses by which means there was space for small triangular raised brick planters. The result was considered 'an eminently economical use of space, and a pleasantly urban and humane street'. The living room had a large picture window that occupied most of the width of the back of the house, with a door opening out onto a small garden, which, by means of being staggered, created a triangular terrace 'where sitting out of doors can be a comfortable and private affair, not overlooked from neighbouring houses'. The blank wall of the adjoining house faced south, being perfect for growing fruit and roses, giving the living room 'the valuable sensation of warmth and cheerfulness that can be given by an external sunlit wall'. It is clear, however, where this house forms part of a larger development with gardens backing onto each other, or connected to a common garden as proposed by Tunnard, that only half the number of houses concerned would have such an ideal orientation. The proposals for the individual gardens (c. 15 x 35/40 feet) included, besides the terrace, a lawn area, with a flower border and small kitchen area. Gardens were partly hedged for additional privacy, while the parts further away were surrounded by mesh wire fences. Each garden had a shed alongside which there was immediate access to the communal garden.

A Master Plan for London

The MARS Group's Town Planning Committee succeeded after four years in publicising its 'Master Plan for London' in *AR* in 1942.[50] Le Corbusier's *Ville Contemporaine*, which Tunnard had hoped would 'become a reality',[51] had been a purely theoretical exercise. However the MARS Group's plan for London came after extensive bombing by the Luftwaffe, and when practical solutions for the extensive rebuilding that would be necessary after the war were demanded. The general reaction to its highly theoretical nature, even from architects and planners, was thus mystification. Thomas Sharp thought the plan 'wild … and bad'. Lionel Brett (1914–2004), himself a member of the Group, expressed his doubts about the realism of the proposals.[52] He also perceived a degree of ambiguity in the presentation of the landscape ideas, the draughtsmen for which: 'have been guilty of those pleasant squiggles which contrasting with the geometrical blacks

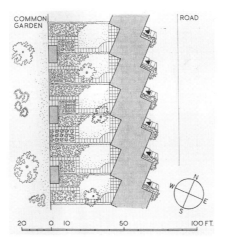

Figure 6.7 (a–c) Tunnard's proposals for the All-Europe House showed terraced housing with private rear gardens, bordering onto communal open space. Drawn by Frank Clark.
(Source: *JRIBA*, 46 (1939), pp. 815 and 817)

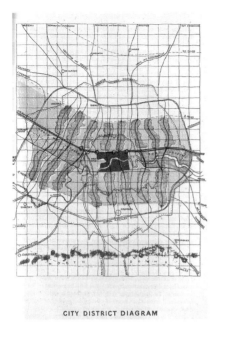

CITY DISTRICT DIAGRAM

COMPLETE UNIT DIAGRAM   Superimposed over North-East London

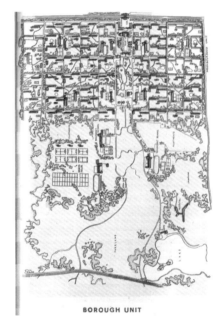

BOROUGH UNIT

Figure 6.8 (a–c) The MARS Group proposals for the reconstitution of London after
World War II shown at various scales reveals the predominant importance of
the greenspace network.
(Source: Fry (1944) Figs. 15, 14 &13)

of our plan should indicate vaguely to the outsider vegetation already existing or vegetation to be'. However, it wasn't clear if the squiggles indicated a landscape garden treatment, or visually less pleasant recreation grounds: 'Now this *might* be mile on mile of Christopher Tunnard; but equally it might be mile on mile of Paddington Recreation Ground.' The latter was well-known as the earliest (1888) public recreation ground in London, packed tight with a cricket ground, football ground, a cycle and running track, tennis courts, 'children's pleasure ground', and outdoor gymnasium areas.[53]

Tunnard himself seems to have cooled from his extreme CIAM-inspired position of four years earlier. The tenor of his revised thinking can be detected in the title of an article that followed the MARS plan: 'When Britain Plans … Today's Utopias Will Not Be Needed'. The planning for the rebuilding of London was actually carried out by Patrick Abercrombie (1879–1957) who in 1915 had been appointed Lever Professor of Civic Design at Liverpool University. Then in 1935 came a move to University College, London. It was here, after the Second World War, that he produced *The County of London Plan* (1943) and *The Greater London Plan* (1944).

Abercrombie was no socialist, but a liberal reformer who cared deeply about improving life for Britain's citizens through planning, as well as for the traditional values and culture of both town and country. Britain, with the world's largest city, and several more of very considerable size, faced problems shared by few other developed counties. Its cities were overcrowded, with a legacy of extensive slums, and decentralisation had long been accepted as necessary, giving rise to ideas for garden suburbs. A lack of direction from central government had resulted in phenomena like urban sprawl as development took place along highway frontages, and there was despoliation of beauty spots with retirement homes. The question, for Abercrombie and his contemporaries like Thomas Sharp, was how decentralisation, and the proper housing of the population, could take place without ruining the glory of England, its countryside. It was a question of judgement, of control and the just allocation of land use.

Abercrombie's prescription for London was a careful balance of several ideas, including 'decongestion' by housing redevelopment at lower densities without destroying the identity of existing neighbourhoods ('villages'); replanning the highways network; an extension of the public open space network; a green belt around London making a clear distinction between town and country, and new towns beyond the green belt to absorb those displaced by slum clearance. The open-space strategy was based on 'open space standards' that provided it in sufficient quantity at convenient distances from dwellings, in fact the same starting point as Tunnard's work for MARS. One important innovation was, though, the concept of a hierarchy of open space, of neighbourhood parks up to regional parks, with activities becoming increasingly countrified at the larger scale. The chief virtue of Abercrombie's plan was the coordination of achievable objectives, and it was substantially acted upon after the war.

Tunnard had once sneered at the Council for the Preservation of Rural England (CPRE) for being a 'false tradition', and because 'sterilisation can only act as a brake on progress towards effective planning'.[54] He may even have known that Abercrombie had been closely involved in its founding in 1926, becoming its first Honorary Secretary. However, Tunnard's doubts about CIAM-inspired town planning must have crystallised in 1942 when he saw the publication of the MARS plan and also heard Gropius's circle at the urbanism conference at Harvard. It was his misconceived early ideas on the 'social landscape' that Tunnard referred to when he wrote in a letter in 1946: 'I have enough sins on my conscience already.'[55] The humanistic planning advocated by Joseph Hudnut and Lewis Mumford, and practised by Abercrombie, now became much preferable. His closeness to Hudnut has been mentioned above. He also came to admire Abercrombie, by then knighted, acknowledging 'various suggestions' from him in *The City of Man* (1953), and referring to him as 'perhaps the greatest living exponent of the art' of civic design.[56]

Experimentation and collaboration

Though so many aspects of Tunnard's thinking changed in the course of the 1940s, there were certain fundamentals that he held throughout. Amongst these were the need, as he saw it, of continuous experiment, and of collaboration between professionals. Indeed, these were the preconditions to an artistic approach which would be aesthetically satisfying.

Experiment

Tunnard knew of and was much enthused by the publication *Circle: International Survey of Constructive Art* (1937). Its stance was Utopian, developing a new, totally non-figurative art serving social ends. Tunnard would have rejected this in later years, but he remained faithful to the conviction that new ideas and new art come from experimentation and the interplay between related arts.

There is no doubt that Tunnard's constructive views were genuinely held from the start. He quoted Walter Pater: 'Failure is to form habits.' Also George Bernard Shaw: 'Consistency is the enemy of enterprise.'[57] The opening words of the preface of *Gardens in the Modern Landscape* ran:[58]

> Tradition in art is one thing – experiment another. Yet in the art of garden and landscape design the two are easily reconciled.

Further on he advocated 'experiment with gardens' in order to 'remake our immediate surroundings into areas of imagery and order', and elsewhere he asserted that 'outworn systems of aesthetics and formulas of design will then make way for the experimental technique, resulting in new forms which are expressive of our own time and of ourselves'.[59] His new way of 'structural' planting would have been refined through experiment.

Joseph Hudnut would have understood. He made uncertainty a basic principle of his educational programme, for example.[60] Hudnut and Tunnard, in finding growing differences with Gropius and his circle, were playing out, in their own sphere, the philosophical debate of historicism versus liberal democracy given prominence by Karl Popper (1902–1994). In his *Poverty of Historicism* (written in 1936 but not published till 1944/5) and *The Open Society and Its Enemies* (1945), Popper developed a critique of historicism which, he said, was based on a belief that the future is predetermined and that events unfold inexorably and inevitably towards it. Setbacks have to be brushed aside, and those who argue against the tendency of history have to be ignored or silenced to enable society to reach its goal more expeditiously. This led to the authoritarianism and totalitarianism embodied in both fascism and communism.

Popper argued that, on the contrary, the future is always unknown, but that did not prevent planning. In his idea of a liberal democracy, which he called the 'Open Society', experiments would be made in social policy, monitored, and the policy adjusted when necessary in a never-ending quest for improvement. That approach was seen in advice once given by Lewis Mumford to a US Senate committee on housing and urban renewal to 'experiment with small measures and small units' until such time that government or society could better plan and organise for an uncertain future.[61]

Many CIAM members would have fitted the description of 'historicists'. This mode of thought led to an inability to deviate from an approach to architecture or civic design once established, and accounted for the repetitiveness of much of postwar architecture in both the USA and the UK. Tunnard indicated in his foreword to the 1948 edition of *Gardens in the Modern Landscape* that he had no sympathy for such people:[62]

> May one say with fairness that there are too many architects and others who adopt a 'modern' style without regard to its origins or philosophy? These are the people who are defeating true modernism … If the current mannerist style continues, its death will come from public indifference.

His own position remained constructivist; he had expected the thinking of a decade ago to have moved on:

> The author's attitude toward modern art, architecture and landscape architecture has also changed somewhat as a result of seeing more examples … the movement is avowedly experimental and no one remotely connected with it can be expected to stand pat on opinions formed at an earlier stage of development.

He had not forgotten about experimentation in *The City of Man*: 'Many of us who are concerned with city planning would like to see much more experimentation.'[63] However, he wrote less about its necessity in finding new forms of expression as he himself moved away from landscape design and towards more abstract ideas in civic planning.

Collaboration

The constructivist ethos of collaboration had been embodied in the editorial team of *Circle*: the Russian sculptor Naum Gabo, the painter Ben Nicholson, and the architect Leslie Martin. It was also a theme that Tunnard recognised from a previous 'constructive' period in landscape design, when the creators of the landscape garden saw painting and literature as sister arts, a theme from Christopher Hussey's *The Picturesque* (1927).[64]

Tunnard thought that in his own time '[t]he relationship between the arts has become closely knit, as in all previous great periods of artistic endeavour'.[65] By this he meant architecture, painting, sculpture, music and the industrial arts, but not yet the art of gardens. This was in need of 'the invigorating modern spirit', and he particularly lamented the absence of the sculptor, the best of which 'are designing for open spaces', and the painter, whose 'conception of form and colour is essential to a modern appreciation of garden planning'.

In discussing his 'artistic approach', he thought it would be pleasant to think that[66]

> when the landscape artist is allowed to return to the garden he will bring with him the inspiration, if not the active co-operation, of the graphic and plastic artists, who will be instrumental in forming his own taste as well as that of the age in which he lives.

As a parallel, he cited 'the best of contemporary architecture is closely related to the best of modern sculpture and constructivist painting because architects, sculptors and constructivist painters are in written or personal contact with one another' through *Circle*.

He also saw that the future of planning should be in collaboration. As was normal amongst modern designers at the time, he ridiculed the garden cities for their cul-de-sacs, avenues of cherry trees, the miles of hedges, and the emphasis upon 'pretty-pretty' effects by the garden designer in large private gardens. In order to perform a revolution[67]

> The town planner as co-ordinator cannot do without the help of the landscape architect, the engineer, and the architect, whose functions through the years have become interdependent and interwoven.

Furthermore the designer and gardener needed to reconsider their contribution in the planning sphere:

> The landscape architect's part in town planning (and his should be a very great rôle indeed) must be one of service to the site and the people who live on it; until now he has been occupied in dispensing decorative favours instead of providing the basis for a new life in Nature.

When he recounted his work for Chermayeff on his garden at Bentley Wood, he entitled the article: 'Planning a Modern Garden: An Experience in Collaboration'. He was to offer an axiom: 'Modern landscape design is inseparable from the spirit, technique, and development of modern architecture.'[68] When he arrived at Harvard, and found that the GSD was committed to interdisciplinary working between architects, landscape architects and planners, he must have thought he had alighted in the promised land. Almost a decade later he was still extolling its potential: 'When the three professions can be brought together in the same studio and on the same project, there is a good chance to develop a new kind of artist.'[69]

An apposite quote from John Dewey's *Art as Experience* (1934) was employed in Tunnard's article, 'The Conscious Stone':[70]

> The separation of architecture … from such arts as painting and sculpture makes a mess of the historical development of the arts.

He affirmed that[71] 'no creative person who is familiar with great art can be content with the current separation of architecture, painting and sculpture. Their re-integration is the sublime responsibility of today's artist,' adding that 'the separation of the arts will become a separation of art and life … to be modern now is not to be too "modern". It is, rather, to be blessed with humility and charged with the inexhaustible strength of humanism.' Art, for Tunnard, included not just architecture and landscape architecture, but sculpture, painting, music, ballet, and all the arts. The country, Tunnard urged, needed a national civic art programme, similar to the Public Works Arts project; in fact, as early as 1953, he was corresponding with Congressman Charles Howell about legislation for a national arts commission.

The theme of painting and sculpture as arts in the city was expanded upon in *The City of Man*. Having provided much historical evidence for the fact that 'where the inspired touch has lingered urban form has been enriched', he lamented that recently 'we have not allowed the artist his place in the city, either as the originator of civic design … or in his capacity as decorator'.[72] The reasons he gave were the attitudes of businessmen and architects, represented by advertising hoardings and functionalism respectively. 'In order to put the artist back into the streets', he wrote, 'a new client must be found', and that had to be Government.[73] The state could commission artists, architects, decorators, craftsmen and musicians creating the mood for private initiative, too.

In his own work, he ceaselessly sought interdisciplinary working, no longer because of some mystical sense that the arts combining would automatically create new forms and beauties, but because he believed in collaboration, someone who saw that the edges of disciplines were also their joins. Throughout his time at Yale he tried to promote greater cooperation between design professionals and environmentalists. In 1958 at a National Trust for Historic Preservation meeting, Tunnard promoted what was then a wildly futuristic idea, that preservation should include the broad heritage of architecture, planning, and rural landscape.[74] Responding to a 1967 questionnaire from Raymond F. Dasmann of the Conservation Foundation, Tunnard stated that 'no discipline can stand isolated', but he went on to say that 'we are far from achieving that "shared" environment which could substitute for the battle for priorities on the face of the earth which seems about to destroy us'. And 'in the university environment itself', Tunnard explained, no doubt reflecting on his difficulties in organising his interdisciplinary planning programme, 'it is well to remember that intellectual confrontation between members of discrete and rigorous discipline are important, and no ordinary consensus will easily supplant their virtues in education'.[75] It was in this world of professional isolation that Tunnard's pleas for interdisciplinary cooperation were again way ahead of his time.

In the mid-1960s, his involvement with several nascent environmental, landscape, and historic preservation programmes provided opportunities for him to promote his interdisciplinary approach. The 1965 White House Conference on Natural Beauty and Lady Bird Johnson's campaign for beautification confirmed many of Tunnard's theses – that beauty and especially natural beauty should be a public concern – but the conference's emphasis still was not as interdisciplinary as he hoped it would be. As a member of the first session of the Advisory Council on Historic Preservation, Tunnard encouraged an inclusive approach in historic preservation. In 1968 he suggested the idea of conference to bring together these related professions to discuss their common cause and action. There is 'a need', he said, 'for the historic preservationists and the nature conservationists to get together – of what avail to preserve an old building on the edge of a polluted river, etc'.[76] He cited examples of individuals who understood these connections; a wife preserving a tavern and a husband trying to conserve the woodlands in Ridgefield, Connecticut, but he was still questing for national attention to the problem.

Blending the built and natural world was another theme recurring in Tunnard's work in his years at Yale. Today such a theme seems commonplace, but in the United States from the 1940s until the early 1970s, a wide chasm existed between design professionals, like architects and landscape architects working in the built environment, and nature conservationists. Even as the environmental movement gathered steam in the 1960s, its emphasis was primarily on the protection of natural resources, not necessarily on the enhancement of urban living areas. Landscape architects were not in the forefront of this movement and historic preservationists then scarcely considered the settings for individual buildings, much less their vistas and impacts on the environment.

Tunnard's interest in and analyses of highway designs may best reflect his remarkably broad and open-minded approach to planning as well as his ability to blend man-made engineering structures with the environment. Tunnard accepted the car as essential for its 'relative flexibility' in meeting a 'dispersed pattern of travel desires', which the public clearly wants.[77] The outstanding section on highway design in *Man-Made America* entitled 'The Paved Ribbon: The Esthetic of Freeway Design' showed how the highway system, especially the recently begun interstate system, could be 'a national monument of enduring beauty'.[78] The design thesis was that 'the paved ribbon should neither destroy the landscape nor be hidden in the landscape. Rather, it should accentuate its character by a firm, yet sensitive, alignment'.[79] The authors' discussion of the plastic harmony of the highway illustrates their remarkable visual sensitivity to transform asphalt lanes into 'sculpture and dance':[80]

> to the eye of the moving observer, the highway slab and its shoulder form an unwinding ribbon of parallel lines, swinging and changing into various horizontal and inclined planes, standing out in stark white or black against the soft, warm colours of the landscape. As it turns and changes directions, as it rises and falls over hills and valleys, as it diverges to accept a stream or pulls together to enter a city, the paved ribbon assumes qualities of an abstract composition in space, which gains in richness because it is not only passively seen but actively traversed by the driver, who experiences visual as well as kinesthetic sensation of tilting, turning, dropping, and climbing.

And, indeed, Tunnard and Pushkarev were able to transform the radii of curves, changes in grades and profiles into sculptural road alignments, which could blend into the landscape, provide visual amenities for the driver, and reduce accidents. In fact, the reader gets so transfixed by the graceful sculpture of the road as it coasts through countryside and city that one almost forgets the polluting cars and trucks roaring along miles of asphalt paving. The same blending of the creative and the practical as well as of man-made structures and their environments occurred in the discussion of the aesthetics of commerce, industry, and housing in *Man-Made America*.

City planning and traffic engineering

The Highways Act of 1956 initiated the Interstate Highway Program, and major urban freeway projects were coming to completion by the late 1950s. The Bureau of Highway Traffic (BHT) had been established at Harvard in 1927 in order to explore the then emerging problem of urban traffic congestion.[81] In 1938 the BHT moved to Yale where it was provided space within the Department of Economics. It offered a certificate (unrecognised by the University) following a one-year graduate programme in traffic and highway engineering. Many of the leaders in the transportation world had been through the BHT; indeed, the Institute of Traffic Engineers (ITE) was for many years dominated by graduates of the BHT.

The planning profession, both those trained in the Beaux-Arts tradition, and those taking an interest in the sociology of cities, were repelled by the work of the highway engineers. However, their counterparts in the highway departments had little sympathy for their planner colleagues, regarding city planning as a loose discipline, with 'city beautiful' objectives being quite impractical in the modern world. Major differences thus appeared between the two professions. However, the Connecticut Life Insurance Company sponsored a modest meeting between planners and highway engineers in Hartford, CT, which had the result of initiating a national conference. The American Municipal Association and the American Association of State Highway Officials joined in holding a conference on Highway and Urban Development in 1958 at Sagamore, NY. A committee at this conference drafted a statement the purpose of which was to 'smooth out' the most difficult differences that were being expressed by engineers, architects, and planners about each other. One of the conclusions was: 'it would be helpful to send engineers to seminars on city planning'. The Bureau's representative at the conference afterwards asked Fred Hurd, Director of the Yale BHT, if a programme placing an engineering slant on city planning could be developed.

It was a mark of Tunnard's dedication to the principle of collaboration and his belief in overcoming conflict through dialogue that he took to this idea with such enthusiasm. He and Hurd devised a suitable curriculum (one year at the BHT and a second one at City Planning) and had this accepted by the University authorities. As it happened, two European students at the BHT had already approached Tunnard to see whether they might join the City Planning Program for a year. The University agreed to accept a year's courses at the BHT as being electives in a Master's Degree conferred through the School of Art and Architecture. The two students were taken on as a trial run, and the following year BPR-sponsored students began to arrive. The 'Joint Program' lasted for about a decade from 1958.

It was seen as a curious hybrid by most. Education tended to class subjects as either a science or as an art. Sciences like physics, chemistry and engineering were 'hard', and literature, art history, design and city planning were 'soft'. The cleavage ran deep. Tunnard was definitely on the 'soft' side of approaches to planning. In the classroom he called for the intelligent integration of man-made interventions and the natural environment. He called for civilised standards of design which were somehow tied to the human being's responsiveness to his surroundings. He studied the Highway and Environment by asking drivers to describe what was seen and how it made them feel.[82] In providing students with the opportunity to see issues from alternative viewpoints, the Joint Program was his contribution to interdisciplinary working and a broader understanding.

The students on the Joint Program thus found themselves in a schizophrenic existence – trained for several hard years to deal with concrete, soil mechanics, stresses and strains, they suddenly found that they were expected to discuss participatory decision making, design concepts and city politics. Instead of the technical manuals at the BHT and *The Highway Capacity Manual*, they were expected to read Tunnard himself, and on topics like rational-comprehensive planning and advocacy planning. The Yale experience was a true cultural shock.

Civic design

'Should architecture be considered an art or a science?'[83] Tunnard could see why the Beaux-Arts approach was considered excessively the former, but was now seeing that the technical approach, with analysis and calculation of people in the mass overriding individual human wants and suppressing creativity, had become excessively the latter: 'carrying the slogan, "form follows function", to its logical conclusion has led many architects into an exaggerated pseudo-scientific attitude toward building'. He saw right-thinking planning as 'functioning where art and science meet', fulfilling a mix of social, scientific and aesthetic functions. He saw himself as someone who could help bring planning back into balance, but with the inexorable rise of the technical approach, that meant being the champion of civic design as an art. With his long interest in art, this was a role he did not find at all distasteful.

A word on terminology is helpful here. The term 'planning' has long been ambiguous. One definition is the making of plans, i.e. showing the intended form and disposition of the physical elements of a city, the traditional art practised by Baron Haussmann in Paris and the City Beautiful movement in numerous cities in North America. Another is the making of development or master plans, documents crammed with statistics, analyses and policies, but often amounting to no more than wishful thinking and generally ignored. Officials engaged in such planning were calling themselves 'city planners', so Dean Hudnut toyed with 'architecture-of-cities',[84] and Tunnard preferred 'civic design', for planning 'with a conscious hand'.[85] Both believed that better models of decision making could allow the groundwork contained in master plans to inform civic design that citizens would identify with and be proud of.

Urban sharawadgi

Hubert De Cronin Hastings had resumed editorship of *AR* when Jim Richards was called up for the war effort. He derided both the Garden City movement and the MARS Group's 'new Jerusalem' of 'all open space and white concrete'.[86] The problem for the latter was that the former was at least human-scale and could be imagined as a lifestyle, whereas tower blocks set in parkland were too alien. The

Figure 6.9 Baron Hausmann, 'nonpareil of planners' flattered an emperor, bribed magistrates and bullied landowners to achieve his aims: 'Paris was his pie'. Cartoon by Tunnard.
(Source: *Architectural Record*, 94 (Oct. 1943), p. 47)

answer was to get away from both caricatures by accepting that the key was a meld of many forms of the old with many forms of the new:

> Neither side is anxious to give up its day-dreams so far as to admit that one ideal is as unlikely a realisation as the other; that English cities … will always be an extraordinary hotch-potch of competing elements; that the visual problem is to coax these competitors into a larger harmony.

Some rationale was required that could enable this. Hastings had been impressed by Christopher Hussey's *The Picturesque* (1927), and he saw an application for the aesthetic principles stated by the early theorists of the picturesque in modern city planning. Variety, curiosity, intricacy, contrast, and balance were exactly the qualities needed to humanise the newly built cities in Britain. He was likewise attracted by Sir William Temple's term, sharawadgi, the art of making a design seem as if it had not been designed, but was a work of nature. This seemed appropriate to the intelligent adaptation of cities that had been largely unplanned and which would necessarily visually retain this feel. Using Horace Walpole's spelling of the word, Hastings posed the question: 'how can we achieve an urban Sharawaggi?'

Hastings found two researchers who could contribute more on the landscape theory side. One was Frank Clark, who wrote on sharawaggi;[87] the other was Nikolaus Pevsner, who had joined *AR* during the war, and who had theories on the picturesque.[88] These arcane articles were a surprise to the *AR* readership; by the 1920s the word 'picturesque' had to most architects become indicative of the garden-city approach to urban design, quaintness, and everything that *AR* stood against.

By 1945 Tunnard had turned to planning matters, and understood perfectly the quandary of people like himself who rejected both the Garden City aesthetic and the Corbusian vision from CIAM. He would have been sympathetic to Pevsner and Clark, with his knowledge of the landscape garden and having written 'Asymmetrical Garden Planning: The Oriental Aesthetic', and also knew something about sharawadgi, having used the word and the idea in *Gardens in the Modern Landscape*.[89] He was of course flattered by various mentions by Hastings and Pevsner in their articles, and contributed a letter dated 8 March 1946 to *AR*. He had found a nice quote in Richard Graves's poetry:

> Discordant objects taught to join
> Now form, now break, the varying line;
> With well-ranged lights one mass compose
> 'Till with full strength the landskip glows.

The poem could be read as advocating the 'humanized method of planning' sought by Hastings. Sharawadgi, Tunnard considered, 'is the antithesis of … building in uniform rows'. The 'art of the irregular … horrifies both pure modernists and the treasurer of the building society'. He envisaged the aesthetic as 'one of skylines, colour, applied decoration, foliage and open vistas … of balancing masses against voids'. The mention of masses and voids reflected his interest in Giedion's 'Space Theory'. However, the general sentiment opened the way for the re-introduction of vistas, axes, styles, and decoration, all aspects of the despised Beaux-Arts tradition, but Tunnard argued that 'we must be less suspicious about styles … and accept the best that each can offer us'.

Hastings developed his ideas on the picturesque qualities of towns through Gordon Cullen's drawings in *AR*, eventually resulting in Cullen's book *Townscape* (1961). Tunnard meanwhile was still writing that 'Sharawadgi … may have present-day application' in 1948,[90] but by 1951 was not so sure:[91]

> The idea, which in essence implies an esthetic of careless or disorderly grace, has never found much favour in the United States – perhaps this is just as well; we have enough disorder already and need a stronger discipline than one of studied irregularity to redeem our architectural and civic future.

He seems to have tired of such a purely visual prescription. In *The City of Man* he mentioned 'the theory of the picturesque applied to city planning' in Britain, only to dismiss it: 'the whole idea has been the amusing toy of art historians until now, when it is fast becoming a cult among certain of the younger architects'. An enthusiasm for heterogeneous collections of buildings might be one form of visual appreciation but it could lead to inaction: 'you are more likely to finish by defending the slums and the *status quo* than proposing any definite town planning system'.[92] It seems that he had conceded that the picturesque was not a sufficient prescription for humanised civic design, and he had been drawn to the conclusion that an integrated multi-disciplinary approach to planning was required, and that it should include deliberate interventions on behalf of art.

The creation of beauty

To Tunnard, the preconditions for creating beauty were imagination, experiment and collaborative working. In the 1930s, like most designers, he had been persuaded by Adolf Loos's assertion in 1897 that 'To find beauty in form instead of making it depend on ornament is the goal to which humanity is aspiring'.[93] 'For Loos', he had written, 'beauty in a work of art was attained by the completeness of its utility and a high degree of harmony of its parts.' The search for decorative beauty was 'profitless'. Instead, beauty was a 'by-product of the creative attitude to garden planning'.[94] Designers do not aim 'at the creation of beauty, as in the past, but at creating the work of art. Our conception of the latter transcends the idea of beauty, although it accepts this quality as a logical accompaniment of the artistic fact.'

Without abandoning the preconditions above, he clearly by 1948 thought very differently about the creative act. He eliminated the paragraph on beauty being a by-product of the creative process from the second edition of *Gardens in the Modern Landscape*,[95] and was soon saying the opposite: 'If we continue to hope for beauty as a by-product of design, good buildings will not be the result.'[96] Hence the designer 'Must include … the positive attempt to create beautiful surroundings. Beauty does not take care of itself.'

The difficulties were that, at that time, architects and planners appeared uninterested in the task of creating beauty, and the public showed little interest either. Tunnard lamented that:[97]

> In city planning, sociology, engineering and pressure salesmanship are rated higher than esthetics. Whilst this remains true, can you blame people for not being interested or informed?

Tunnard had respect for public taste; it behoved planners to remember that cities were built by and for the public. In this he was certainly of a more democratic persuasion than most Modernist planners:[98]

> Public taste is not the ephemeral thing it is supposed to be by disappointed architects. If people do not like a certain building it is more likely the building that is at fault, not the people.

This was a very different attitude from his criticism of the planners he encountered over Bentley Wood 16 years before! He also felt that the client, often a city corporation, needed to take interest itself in decision making, and not abdicate it to its expert advisors.

Meanwhile, in Tunnard's view, the city planner was 'neglecting esthetics as his strongest weapon … The architect, who once was the guardian of urban esthetics, has given up trying.' This was largely a consequence of recently trained architects having become excessively technically orientated in meeting various standards for light, air, sanitation and so forth. This was driving the practice of architecture away from meeting spiritual and aesthetic needs. 'We have forgotten art in order to be comfortable, and in pursuit of that fallacy we are becoming more uncomfortable every day.'[99]

By 1948 Tunnard was using the word 'beauty' in talks and articles. His ideas on a new landscape theory included 'a positive drive toward the creation of beauty, not as a by-product, but as an integral part of out design'.[100] At a MOMA symposium of the same year on 'What is happening to Modern Architecture?' Tunnard queried whether modern architecture lacked something: 'dare I mention the word, "beauty"?'[101] It was a surprising decision to use the word openly. Most architects and landscape architects would have been taken aback to hear a speaker talk in this way. They would have been more comfortable hearing about 'aesthetic quality', or 'landscape quality'; but 'beauty' smacked of the Beaux Arts, and sounded unprofessional in the Modernist era.

Tunnard's opportunity to explain why beauty needed to be discussed and how it could be created came with *The City of Man* (1953), subtitled *The Recovery of Beauty in the City*. In his day, he observed:[102]

Literature in the field reveals an almost exclusive reliance on technics, coupled with severe and often ridiculous moral condemnation of the city and its culture. The reader must search hard to find a recognition of Art as a power in the creation and regeneration of cities.

He described the book as 'an attempt to fill this lacuna'. More specifically he wanted a revival of civic design, the art of designing physical changes to cities that not only satisfy social and economic aims, but express the life of the city by spatial and visual means.

In 1954 at least Josep Lluis Sert (Stubbins's successor as Dean at Harvard) recognised that perhaps an open discussion of beauty was due:[103]

> It is a little difficult today to deal with this aesthetic factor because people may say you are going backwards, using some of those same words we heard in schools many years ago as part of the program the Beaux-Arts was trying to promote. But it is not true … There are some things that have been eternally in architecture, regardless of styles, regardless of time. Those are the factors that tie man to everything that is beautiful, to which man normally reacts and appreciates, which contribute to make a better living, a better environment for man; that is the key word.

However, a great impediment to a recognition of beauty as an aim was the legacy of Gropius's educational methods, which of course Tunnard had seen first hand, in particular the premium on originality. Gropius had claimed that:[104]

> a student is so absorbed by studying music composed by others, poetry written by others, and architecture, painting and sculpture created by famous men of the past, that he rarely finds a chance to try his hand at *making* poetry, music or art of his own invention.

Tunnard thought that each student attempting to prove his original genius resulted in visual clashes: 'very few buildings had the calm authority of a work of art'.

Furthermore, in terms of civic design, '[t]he striving for originality for its own sake, the cult of the new for its own sake, prevents the tradition of quiet anonymous building from continuing use on the part of our better designers'.[105] As an example of how ill-considered buildings could reinforce or ruin the qualities of others, he revealed his outrage at how Independence Hall had been treated:[106]

> nothing is more ridiculous than the beautiful Independence Hall in Philadelphia, one of our very best architectural inheritances, dwarfed by the Curtis Publishing Company and other tall buildings around.

This tendency 'denies us the pleasures of a quiet street architecture and the unassuming court or square'.

Tunnard saw that Gropius's opposition to architectural history in order to prevent students borrowing from previous masters was a mistake. 'The esthetic sense must be trained or it will wither or become perverted.'[107] Of his new opinions[108]

> [m]ost important perhaps is the conviction that creative art has a firmer foundation when based on the accumulation of acquired knowledge rather than intuitiveness alone … The free, untrammelled creator may be an engaging personality, but he may also be out of touch with the needs of the times, and commit some frightful blunder when faced with a situation requiring exact economic, artistic, or historical knowledge.

Tunnard thereby rejected the essentially Romantic model of the source of creativity, as first famously espoused by J.J. Rousseau, and had nailed his mast to the 'Classical' model. This can briefly be characterised as follows. The great masters of the past had themselves initially studied under a master to learn the technique. Complete mastery of technique, once achieved, became the freedom of the artist to convert his ideas into paint, stone or space. There would be no question of copyism or sterility as long as the idea behind a design stemmed from the needs and conditions of the time.

For reasons such as this, Tunnard thought, a study of history was essential:

> The more forward-looking practitioners regret this gap in their training and many have now begun to study the methods of past times in order to salvage what may be useful to them in cultivating their artistic growth.

He advocated that the student should travel through time and space in order to expand his horizons, and this made history and study abroad very desirable:[109]

> the current emphasis on intuitiveness and self-expression is very limiting. If the student once knows good architecture he is on the way to creative activity.

Education in the aesthetics of the city should not be limited to architectural students. Politicians, the public and planners would all benefit from a greater awareness. 'The indiscriminate bringing together of buildings of different character in the modern city calls for education in esthetics by and for the city planner'.[110] The public had been indifferent to visual anarchy but was learning fast.[111]

Tunnard proposed the establishment of civic art commissions, so that art and design could be incorporated in public decision making; he gave speeches entitled 'Waging War on Ugliness,' and in his days on the New Haven Plan City Commission, he decried the city's low-quality new buildings, 'buildings smirched by compromise,' and urged the city to respect its architectural heritage.[112] He argued for the retention of the city's important historic buildings, like its main Post Office, and showed how simple design principles like a wall of buildings along the city's central Green could stress the significance of that space.

Figure 6.10 Tunnard emphasised the importance of art in the city and showed Jules
Coutan's statue of Mercury above the entrance to Grand Central Terminal,
New York City. Drawing by John Cohen.
(Source: Tunnard, with Reed, *American Skyline* (1955), p. 18)

Cities as works of art

For Tunnard, the city should be a collective work of art. The civilising role of
aesthetics was paramount, providing the underpinning of most of his work in
planning. He thought like an art lover whether as a practising landscape architect,
a writer or an advocate of aesthetic considerations in the planning of man-
made and natural environments. All his books, but especially *The City of Man*
and his last book, *A World With a View*, brought out his interest in stirring the
'esthetic conscience' to create fulfilling and stimulating natural and man-made
environments.

Hence the civic designer must 'revive the visual approach'. He will be[113]

> the creative designer ... a visual expert, an artist in the form of cities, and
> aware of the contribution which others [like natural and social scientists] must
> make if we are to live in communities which achieve the integration of art
> and life. He must know what tradition means ... He must develop the quality
> of imagination which can seize on the insignificant-seeming things and make
> them into magical touchstones of urbanism; but he must not be arrogant ...
> With this democratic ideal, ... the creative designer will achieve the lasting
> triumph in that market place beyond economics, the city born of art.

Tunnard believed in city planning as an art form, one that should provide aesthetic satisfactions like all the other creative arts:[114]

> Civic Design which is so closely a part of architecture and the allied arts has a tremendous power, the power to move us deeply.

Furthermore, as a social and public art as the setting for everyday life, it should nurture the other arts. He looked forward to it being a 'method of coordinating all the creative arts which must be given urban expression if we are to achieve an integration of art and life'.

Some thought that Tunnard was trying to revive the City Beautiful movement. Not for a moment did he believe that that would be right, though he did see that in some respects his concept of a revived civic design would reassert some older modes of thought. An example was the formulation of tests and measures against which the practice of civic design could be gauged. The original picturesque theorists had defined the qualities of a landscape that determined the degree of the picturesque. In a similar way Tunnard nominated the desirable qualities of the civic scene as accent, surprise, ornament, order, repetition, and monumental effect.[115] 'All these elements can be consciously applied to make our cities more interesting in form and detail.'

Monumental scale, he believed, was particularly suited to the vast cities of America, and their central business districts.[116] Tunnard approved of the advances made by the City Beautiful movement of the early twentieth century in coming to terms with the scale of cities, and advocated that this theme was continued through 'grand design'.[117] He also approved of Baron Haussmann's achievement in Paris: 'in seizing strategic points and opening up their approaches he taught us to "make no little plans".'[118] Even more impressive, he thought, was Jacques Gréber's avenue linking the City Hall and the Art Museum in Philadelphia.

In Tunnard's day the business of the planner was largely producing two-dimensional land-use diagrams, and architects were (and still are) fond of producing diagrams that indicated movements of people through the spaces of a building or city. He disliked such two-dimensional thinking as simplistic and for its presumption that people can be coerced into behaving as per the plan. He thought that planning should have passed the stage of the land-use map:[119]

> one method of planning with which we have been familiar now for many years – the two-dimensional diagram of land allocation with perhaps some social emphasis on housing and mechanical emphasis on traffic facilities is not going to satisfy many interests in the city from now on.

Familiar with the joys and unpredictable uses of spaces in older European cities, he was similarly unimpressed by design from flow diagrams:[120]

> We must learn not to create space patterns from space-flow diagrams for

Figure 6.11 The Benjamin Franklin Parkway, Philadelphia, designed by the French city planner Jacques Gréber in 1918, was upheld by Tunnard as an example of grand design.
(Source: Tunnard, with Reed, *American Skyline* (1955), p. 160)

"In proposing his plans the town planner should take into consideration the possibilities for their achievement."

Figure 6.12 In Tunnard's day the business of the planner was largely producing two-dimensional land-use diagrams, but he disliked this as simplistic. Hudnut emphasised that planning was a political as much as a technical skill. Cartoon by Tunnard.
(Source: *Architectural Record*, 94 (Oct. 1943), p. 46)

people to follow in their daily lives, but to create space in which people can form their own patterns.

He considered that an aesthetic based solely on two-dimensional spatial relationships and materials was too austere and could not satisfy public taste. He had much sympathy with 'a new generation tired of our endless streets with their wretched sameness':[121]

> No wonder they crowd Stratford-on-Avon or Williamsburg, where picturesqueness, detail, glimpses of history, architecture, or anything else they can find there offer a welcome change from their deadeningly remorseless surroundings.

Henry Hope Reed had no doubt pointed out how style and ornament gave buildings individuality, incident and visual interest. Tunnard thought it was time to challenge the Modernist rejection of ornament. 'Latterly the wave of neo-Puritanism has made visual elegance unpopular.'[122] He now saw that detail and variety were extremely important to public satisfaction. 'We have forgotten the role to be played by the artisan. Workmanship and detail must be revived … if it is missing, we notice it.'[123]

Furthermore, ornament could be more than just frivolous clothing to a building; it could help to give important buildings and scenes symbolism and meaning:[124]

> Questions of memory, hope and purpose enter into our vision of cities and that is where art and knowledge of art are so important. In training ourselves to see the city and its relationships, we must also take into account social and philosophic problems of symbolism, for instance, and what the city means to its people in its visible form.

Creative urbanism

By 1951 Tunnard was proposing a model of decision making in planning which he dubbed 'creative urbanism'.[125] It concerned the respective roles of client, technical expert and civic designer. The title of his article 'Civic Designer, Urban Analyst and Public Client' pursued the theme which was also incorporated into *The City of Man*.

Civic design had been the business of City Beautiful and Garden City planners like Frederick Law Olmsted, as at the World's Columbian Exposition in Chicago; Daniel Burnham, also in Chicago; and Raymond Unwin, at Letchworth. The purpose of a planning scheme was determined by the client, often acting on philanthropic impulses; the town planner was not expected to be involved in determining the broad objectives of a scheme, merely how they could be made real. At least this had clarity:[126]

"Each in his narrow cell forever laid."

Figure 6.13 Joseph Hudnut lamented that 'Heaven only knows how many Master Plans are buried in the Library of Planning at Harvard'. Cartoon by Tunnard. (Source: *Architectural Record*, 94 (Oct. 1943), p. 45)

In the early years of the present century the function of the professional town planner was still fairly well defined. He was, although not always called so, a civic designer.

However, their role in coordinating the physical form of cities had been undermined after the First World War by experts who interceded between the civic designer and the client:

When town planning became a function of government after 1910 the civic designer was put in an anomalous position. The sociologist, the social engineer, the economist, the lawyer and the political scientist – program-makers for physical planning and housing – began to take over some of his former design functions. Where facilities were to go, how the site was to be planned, types of street layout and even appearance were often predetermined. Specialists began to appear – highway traffic engineers, housing consultants and industrial experts reserved whole areas to themselves which the civic designer had once considered his own … The civic designer and his patron had become separated by a spongy layer of 'experts' which was absorbing much of the power of both older parties.

This process had resulted in a common perception of Civic Design as something which comes after 'planning'.[127] As early as 1946 he was observing that[128]

> now that the world is about to build again in quantity, there seems to be a limited place for aesthetic analysis, as a help to town planners and architects to see things in the round. But we must learn to link aesthetic with social problems. The dangerous rationalization that fine building will make a fine society, so dear to the architectural mind, must be forgotten.

In the second edition of *Gardens in the Modern Landscape* he was repeating that[129]

> Architecture and physical planning have never shaped society … Architects and allied technicians must go into community planning – they are badly needed – but … they should not try to dictate its final form. We must beware of the approach of the technocrat, of anti-intellectual reliance on 'intuition', of metaphysical formulae and of the so-called biological or 'organic' approach … which does not belong in the socio-economic process of town planning.

Tunnard regretted that modern architects, exalting technique and economy, 'verge close to being technocrats'.[130] The technocrat, he explained, is a man who 'believes in an elite group of specialists to run things for us'. Highway engineers had been allowed to 'build Chinese walls that separate neighborhood from neighborhood'. The result had been ugliness and congestion. 'We train too many "practical" men – what errors are committed in the name of practicality! – and too few artists.' The role of civic designers was evident:[131]

> Civic Designers must function as guardians and promoters of everything to do with vision. There are plenty of other technicians to worry about whether or not the heating functions or the plumbing works.

He also had strong views on the proper contribution of the sociologist. If it was not true that 'fine building makes a fine society', the obverse was not true either. Good social aims do not necessarily make good buildings, and the hope that 'the just social program will automatically result in "good" solutions is destroyed by experience'.[132] The answer to his question, 'can social needs be automatically objectified in specific urban forms?' was thus in the negative.

The social scientist can propose social policies, but 'has not yet been able to tell us what would be a favourable urban atmosphere'. He should be uniting his insights with the creative mind of the designer, and was:[133]

> not able to help directly in the conditioning of the urban environment except as clinical experts. The civic designer, on the other hand, because he is a creative person may be able to help more directly in creating the amenities

of life because his approach and the results of his approach will actually condition the life that goes on in cities. He has to start where the social scientist leaves off.

Tunnard's response to the rise of the sociologist and technocrat was his new model of decision making. He emphasised that it was the client's role to be decision maker, not anyone else's. The client represented the public, and the designer, informed by researchers and scientists, should be responsible for offering physical solutions that worked technically, socially and aesthetically. So instead of civic design being a mere presentational activity following the more serious business of the deliberations of sociologist and engineer, it would interact with the technical studies through a process of pooling and fusion of ideas, integrating and reconciling them, until a balanced set of recommendations was in a fit state to be put to the client's officers who would test the ideas against the aims of the project.

This proposed process of decision making is historically of interest as a precursor of other writings in the 1960s, a most productive decade for planning theory. The most influential paper asserting the primacy of the client stated:[134]

> [W]e maintain that neither the planner's technical competence nor his wisdom entitles him to ascribe or dictate values to his immediate or ultimate clients. This view is in keeping with the democratic prescriptive that public decision-making and action should reflect the will of the client; a concept which rejects the notion that planners or other technicians are endowed with the ability to divine either the client's will or a public will.

Another issue in planning theory was 'the science of muddling-through' versus 'rational-comprehensive' planning. Adherents of the latter, believing in broad goals and drastic action, were the spiritual heirs of socialism and the CIAM approach. 'Muddling through' was much closer to Karl Popper's proposal for incremental changes to be made, the results assessed, and then further changes made. Its chief advocate in planning was Charles Lindblom, a fellow professor of

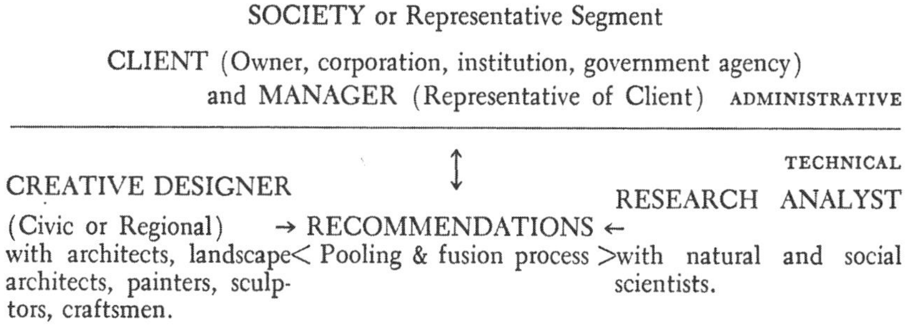

SOCIETY or Representative Segment

CLIENT (Owner, corporation, institution, government agency)
and MANAGER (Representative of Client) ADMINISTRATIVE

                                ↕   TECHNICAL

CREATIVE DESIGNER   RESEARCH ANALYST
(Civic or Regional)   → RECOMMENDATIONS ←
with architects, landscape< Pooling & fusion process >with natural and social
architects, painters, sculp-   scientists.
tors, craftsmen.

Figure 6.14 Tunnard's diagram of how the process of 'Creative Urbanism' should work.
(Source: Tunnard, *The City of Man* (1953), p., 366)

Tunnard's at Yale, whose Chair was in Economics and Political Science. Tunnard's sympathies would have been with Lindblom, just as they had been with Hudnut and Gaus, though in fact he wrote less on the process of planning as he came to concentrate on the form of cities and preservation issues towards the end of the 1950s.

Obviously student projects could not replicate real-life decision making, but Tunnard's description of his course shows that he carried his ideas through to the classroom:[135]

> [The student] is encouraged to develop a concept of the city in all dimensions and to present his solutions in a clear, an imaginative and graphic manner, backed up by the techniques of survey and research essential to all city planning activity. The valued cooperation that public and private agencies afford us from time to time teaches him to understand the needs and demands of other people and to realize that the city must always reflect the work of many hands. It is hoped that this broadly humanistic attitude to the city and its problems is brought out.

Intangibles and values

The technocratic dominance of planning that Tunnard warned against increased, if anything, in the 1960s as computers increased in capability. Mathematical models were developed on the analogy of gravitational attraction between populations and attractors like central business districts or industrial areas. The pull diminished with the distance between them. Hence socio-economic information could be linked to traffic generation, and the planner could juggle with the size of new communities, employment generation and the required capacity of highways.

Land use and transportation plans, using such models, were highly mechanistic, and there was little scope for imagination, design or heritage values. However, their advocates argued for models and analysis to take over some of the role formerly given to creativity; for example, C. Britton Harris, a city planner at the University of Pennsylvania, stated:[136]

> The basic difference between two large groups of planning-oriented professionals appears to hinge on the use of models in planning, but this may be in part a superficial manifestation. It would appear that some imaginative, creative, and wilful planners view with distrust and dismay not only the growing paraphernalia of analysis with its mathematical involutions, but even the growing role of analysis itself. Such distrust, if it exists, is not based widely on any hostility to knowledge. Nor is it based entirely on an unsophisticated view of analytic method: otherwise it would be hard to explain the obvious romantic attraction which computer technology exerts throughout the profession. It seems much more likely to be based on the implicit assumption that analysis in the ascendancy would not aid, but replace, the wilful and self-directed control of man over his urban-metropolitan environment.

Harris used, as Tunnard had, the conflict between traffic engineers and city planners to make his position clear:

> [M]odels are considered as theories which, in part, serve as substitutes for experiment, and which are designed to answer questions about how the real world will react to changes in conditions and policies. Examining the questions which a transportation planner and a city planner are apt to ask, we find that neither one at present asks enough questions to bridge the gap between their viewpoints. This is certainly not a shortcoming of the models, but rather of the planners' respective professional limitations and biases. Finally, it is suggested that neither profession can achieve a successful solution of its problems without a joint effort to improve the construction of theories through model building, so as to answer entirely new questions of overwhelming importance.

Judgements of whether expenditure on highways should take place, or which projects should take precedence, were guided by 'cost-benefit analysis'. This compared the cost of construction to the benefits of reduced travel times.

Dealing with intangibles

The critics of cost-benefit analysis pointed out that it ignored all factors that were not quantifiable in monetary terms. Tunnard was to recall that traffic engineers had ignored visual aspects:[137]

> Only a few years ago a leading traffic engineering consultant refused to take part in a visual study of a proposed highway, because, he said, aesthetic factors could not be measured. He has since changed his opinion, acknowledging that at least these factors should be given some weight. It is significant, too, that the United States Highway Research Board, since the passage of the Highway Beautification Act of 1965, has funded studies on the aesthetic aspects of highway design for objectives other than that of traffic safety.

Those who wished aesthetics, historical values, nature conservation interests and so forth to be taken into account had three lines of argument. Some proposed the notional costing of intangibles, for example trees, on the basis that this was the only way to have them incorporated directly into the cost-benefit analysis. However, the basis of notional costings has never been entirely convincing. A second way was to define 'constraints' on sieve maps, which would require a legislative backing. For example, national park, nature conservation and archaeology interests in the UK were all mapped and treated as inviolate except in unusual circumstances. A third approach was to present the decision maker with the full consequences of decisions on a balance sheet and thus confront him with his own value judgements.

The sieve-map approach was essentially that adopted by Ian McHarg in his *Design with Nature* (1969). It clarified the principal values affected, and overlayed them graphically, so that, say, highways might be located through the white areas. On the other hand, it could not differentiate between the relative importance of values, and the boundaries drawn could be arbitrary. The balance-sheet system, on the other hand, was not a design tool, but enabled options to be assessed by identifying all interest groups and quantifying all known impacts in their own terms, and if that were not possible, providing a brief explanatory text. It was thus a combination of cost-benefit analysis and environmental-impact assessment. The 'Leitch framework' employed for assessing highway proposals in the UK from 1977 was in this form.[138]

During the 1960s and 1970s Tunnard became involved in national and international bodies concerned with heritage preservation. The White House Conference on Natural Beauty of 1965 was followed in 1967 by a spell on the President's Advisory Council on Historic Preservation. He was also active in the USA's National Trust for Historic Preservation, and the International Council on Monuments and Sites. The Division of Cultural Heritage of the United Nations Economic, Social and Cultural Organisation (UNESCO) asked him and John C. Pollacco to conduct a technical assistance mission to Jamaica between September 1968 and April 1969, and afterwards to the Kathmandu valley in Nepal, and the stupas at Pramanan and Borobudur in Indonesia.[139]

Seeing decision making at these elevated levels seems to have persuaded Tunnard that the fundamental problem for preservation and conservation was not faulty decision-making tools, but that decision makers too easily ignored 'basic human esthetic needs'. He sought through his book, *A World with a View* (1978) to address 'the absence of an esthetic conscience in man's dealing with his environment'.[140]

His appreciation of art, culture, and beauty in society, undoubtedly strengthened in his many years of scholarship, was certainly challenged as he tried to introduce it in many difficult planning situations. Having done his best at grappling with planning, one senses that Tunnard felt freed in *A World with a View* to return to his consuming interests in aesthetics and how art and culture can help produce a civilised and beautiful world. Ian McHarg had argued for an ecological imperative to counterbalance purely financial considerations; but Tunnard here made a direct plea for recognition of cultural values in the landscape.

He saw that conservation was more than ensuring a clean and healthy environment. However, what right had natural beauty, rare species and architectural excellence to protection? These values had no absolute right for their own sake. Tunnard argued that the way to convince decision makers of their importance was to illuminate the nature of aesthetic values and show how meaningful they were to the public; to replace confrontation by persuasion, in the hope of coexistence rather than conflict, and curation rather than exploitation:[141]

> [I]t is absurd to think any longer of the natural versus the man-made in terms of environmental values, any more than it is necessary to think of antagonism between the past and the present, which ideally should merge in the consciousness of man. Man must take on the role of custodian of nature

and of the past; he is the sole animal who understands the contributions of civilisations other than his own, contributions psychologically important to his own welfare. Coexistence has become a vital concern of present-day society – coexistence with nature and the rest of the cultural patrimony contained in the past.

His hope was that greater understanding of the aesthetic values of society would help to bridge 'the yawning chasm between unbridled exploitation of technology on the one side and full development of the cultural patrimony on the other'.[142] A chapter was devoted to 'Landscape and Scenic Preservation'.

The book's subtitle – *An Inquiry into the Nature of Scenic Values* – introduces the reader to a then unfamiliar approach, a discussion of values.

Values

Tunnard's long interest in 'cultural patrimony' had taught him that assessment of the landscape involved the landscapes of the mind. Although the visible landscape was the most obvious aspect of scenery, many other factors gave mental satisfaction. He instructed the reader how to enhance the 'invisible realities' such as an understanding of geology or ecology, an appreciation of the rarity or natural wildness of a habitat, a respect for a religious site and a feeling for history.[143] The botanic garden, for example, 'induces scientific curiosity, and often … it encourages esthetic sensibilities … Like nature reserves and wilderness areas, they form oases that testify to man's determination to husband nature.'[144] He showed how art and literature too, in crafting imaginative worlds, have influenced conceptions of the physical world. He explained the many aspects of 'scenic values':[145]

> All elements of society must come eventually to realize that scenic values are an essential part of the cultural life of nations, that their desecration is a crime against the people, and that they can be cherished and enhanced only by the development of aesthetic judgment. Further, it must be realized that this kind of judgement can be applied to all the arts and sciences, for as the philosophers tell us, their ultimate satisfactions are aesthetic ones.

'The landscape is a storehouse of impressions, of knowledge, of loyalty', he wrote.[146] He quoted the art historian, Bernard Berenson, who pointed out in *Seeing and Knowing* (1953) that looking involved both retinal seeing and conceptual comprehension, so that perception was partly a function of previously-held images. Tunnard also quoted Constable's opinion that 'we see nothing unless we understand',[147] and Thomas Henry Huxley's observation that 'To a person uninstructed in natural history, his country or seaside stroll is like a walk through a gallery full of wonderful works of art, nine-tenths of which have their faces turned to the wall.'[148] Tunnard commented that memory and familiarity were important too:[149]

'[M]emory' (hence history) enters the picture and similarities between objects and events are related to the situation of the moment. Thus identification may include more than the senses perceive at the time. Such a concept would give much more importance to already-seen landscapes in the evaluation of views.

A determinant of the aesthetic value felt by any individual was, then, knowledge and understanding of the scene in question: 'Our view of the landscape is conditioned by familiarity.'[150]

At the White House Conference on Natural Beauty in 1965 Tunnard commented that there would be different perceptions of beauty by different people.[151] He had earlier made this point in *Man-Made America*:[152]

[A] mountain range may receive the attention of the hydraulic engineer or of Gutzon Borglum, of the skiing enthusiast or of Robert Frost – each will see it differently: as a utilitarian, a hedonist, a conceptualist, or a moralist, whatever he may be, connecting the phenomenon with his own intuitions and ideas.

Figure 6.15 Bronx River Gorge, now within New York Botanical Garden, included as 'Wilderness in town'.
(Source: Tunnard, *A World with a View* (1978), p. 25)

Tunnard's humanistic approach contrasted with that adopted by most of those who developed 'landscape evaluation' in the 1960s and 1970s. They placed reliance upon mathematical modelling, believing that beauty in the landscape, or 'landscape quality', was an objective reality that could be scaled. The theory, if it can be elevated to this description, behind this assumption was based on Modernist and neo-Platonic assumptions, so that beauty was derived from form, and form was a by-product of the cosmic laws by which the universe operated.

The supporters of landscape evaluation, whilst recognising that beauty was objective, conceded that the only means of detecting it was the human. The right conditions were for the human mind to be passive, an empty vessel, unquestioning and awaiting stimulus from its environment. The purity of the response could be affected by subjective influences such as background, training and mood, giving deviations from the 'correct' or 'normal' response. Detached yet sensitised experts like the researchers themselves would be more able to free up the mind to get in tune with the Universe, and would be the best hope of ascertaining beauty reliably. Because their responses would be more objective, the results could be treated mathematically. Complex regression analysis formulae were developed in order to model and predict 'landscape quality' based on the components visible in the landscape.

Just as Tunnard had rejected 'pseudo-scientific' approaches to building and planning in the 1950s, he now showed no inclination to follow academic fashion in landscape evaluation either. He rejected 'semi-scientific classifications', saying that 'the whole question of quality somehow eludes this labelling process'. He also was unconvinced by Jay Appleton's 'prospect-refuge' theory expounded in *The Experience of Landscape* (1975). He observed that none of these technical experts were *vedutisti* – painters of views – a background that might have given them true insight.[153]

The wheel came round, and by the time of *World with a View* his position had come to be shared by others. One criticism of the 'objective' adherents was their refusal to admit to the subjectivity that underlay the design of studies and their assessments. 'Evaluators themselves generally assumed that they were dealing with scientific facts about landscape esthetics, not just with their own scenic values.'[154] Wittingly or unwittingly, 'academics as well as planners parade their own tastes as survey results'. Another author pointed out that no study could assume from the outset that there is necessarily a consensus on what is beautiful and attacked the reliance on mathematical analysis.[155] Despite a rearguard action by the 'objective' camp, the humanistic approach became accepted in the 1980s.

Furthermore, values – which can be complex and potentially variable – became the currency of international efforts at landscape conservation in the 1990s. The postwar approach, based on the search for universal principles which could then be enshrined in charters, faltered. This was most clearly seen in the development of the cultural landscapes approach, a movement that might have taken any one of a number of statements by Tunnard as its manifesto.[156]

Notes

1　Tunnard, *American Skyline* (1955), p. 197.
2　Sharp (1936), p. 88.
3　Eden (1935), 'The English Tradition in the Countryside II', pp. 147–9.
4　Ibid., pp. 198–201.
5　Tunnard, *Gardens in the Modern Landscape* (1938), pp. 9–61.
6　Ibid., pp. 129–32; the seven drawings were by Letitia Hicks-Beach.
7　Ibid., p. 6.
8　Tunnard, *Gardens in the Modern Landscape* (1948), p. 8.
9　Ibid., p. 5.
10　Hudnut (1949).
11　Pearlman (2007), p. 173.
12　Tunnard, *The City of Man* (1953), 333.
13　Pearlman (2007), pp. 36–7.
14　Anon., 'What Is Happening to Modern Architecture', as cited by Pearlman (2007), p. 175.
15　These were by John Cohen (b. 1932), at the time studying at the Yale School of Fine Arts, and who went on to be a photographer and film maker of note.
16　Tunnard, *American Skyline* (1955), p. 16.
17　Tunnard, *Gardens in the Modern Landscape* (1948), 5.
18　LI Archives, Box 6; Christopher Tunnard (ed.), 'Garden and Landscape' (printed catalogue of ILA exhibition held in June 1939), p. 5.
19　Tunnard, *American Skyline* (1955), p. 15.
20　Ibid., p. 195
21　Tunnard and Pushkarev (eds), *Man-Made America* (1963), p. 439.
22　Tunnard, *The City of Man* (1953), p. 354.
23　Ibid., p. 354.
24　Tunnard Papers, Box 12, folder 198.
25　Tunnard, *A World with a View* (1978), p. 156.
26　Tunnard Papers, Box 3, folder 39.
27　Tunnard and Pushkarev (eds), *Man-Made America* (1963), p. 425.
28　Tunnard Papers, Box 22, folder 341.
29　Sir James Richards remembered that Tunnard had joined MARS soon after its start, though this was unlikely to have been as early as 1934.
30　Richards (March 1938), 'Modern Architecture and the Public, The M.A.R.S. Exhibition'.
31　Sharp (ed.) (1967), p. 14.
32　Korn and Samuely (June 1942), 'A Master Plan for London', p. 143; Korn gave Tunnard's name as one of the active participants in the committee. Fry (1944), p. 86, repeated this.
33　Marquis (1957), gave him as chairman of the Open Spaces Committee from 1938.
34　Tunnard (May–June 1956), 'The Conscious Stone', p. 22.
35　Tunnard Papers, Box 37, folder 600, labelled 'Landscape Architecture 2'. This included notes on the Amsterdam Bos, London County Council population statistics 1934–6, a European survey by the Building Centre Committee of 1936, and a letter from Arthur Ling of 23 January 1938 with useful statistics.
36　Tunnard, *Gardens in the Modern Landscape* (1938), pp. 137–41, 166.
37　Korn (June 1938), 'A New Plan for Amsterdam'.
38　Bijhouwer (1937), 'Het Amsterdamsche Boschpark'.
39　Tunnard, *Gardens in the Modern Landscape* (1938), p. 163.
40　Anon., *L&G* (Spring 1939), pp. 37–8.
41　Peter Youngman was present too. In Harvey (1987), p. 110, he remembered that Tunnard 'would talk knowledgeably and enthusiastically about Corbusier and Bauhaus, and contemporary art'.

42 Tunnard, *Gardens in the Modern Landscape* (1938), pp. 137–41, 149.
43 Ibid., p. 95.
44 Ibid., p. 65.
45 Ibid., p. 164.
46 Roth (1940), pp. 71–90, provides further information.
47 Tunnard, *Gardens in the Modern Landscape* (1938), p. 155.
48 Denby (1938), p. 70 and 71.
49 Anon. (26 June 1939), 'The All-Europe House'.
50 Korn and Samuely (June 1942), 'A Master Plan for London'.
51 Tunnard, *Gardens in the Modern Landscape* (1938), p. 126.
52 Brett (9 July 1942), 'Doubts on the MARS Plan for London', pp. 23–5.
53 James B. (sic), *The Playground of Paddington; How We Secured It – To Whom We Owe It* (1902).
54 Tunnard, *Gardens in the Modern Landscape*, 1938, p. 133 and 161.
55 Letter to the editor, *Architects' Journal*, 8 March 1946.
56 Tunnard, *The City of Man* (1953), pp. x and 330.
57 Tunnard, *Gardens in the Modern Landscape* (1938), p. 67 and 96.
58 Ibid., p. 5.
59 Ibid., p. 107, 108 and 136.
60 Pearlman, Inventing American Modernism, 79.
61 Wojtowicz, 'City As Community: The Life and Vision of Lewis Mumford'.
62 Tunnard, *Gardens in the Modern Landscape* (1948), 5–7.
63 Tunnard, *The City of Man*, 220.
64 Tunnard, *Gardens in the Modern Landscape* (1938), 10–11.
65 Ibid., p. 75.
66 Ibid., p. 95.
67 Ibid., p. 138 and 165.
68 Tunnard (January 1942), 'Modern Gardens for Modern Houses', p. 58.
69 Tunnard (April 1949), 'Art and Landscape Design', p. 110.
70 Tunnard (May–June 1956), 'The Conscious Stone', p. 22.
71 Ibid., p. 24.
72 Tunnard, *The City of Man* (1953), pp. 290–1.
73 Ibid., p. 299.
74 Tunnard Papers, Box 12, folder 194.
75 Tunnard Papers, Box 4, folder 59.
76 Tunnard to Ann Satterthwaite, 23 January 1968.
77 Tunnard and Pushkarev (eds), *Man-Made America* (1963), p. 160.
78 Ibid., p. 169.
79 Ibid., p. 209.
80 Ibid., p. 177.
81 De Angelis (1991), 'Christopher Tunnard: The Transportation Connection at Yale'.
82 Tunnard (1971), 'Highway as Environment'.
83 Tunnard, *The City of Man* (1953), pp. 211–12.
84 Hudnut (October 1943), 'The Political Art of Planning', p. 46.
85 Tunnard, *The City of Man* (1953), p. 313 and 330–47.
86 Hastings (January 1944), 'Exterior Furnishing or Sharawaggi', p. 5.
87 Clark (May 1944), 'Lord Burlington's Bijou, or Sharawaggi at Chiswick', p. 126, caption.
88 Pevsner (November 1944), 'The Genesis of the Picturesque'.
89 Tunnard, *Gardens in the Modern Landscape* (1938), p. 61.
90 Tunnard, *Gardens in the Modern Landscape* (1948), p. 7.
91 Tunnard (January 1951), 'The Original Sharawags', p. 28.
92 Tunnard, *The City of Man* (1953), p. 224.
93 Tunnard, *Gardens in the Modern Landscape* (1938), p. 73.

94 Ibid., p. 95 and 107.
95 Compare Tunnard, *Gardens in the Modern Landscape* (1938), p. 94, with Tunnard, *Gardens in the Modern Landscape* (1948), p. 93.
96 Tunnard, *The City of Man* (1953), p. 213, 346 and 372.
97 Ibid., pp. 343–5.
98 Ibid., pp. 359–60.
99 Ibid., p. 332.
100 Tunnard (April 1949), 'Art and Landscape Design', p. 108.
101 Anon., 'What Is Happening to Modern Architecture?', as cited by Pearlman (2007), p. 175.
102 Tunnard, *The City of Man* (1953), p. xx.
103 Floyd (1989), p. 102.
104 Tunnard (May–June 1956), 'The Conscious Stone', p. 23.
105 Tunnard, *The City of Man* (1953), p. 337.
106 Ibid., p. 377.
107 Ibid., p. 347.
108 Tunnard, *Gardens in the Modern Landscape* (1948), pp. 5–6.
109 Tunnard, *The City of Man* (1953), p. 221.
110 Ibid., p. 343.
111 Ibid., p. 350.
112 Tunnard Papers, Box 13, folder 204.
113 Tunnard, *The City of Man* (1953), p. 385.
114 Ibid., p. 332.
115 Ibid., pp. 339–42.
116 Ibid., p. 315.
117 Ibid., p. 324.
118 Ibid., p. 310.
119 Ibid., p. 350.
120 Ibid., p. 344.
121 Ibid., p. 384.
122 Ibid., p. 353.
123 Ibid., p. 344.
124 Ibid., p. 376.
125 Tunnard (October 1951), 'Creative Urbanism'.
126 Tunnard, *The City of Man* (1953), pp. 364–5.
127 Ibid., p. 331.
128 Tunnard to the editor of *AR*, 8 March 1946; copy in Tunnard Papers.
129 Tunnard, *Gardens in the Modern Landscape* (1948), p. 7.
130 Tunnard, *The City of Man* (1953), pp. 333–5, 384.
131 Ibid., p. 346.
132 Ibid., pp. 355–6.
133 Ibid., pp. 331–2.
134 Davidoff and Reiner, 'A Choice Theory of Planning', cited in Faludi (1973), p. 22.
135 Tunnard with Pearce (eds) (1954), 'City Planning at Yale'.
136 Harris (1960), p. 272.
137 Tunnard, *A World with a View* (1978), p. 108.
138 Leitch (1977).
139 Tunnard, *A World with a View* (1978), pp. 168–78.
140 Ibid., p. xi
141 Ibid., p. 185.
142 Ibid., p. 185.
143 Ibid., p. 179.
144 Ibid., p. 24.
145 Ibid., p. 184.

146 Ibid., p. 2.
147 Ibid., p. 179.
148 Ibid., p. 2.
149 Ibid., p. 32.
150 Ibid., p. 1.
151 Tunnard (1965), 'On Education', p. 526.
152 Tunnard and Pushkarev (eds), *Man-Made America* (1963), p. 6.
153 Tunnard, *A World with a View* (1978), p. 123.
154 Lowenthal (1978), 'Finding Valued Landscapes'.
155 Jacques (1980), 'Landscape Appraisal: The Case for a Subjective Theory'.
156 Jacques (Winter 1994), 'The Rise of Cultural Landscapes'.

7 From Wisley to *A World with a View*: the metamorphosis of a landscape architect

'What became of Christopher Tunnard?' was a frequent question when his acquaintances in England were interviewed fifty years on. In England his contribution had been the first writings on Modernism in landscape architecture in the English language. In America he ceased to be Canadian or English, and became American; he converted from being a landscape architect to being a city planner; he became critical of how Modernism had developed; and he espoused the historical approach and historic preservation. It was as if Tunnard had inhabited two different worlds.

Tunnard's place in the history of garden design began to be acknowledged in the late 1980s. Jane Brown gave him several pages in *The English Garden in Our Time* on the strength of *Gardens in the Modern Landscape* (1938) and his work in England.[1] Tunnard was also written up from an English perspective in *Landscape Design* with the regret that at Yale 'Tunnard seems to have become swamped by the American system'.[2] Brown then included him in a book on influential gardeners.[3] This was reviewed in *The New York Times* with the information that 'he left England in 1939 and spent much of the rest of his life in the United States, mostly at Harvard, writing and teaching'.[4]

Henry Hope Reed, his collaborator in the 1950s, thought that this required some correction:[5]

To the Editor:

It was refreshing to see Caroline Seebohm's mention of Christopher Tunnard in her review of 'Eminent Gardeners' by Jane Brown (March 17). As one who knew and worked with him, may I offer a few comments?

Christopher Tunnard, who first came to this country in 1939, did teach at Harvard briefly before serving in the Canadian Army. The greater part of his career, from 1945 to 1975, when he retired, was as professor of city planning in the Yale School of Architecture. There his concepts underwent considerable change. From the modernism of his youth he turned to our classical heritage, being one of the first in the postwar era to do so. In 1952 he and Lamont Moore of the Yale University Art Gallery staged a landmark exhibition that acclaimed the role of the classical in embellishing the city. In *American*

Skyline – I was privileged to be his co-author – he underscored the need for the preservation of our man-made heritage.

For those who have espoused our traditional heritage in the arts, Christopher Tunnard, despite strong opposition, was the leader and guide. When this nation once again accepts the classical, he will be recognized as having been a major force.

HENRY HOPE REED New York

Tunnard's many other colleagues and students in America had not forgotten him either, and Ralph Warburton, the architect and planner, honoured him with an obituary.[6] Ten years later he prepared a lengthy bibliography.[7] In 1989 William W. Wilson remembered *The City of Man* as 'at once urban and community history, a celebration of the humane environment, a condemnation of modernist self-indulgence, and a recovery of neoclassical civic design' when appreciation of Classical heritage was at its lowest ebb.[8] Several of the papers to a transatlantic congress in Oxford organised by the Association of Collegiate Schools of Planning and the Association of European Schools of Planning in 1991 drew inspiration from Tunnard's work, and the failure to publish was a lost opportunity of great magnitude. Meanwhile Lance Neckar, intrigued by the fact that the same man had also written the seminal 'manifesto' on Modernist landscape architecture, started casting about for materials on Tunnard's early career. Interviews, careful study of *AR*, a round-up of reviews of the first edition of *Gardens in the Modern Landscape*, comparison with the second edition, inspection of the Tunnard Papers, and attendance at the Berkeley symposium on 'Modern Landscape Architecture [Re] Evaluated' led to a piece that laid the groundwork for many of the issues examined more closely in this book.[9]

Neckar's article observed that Tunnard's principles had undergone a seismic change in the late 1940s. Indeed Tunnard was an interesting example of the first generation to have serious doubts about the direction of Modernism as it was then developing. William Arthur Eden, his contemporary in England, underwent a similar metamorphosis and became the Head of Historic Buildings at the London County Council. His work on Marble Hill placed him amongst the 'neo-Palladians' of the 1950s. Tunnard's conversion, abetted by Reed himself, went further than buildings, into planning and historic preservation, territory which led him into isolation from most of the rest of academic planning.

Deeper and more personal still was a shift in Tunnard's philosophical views. He never joined any political or philosophical organisation, as far as is known, but the principles underlying his writing are not hard to discern. In his latter years in England he was content to accept the left-wing positions on offer at the time; for example, in his work for the MARS Group and his vigorous opposition to Nazism; in this he was no different from a vast swathe of English intellectuals. Some of his ideas were thus harsh and unyielding, for example on private open space. However, the late 1940s saw a mellower Tunnard who always saw questions and issues from the point of view of the individual. The word 'humanistic' has been used several

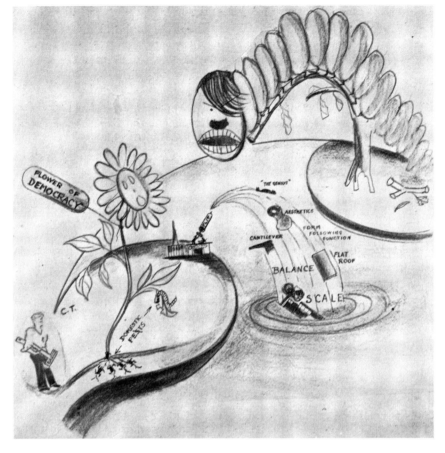

Figure 7.1 Whilst at Harvard Tunnard confirmed his anti-Nazi position with this cartoon
in *Task*, putting the efforts of Modernist design in perspective.
(Source: Harvard GSD)

times in this book. While there is no evidence that he belonged to any humanist organisation, he was certainly of this bent, shown in his own writings and in
the affinity he had with those of well-known humanists like John Dewey, Julian
Huxley, and Karl Popper.

Despite such changes in conviction, though, certain traits ran through his life's
work. He was forever anxious that his insights should be useful. In the design
sphere this took the form of proposing design principles and forms that would be
suitable. Fascinated by the shapes, lines and spaces equally of the winding river
valley and the city square, he saw culture, architecture, and human activity as integral to his endeavour. His adherence to the historical method showed his belief
both in the explanatory power of historical analysis, and in a more metaphysical
appreciation that the past is the springboard for the present and the future. Having

learnt from Frank Clark that there was a commonality amongst the arts at any moment in history, he was a constructivist in his own mind till the end.

This may go some way to explain his ever-present optimism and his ability to see the positive benefits of change – 'his creative and enthusiastic human hopefulness,' as Professor John Gaus of Harvard noted.[10] He was unusually open-minded and willing to test his ideas against the art and ideas of others. He could discuss Jack Kerouac, H.G. Wells, and Camillus and at the same time juggle the formulae of highway engineers with the theories of philosophers like Josiah Royce and Arthur Schopenhauer. At conferences he would pull together such varied participants as the public relations guru Edward Bernays, a Stop & Shop supermarket executive, J. Walter Thompson, economists, and Steen Eiler Rasmussen, the Danish architect and architectural historian.

Tunnard had found in Frank Clark the only other landscape architect in Britain who was attuned to the Modern Movement. They obviously inspired each other, and it is now impossible to determine with any precision their respective responsibilities for *Gardens in the Modern Landscape*. In keeping with his far greater commitment and ambition, it was Tunnard who pushed forward with the articles and then the book. The credit that he gave to the other man was merely: 'the author's thanks are due to H.F. Clark for help in the preparation of the text and illustrations and for plans'. Several of Clark's friends and his wife were under the impression that he made a very substantial contribution to the book. When remonstrated with for not taking more credit, Clark, quite in character, would say: 'Well, if it hadn't have been for Christopher …'.[11]

Together they espoused Modernism to the pre-war landscape profession in England, to its general bafflement. George Dillistone, boasting '30 years of garden design', asserted in 1939 that 'there is little or nothing in the design of a structure, except the position of its entrance, exit and outlook, that can possibly exercise any material influence on the garden design … To talk of a new "style" in gardens is merely absurd.'[12] However, younger members remembered that Tunnard 'would talk knowledgeably about Le Corbusier and Bauhaus and contemporary art. I didn't understand much, but found it far, far more exciting than Mawson or even Lutyens.' Geoffrey Jellicoe 'knew he had a message to give to the younger generation which I couldn't at that time understand'.[13] In fact, Jellicoe did not feel the truth of Modernism until 1951, when he was at a sculpture exhibition in Battersea Park.[14]

The influence that Tunnard had on Garrett Eckbo, Dan Kiley and James Rose has been debated. They actually left the GSD as he arrived, so the most that can be said, perhaps, is they gained in righteousness and confidence on seeing his book.[15] Eckbo, at least, acknowledged Tunnard's strong influence.[16] However, there is no doubt about his inspirational role in Lawrence Halprin's (b. 1916) becoming a landscape architect.[17] Halprin had initially been fascinated by Frank Lloyd Wright and went to a library to learn more about him. There he found books about architecture, landscape architecture and finally Tunnard's *Gardens in the Modern Landscape*. The next day, Halprin went to a professor with his discovery and asked: 'You know, I've discovered there is this fascinating thing called landscape architecture. Do you know anything about it?' While the professor did not, he referred Halprin to one who did. Impressed by his evident enthusiasm, the professor sent Halprin with a scholarship to Harvard University, where he studied under Tunnard himself. His summary of Tunnard's influence on him was that he had been taught 'to design well and make an aesthetically and socially better environment for people to live in and thus in the broadest sense improve the modern world'.[18]

Gardens in the Modern Landscape was the foremost text for landscape architectural students into the 1950s, and thus inspired a generation of the profession across the English-speaking world. Ian McHarg (1920–2001), a Scot who had served as a paratrooper in World War II, enrolled at Harvard University GSD in 1950, earning Master's degrees in both Landscape Architecture and City Planning. Holmes Perkins had meanwhile become dean of the Graduate School of Fine Arts at the University of Pennsylvania and in 1954 attracted McHarg back from Scotland to Philadelphia to establish the Department of Landscape Architecture and Regional Planning. In 1955 McHarg wrote to Tunnard at Yale:[19]

> The person unquestionably most competent to teach landscape architecture is yourself, and you do not offer any graduate instruction in this field … You will recall that at Harvard through the student council, I sought to have you return there to direct landscape instruction; you know of my admiration for your original contribution to landscape architecture.

In 1958 McHarg wrote again for advice on writings that would be 'most indicative of the path toward design of open space appropriate to 20th century society'. He added hastily that 'Your own book, "Gardens in the Modern Landscape", still remains the best thought on the subject.'

Others have left direct testimony of the influence of the book on them. Richard Clough (b. 1921) began the study of landscape architecture at University College, London, in 1949, and afterwards worked with Sylvia Crowe. Meanwhile the unexpected references to nineteenth-century garden writers in *Gardens in the Modern Landscape* led him to seek out their books, then little valued and inexpensive. Returning to Australia in 1956, he pursued a distinguished career in landscape architecture with the National Capital Development Commission in Canberra and as Professor of Landscape Architecture and Head of School at the University of New South Wales from 1981–6. He expanded his library to a substantial collection on all aspects of garden design, which he presented it to the Historic Houses Trust of New South Wales in 2004.[20]

Having found a conducive intellectual climate at Harvard, Tunnard might have been expected to settle in for a long-term career in landscape education. However, he was evidently converted to a humanistic approach to the work of the designer, saw that the real issues were in city planning, and by a couple of fortunate leaps found himself teaching planning at Yale. Tunnard's acute visual, social and literary sensitivities which helped to make him such an outstanding landscape architect, planner, scholar and writer informed him that Modernism in America was not developing well. Its overly technical approach, its rejection of cultural background and a decreasing ability to generate new and appropriate forms confirmed to him that the Modernist project had faltered.

His response was to think it all through again, with mankind being the focus of attention, and from the viewpoint that the human was a cultural being, with needs that were aesthetic as well as economic and social. He emphasised human values and this meant that he was always cautious about abstract models in city planning, transportation engineering and landscape evaluation. His emphasis upon the creation of beauty in cities was wildly off-beam as far as many of his architect and planner contemporaries were concerned. It took a fellow oddball like John Brinkerhoff Jackson to appreciate the thrust of Tunnard's writings. In 1957 Jackson recalled his dealings eight years earlier, particularly 'the help and encouragement you gave me (and Landscape) when I was first starting the venture. You were in fact the first prospective contributor I dared approach.'[21]

It was not until the late 1970s and early 1980s that the landscape architecture profession became involved in historic or cultural landscapes. In the 1940s, 1950s and early 1960s, historic preservation was still enamoured with the historic mansion and the hoop-skirted guides. Few cities had effective private, much less public, historic preservation programmes. For Tunnard, concerned to blend the new and the old as well as the natural and the man-made, this was indeed a lonely time. Even the articulate Jane Jacobs and analytical Martin Anderson, whose books exposed the human, community, and administrative flaws of Urban Renewal, were mocked by the 'can-do' city planners of this period. In much of his work in this period, Tunnard was usually swimming against the current.

He was in some respects an ally, and in others not, of the enormously influential Lewis Mumford. *The Culture of Cities*, revised and greatly expanded as the better-known *The City in History* (1961), was a winner of the National Book Awards non-fiction category in 1962. Perhaps surprisingly, Tunnard and Mumford had little contact with each other and only occasionally referred to each other. Maybe this was partly because they moved in different circles. Mumford was a New York journalist, fifteen years the senior. It may also have been because Tunnard thought that Mumford's approach, based on Patrick Geddes, was intellectually unsound and was a diversion for civic designers away from the relationships of structures and space.[22] Tunnard had always been suspicious of 'nature worship', as he called it, and of the so-called biological or 'organic' approach that had been promoted by Geddes as a metaphor for city growth.[23] In 1951 he had gone out of his way to debunk Geddes's organic approach to city planning in 'The Leaf and the Stone: Neo-romantic Aspects of Nature in the City Plan'.

Yet Tunnard and Mumford were obviously fellow travellers in their admiration for the city and their quest to improve it. It must have been clear when Tunnard and Pushkarev won the 'science, philosophy and religion' category of the National Book Awards in 1964 with *Man-Made America: Chaos or Control?* that it was Mumford and Tunnard who had their finger on the pulse of the nation, not the official profession. As James DeAngelis was reviewing the 1981 edition of

Man-Made America, he recalled Wolf von Eckardt's summary of that era's extraordinary publications, reminding us of the stature of Tunnard's work:[24]

> *Man-Made America* joined a small but potent shelf of books, all published at about the same time, that brought new insights and some relief. John Kenneth Galbraith showed us that *The Affluent Society* was wanting. Michael Harrington pointed to abject poverty in *The Other America* for shocking evidence. Rachel Carson told movingly in *The Silent Spring* how chemical insecticides and other deadly progress poisons nature's ecology. Lewis Mumford's lifework, but particularly *The City in History*, made us aware of the urban ecology. Jean Gottmann discovered and described the dynamics of *Megalopolis: The Urbanized Northeastern Seaboard of the United States*. Peter Blake charged that these dynamics were turning the country into *God's Own Junkyard*.
>
> William H. Whyte and his collaborators at *Fortune* magazine showed that *The Exploding Metropolis* left downtown in shambles. Jane Jacobs, in her *The Death and Life of Great American Cities*, opened our eyes to the fact that urban revitalization, as prescribed by modern architecture, was killing the cities, and that their true life springs from their old, organic neighborhoods. The revelation shocked the city planners but came just in time to stop cataclysmic 'urban renewal' and launch urban conservation and recovery.

For students, the lectures may not have had the pyrotechnics of favourites like Yale's architecture professor Vincent Scully, but Tunnard's seminars and conferences provided more lasting inspiration and information, which guided the academic and professional careers of many undergraduates and graduate students. By the 1970s Tunnard had developed a devoted following among Yale planning alumni, whilst several landscape architects remembered his influence on them although his formal connections to landscape architecture were long severed.

Several of Tunnard's planning students at Yale became prominent in preservation. Besides Ralph Warburton and Ann Satterthwaite, a contributor to this book, there was also Elizabeth Barlow Rogers, the leading figure in the restoration of Central Park, New York City, in the 1980s. A resident of New York City since 1964, her early publications included *The Forests and Wetlands of New York City* (1971), and *Frederick Law Olmsted's New York* (1972). She was the first person to hold the title of Central Park Administrator, a New York City Parks Department position created by Mayor Edward I. Koch in 1979. She was also the first president of the Central Park Conservancy, founded in 1980. In this capacity she wrote *Rebuilding Central Park: A Management and Restoration Plan* (1987). Her interest in design led to *Landscape Design: A Cultural and Architectural History* (2001) and to her becoming the founding director of Garden History and Landscape Studies at the Bard Graduate Center in New York City between 2001 and 2005.

William Brenner likewise became interested, through Tunnard, in historic preservation in the late 1960s. He joined the newly formed National Institute of Building Sciences (NIBS) in Washington, DC, in 1978. His first major project there was managing the development of the US Department of Housing and

Urban Development (HUD) rehabilitation guidelines. These provided step-by-step technical information for evaluating a residential building's site, exterior, interior, and structural, electrical, plumbing and HVAC (heating, ventilating and air conditioning) systems. First published by HUD in 1984 as the *Guideline on Residential Building Systems Inspection* (1984), it found widespread use and acceptance among architects, engineers, builders, realtors and preservationists. As a consultant for HABS/HAER, he conducted the Army Material Command historic survey, covering more than 40,000 buildings and structures and hundreds of historic sites at Rock Island and Watervliet Arsenals, White Sands Missile Range, and about 70 other military bases.

It was not until the late 1960s and the 1970s that many of the ideas that Tunnard had been discussing over the years were finally recognised as legitimate

Figure 7.2 Tunnard became professor emeritus in 1975; here depicted with his wife Lydia on holiday at Villa d'Este, Cernobbio, Lake Como, Italy.
(Source: Yale, Tunnard Papers, box 42, folder 699)

public concerns. Then when many of the simplistic hopes of Urban Renewal for reviving inner cities were dashed, a new appreciation of diverse social, cultural, health, and environmental and societal issues emerged. Protection of the environment, support for the arts and humanities, greater citizen participation, historic preservation of not just single buildings but districts as well, were now on the public agenda. Tunnard's long-held interest in viewing the natural and man-made worlds as one, in integrating culture and aesthetics into all aspects of public and private developments, and in having conservationists and historic preservationists work together was slowly accepted. After decades of intellectual isolation, his final years brought him the satisfaction of seeing growing public interest in his long-articulated ideas.

Tunnard's seemingly fearless questioning so often placed him in the avant-garde on an issue in a period when single problem solving took on ever more hardened, specific dimensions. His complex and subtle mode of inquiry, unleashed from the dogmatic tyrannies of style and narrow problem solving, is also his legacy to designers and planners as they perilously undertake to transform our own world with a view.

Notes

1 Brown (1986), pp. 123–34.
2 Welsh (October 1987), 'Tunnard: The Modernist with a Memory'.
3 Brown (1990), pp. 115–38.
4 *The New York Times*, 17 March 1991.
5 Henry Hope Reed to *The New York Times*, 5 May 1991.
6 Warburton (May 1980), 'A Worldly View of Tunnard at his Best'.
7 Warburton (1992), 'Christopher Tunnard'.
8 Wilson (1989), p. 299.
9 Neckar (1990), 'Strident Modernism/Ambivalent Reconsiderations'.
10 John Gaus to Christopher Tunnard, 30 August 1953; Tunnard Papers, Box 6, folder 92.
11 Information from Marjorie Clark; on the other hand, Professor Stearn, who was RHS librarian at the time, is under the impression that 'Tunnard wrote his own books'.
12 George Dillistone, in Mercer (ed.) (1939), pp. 11–14.
13 Harvey (1987), p. 13.
14 Interview, David Jacques with Geoffrey Jellicoe, 19 September 1989.
15 Snow (1969).
16 Walker and Simo (1994), p. 124.
17 Ibid., p. 149.
18 Simo (2000), p. 33.
19 Tunnard Papers, Box 20, folder 316.
20 Martin (Spring 2004), 'The Richard Clough Collection of Garden Books'.
21 Brinkerhof Jackson to Christopher Tunnard, 1 December 1957; Tunnard Papers, Box 11, folder 165.
22 Tunnard (February 1951), 'The Leaf and the Stone', pp. 67–74.
23 Tunnard, *Gardens in the Modern Landscape* (1948), p. 7.
24 DeAngelis (1991), note 9.

Annex A: Brief biographical facts

1910	Born in Victoria, British Columbia
1927–8	Studied Liberal Arts at Victoria College
1928	Father retired to the United Kingdom
1928–30	Horticulture course at the Royal Horticultural Society, Wisley
1930–2	Apprenticeship with Sharp and Company, seed merchants in Sleaford, Lincolnshire
1932–4	Articled to Percy Cane
1934–6	Student member of the Institute of Landscape Architects
1936	Associate of the Institute of Landscape Architects
1936–9	Practice as landscape architect
1936	Moved to St Ann's Hill, Chertsey, overseeing the building of the house
1937	Silver-gilt medal for landscape design at the *Exposition Internationale des Arts et Techniques dans la Vie Moderne* in Paris
1937	Moved to 115 Mount Street, in Mayfair
1938	Modern Architectural Research (MARS) Group Town Planning Committee
1938	BBC television programme with Jim Richards at Alexandra Palace
1938	Publication of *Gardens in the Modern Landscape*
1939	Exhibition for the ILA called 'Garden and Landscape: an Exhibition of the work of the Landscape Architect'
1939	Visiting lecturer in landscape architecture and regional planning at the Harvard Graduate School
1942–3	Conscripted into the Royal Canadian Engineers (honourable medical discharge)
1943–4	Arthur W. Wheelwright Fellowship
1944–5	Associate editorship of *Architectural Forum*
1945	Visiting lecturer at Yale University
1945	Married Lydia Evans
1945–8	Assistant Professor at Yale University
1947	Member of the Connecticut State Site Selection Committee for the United Nations
1948–62	Associate Professor of City Planning at Yale University
1948	Visiting lecturer to Massachusetts Institute of Technology
1948	Republication of *Gardens in the Modern Landscape*
1949	Became a US citizen
1949	Bronze medal from the Federated Garden Clubs of Connecticut for the outstanding civic project
1950	John Simon Guggenheim Fellowship for the study of American cities

1950	One of the first contributors to J.B. Jackson's *Landscape*
1951–65	Director of graduate program in city planning at Yale University
1953	Publication of *The City of Man*
1955	Publication of *American Skyline*
1955	Atlantic Urban Region Conference at Yale
1956	Fulbright Scholarship to study the interrelationships of the arts in civic design, eight months based at the *Institut d'Urbanisme*, Paris
1957	Joint Program in City Planning and Transportation Engineering
1957	Chair, City of New Haven Planning Commission
1958	Joined the National Trust for Historic Preservation
1960	Guest speaker at the World Design Conference in Tokyo
1960	Joined Regional Planning Agency of South Central Connecticut
1962–75	Professor at Yale University
1963	Publication of *Man-made America: Chaos or Control?*
1963	President, New Haven Preservation Trust
1965–9	Chair, Department of City Planning, Yale University
1965	White House Conference on Natural Beauty
1965	US Provisional Committee of ICOMOS
1966	Fellow of the Royal Society of Arts, London
1967	The President's Advisory Council on Historic Preservation
1967	Participating expert in devising the Norms of Quito
1968	Publication of *The Modern American City*
1969	UNESCO mission to Jamaica
1970	Honorary Doctorate of Letters from the University of Victoria
1970	UNESCO mission to Java
1974	UNESCO mission to Kathmandu Valley
1975	Professor Emeritus at Yale University
1978	Publication of *A World with a View*
1979	Died in New Haven, Connecticut
1979	Christopher Tunnard Memorial Fellowship established

Annex B: Tunnard's principal landscape designs

Date	Client	Place	Architect
1936	Mrs Margaret Tillard	The Hooke, Chailey, Sussex	–
1936	F.B. Goldschmidt	'Salcott', Fairmile Park Road, Cobham, Surrey	–
1936	Miss Langer	Printstyle Place, Ashour, Bidborough, Kent	Raymond McGrath
1936	Mrs F.A. Chambers (Dunmoulin)	Thatch Croft, Burwood Park, Walton-on-Thames, Surrey	–
1936	Gerald L. Schlesinger	St Ann's Hill, nr. Chertsey, Surrey	Raymond McGrath
1937	Sir Charles Keene	'Carrygate', Gaulby, Leicestershire	Raymond McGrath
1937	W.D. Keene	Ravenhead, Ingarsby, Leicestershire	–
1937	J.S. Masterson	Pettings Court, Wrotham, Kent	–
1937	Serge Chermayeff	Bentley Wood, Halland, Sussex	Serge Chermayeff
1937	[proposal]	Walton-on-Thames, garden at	Raymond McGrath
1937	[proposal]	Cobham, garden for a week-end house at	Raymond McGrath
1938	Gerald L. Schlesinger	The Hill House, 87 Redington Road, Hampstead, London NW3	Oliver Hill
1939	Randall Bell	10 Palace Gate, Kensington, London W8	Wells Coates
1939	Ideal Home Exhibition	All-Europe House, Ideal Home Exhibition, London	Elizabeth Denby
1940	Snake Hill Cooperative Housing Community	Snake Hill Road Development, Belmont, MA	Carl Koch
1941	Dr John Monks	Monks' Residence, Lincoln, MA	G. Holmes Perkins
c. 1941	Prof. and Mrs Karl Terzaghi	Terzaghi Residence, Winchester, MA	G. Holmes Perkins
by 1941	Carl Koch	4 Buckingham Street, Cambridge, MA	Stone & Koch

1941	US military?	Defence Housing Project, Stamford, CT	Carl Koch
1946?	James Thrall Soby	29 Mount Spring Road, Farmington, CT	Henry-Russell Hitchcock
1946	[proposal]	Museum of Modern Art, New York City	Philip L. Goodwin
1947	[proposal]	Jefferson National Expansion Memorial Competition, St. Louis, MO (member of the team which won Third Prize)	Breger, Hornbostel & Lewis
1948	New London County Historical Society	Shaw Mansion, 11 Blinman Street, New London, CT	–
1949	George Henry Warren, Jr	Warren House, 118 Mill St, Newport, RI	–
1949	[proposal]	United Nations headquarters gardens, New York City	–
1951	University of Arkansas	Fine Arts Center	Edward Durell Stone
1952	Yale University	Yale Art Gallery and Design Center	Louis Kahn

Annex C: Tunnard's writings

'The Influence of Japan on the English Garden', *L&G* (Summer 1935): 49–53.

'Interplanting', *L&G* (Autumn 1935): 110–12.

'Garden-making on the Riviera', *L&G* (Spring 1936): 30–3.

'Garden Design at Chelsea Show, 1936', *L&G* (Summer 1936): 90–4.

'Landscape Design at the Paris International Congress: What other Countries are doing', *L&G* (Summer 1937): 78–82.

'Landscape into Garden: Reason, Romanticism and the Verdant Age', *AR*, 82 (October 1937): 143–6, 151.

'A Garden Landscape, 1740: Pain's Hill', *AR*, 82 (October 1937): 147–50.

'Pictures versus Prospects: The Evolution of the Nineteenth Century Garden', *AR*, 82 (November 1937): 201–2, 207–8.

'A Garden Landscape, 1840: Redleaf', *AR*, 82 (November 1937): 203–6.

'Colour and the Cottage Garden', *AR*, 83 (January 1938): 37–40.

'Science and Specialisation', *AR*, 83 (February 1938): 85–7.

'The Garden in the Modern Landscape', *AR*, 83 (March 1938): 127–32.

'The Functional Aspect of Garden Planning', *AR*, 83 (April 1938): 195–200.

'Asymmetrical Garden Planning: The Oriental Aesthetic', *AR*, 83 (May 1938): 245–9.

(attributed) 'Modern Architectural Research and Landscape Planning', *L&G* (Summer 1938): 101.

'The Case for a Common Garden – Claremont, Surrey', *AR*, 84 (September 1938): 109–16.

Gardens in the Modern Landscape (London: Architectural Press, 1938, 2nd ed. 1948).

'The Suburban Plot, A Standard Garden Problem', *AR*, 85 (January 1939): 41–2.

'Architects' Plants', *AR*, 85 (January 1939): 42; *AR*, 85 (February 1939): 95–6; *AR*, 85 (March 1939): 147; *AR*, 86 (1939): 39, 173.

(attributed) 'Modern Architecture in the Sussex Landscape', *AR*, 85 (February 1939): 61–9.

'The Country Acre: A Typical Garden Problem', *AR*, 85 (February 1939): 96.

'Common pleasures', *AR*, 85 (March 1939): 147–8.

'The Sectional Layout of a Small Plot', *AR*, 85 (1939): 199–201.

'Planning a Modern Garden: An Experience in Collaboration', *L&G* (Summer 1939): 23–7.

'The Adventure of Water', *AR*, 86 (September 1939): 99–102.

'What Kind of Landscape for New England?', *Task*, 1 (1941): 39–43.

'Modern Gardens for Modern Houses: Reflections on Current Trends in Landscape

Design', *Bulletin of the Garden Club of America*, 17 (September 1941): 18–30; reprinted in *Landscape Architecture*, 42 (January 1942): 57–64.

'When Britain Plans … Today's Utopias Will Not be Needed; The Basis is Being Laid in Wartime Organization and Construction', *Task*, 2 (1942): 2–8.

'Portland Improvement', in *Task*, 5 (Spring 1944): 21.

'The American Planning Tradition', *AR*, 98 (August 1945): 37–42 and 126–34.

'The New Plan for Birkenhead', *Architects' Journal*, 104 (12 September 1946): 186.

'Planning in the United States', *Planning and Reconstruction* (1946): 232–40.

'Minerva's Union: Union College, Schenectady, designed in 1812 by Joseph Jacques Ramée, was the first American college to be built to a unified plan', *AR*, 101 (February 1947): 57–62.

'Fifty Years', *AR*, 101 (April 1947): 156.

'The Romantic Suburb in America', *Magazine of Art*, 40/5 (May 1947): 184–7.

(letter to the editor): *AR*, 101 (1947): 156.

'Gardens in Tennessee' (review), *AR*, 101 (1947): 228.

'A Deviation by the Brothers Potter', *AR*, 103 (February 1948): 67.

'The National War Memorial', *Country Life*, 104 (3 September 1948): 486.

'"Reflections on the Course of Empire" and other Architectural Fantasies of Thomas Cole NA', *AR*, 104 (December 1948): 291–4.

'Architecture and Art', *Task*, 7–8 (1948): 84.

'Westport Improved', *Magazine of Art*, 42/1 (January 1949): 8–13.

'Art and Landscape Design: A Talk given to the Ann Arbor Conference on Aesthetics', *Landscape Architecture*, 39/3 (April 1949): 104–10.

'Unmodern County' (review of Murray's *Berkshire Architectural Guide* (1949) by John Betjeman and John Piper), *AR*, 106 (December 1949): 401.

'A City Called Beautiful', *Journal of the Society of Architectural Historians*, 9/1–2 (March and May 1950): 31–6.

'Modern Landscape Design: The Growth of a New Art Form', *Journal of the Royal Architectural Institute of Canada*, 27/8 (August 1950): 251.

'Man-Made America: Scene 2', *AR*, 108 (December 1950): 345–9.

'The Original Sharawags' (review of Osvald Siren's *China and Gardens of Europe*), *Architectural Record*, 109/1 (January 1951): 28 and 30.

'The Leaf and the Stone: Neo-Romantic Aspects of Nature in the City Plan', *Magazine of Art*, 44/2 (February 1951): 67–74.

'Cities by Design', *Journal of the American Institute of Planners*, 17/3 (Summer 1951): 142–50.

'*L'homme et le Jardin*, by André Véra' (review), *Landscape Architecture*, 41/4 (July 1951): 183–4.

'Creative Urbanism', *Town Planning Review*, 22/3 (October 1951): 216–36.

'Civic Designer, Urban Analyst and Public Client', *Community Planning Review*, II/1 (February 1952): 26.

'*Architecture and Town Planning in Colonial Connecticut*, by Anthony N.B. Garvan; *Cities and Towns of Illinois: A Handbook of Community Facts*, by Karl B. Lohmann' (reviews), *Journal of the American Institute of Planners*, 18/2 (Spring 1952): 89–90.

'Fire on the Prairie', *Landscape*, 2/1 (Spring 1952): 9–13.

'Peacocks in Paradise' (review), *AR*, 111 (1952): 124.

'An Artist in the Streets', *Magazine of Art*, 46/2 (February 1953): 67–74.

The City of Man (London: Architectural Press; New York: Charles Scribner's Sons, 1953; 2nd ed. 1970).

'Urban Aesthetics: 1', *Planning* (1953): 48–56.

(with Henry Hope Reed) 'The Temple and the City', *New World Writing. 3rd Mentor selection* (New York: The New American Library, 1953): 98–109.

(editor) 'City Planning: A Pictorial Compendium of Examples and Designs' (unpublished report), (New Haven, CT: Yale University Graduate Program in City Planning, 1953).

'The Future of Frank Lloyd Wright', *Landscape*, 3/3 (Spring 1954): 6–8.

'A Government Bureau of Art', *Journal of the American Institute of Architects*, 21/5 (May 1954): 234–5.

'H-bomb and City Planning', *Architectural Forum*, 101/1 (July 1954): 72.

(with John N. Pearce, editors) 'City Planning at Yale: a selection of papers and projects' (unpublished report), (New Haven, CT: Yale University Graduate Program in City Planning, 1954).

'*Pleasure of Ruins*, by Rose Macaulay; *Follies and Grottoes*, by Barbara Jones' (review), *Landscape Architecture*, 45/1 (October 1954): 44–5.

'The Conscious Stone', *Perspecta: The Yale Architectural Journal*, 3 (New Haven, CT: Yale University, December 1954): 22–5, 78; reprinted in *Craft Horizons*, XVI (May–June 1956): 40–1.

'Regionalism and the South', *Journal of the American Institute of Architects*, 23/4 (April 1955): 178–9.

'Reply to Miss S. Crowe's review of *The City of Man*', AR, 117 (1955): 222.

(editor) 'City Planning at Yale, The Atlantic Urban Region' (conference papers), (New Haven, CT: Yale University Graduate Program in City Planning, 1955).

(with Henry Hope Reed) *American Skyline: The Growth and Form of Our Cities and Towns* (Boston, MA: Houghton Mifflin Co., 1955).

(editor) *The Atlantic Urban Region* (New Haven, CT: Yale University Graduate Program in City Planning, 1956).

'*Outrage*, by Ian Nairn' (review), *Journal of the American Institute of Planners*, 23/1 (Winter 1957): 43.

'Regional studies at U.S. universities, a survey of regionally oriented research and graduate education activities, organized by Harvey S. Perloff' (review), *Journal of the American Institute of Planners*, 24/1 (1958): 44.

'America's Super Cities', *Harper's Magazine*, 217 (August 1958): 59–65.

'Super-City on the Seaboard', *The Rotarian*, XCIV (February 1959): 30–2.

'What Can Be Expected from Regional Planning?', *Connecticut State Journal*, XXVII (May 1959): 5–6.

'Architecture and Planning', *Arts & Architecture*, 76 (October 1959): 24–33.

'The Garden of the Silver Pavilion', *Bulletin of the Garden Club of America*, 49/1 (January 1961): 86–92.

'The City and its Interpreters' (review of *The City in History* by Lewis Mumford), *Journal of the American Institute of Planners*, 27/4 (November 1961): 346–50.

'*The Works of Sir Joseph Paxton, 1803–1865*, by George F. Chadwick' (review): *Landscape Architecture*, 53/1 (October 1962): 61–2.

(with Boris Pushkarev, editors) *Man-made America: Chaos or Control? An Inquiry into Selected Problems of Design in the Urbanized Landscape* (New Haven and London: Yale University Press, 1963; reissued 1967; 2nd ed. 1981).

'The Customary and the Characteristic: A Note on the Pursuit of City Planning History', in Oscar Handlin, ed. *The Historian and the City* (Cambridge, MA: MIT Press and Harvard University Press, 1963): 216–24.

'On Education', *Beauty for America: Proceedings of the White House Conference on Natural Beauty* (Washington DC: US Government Printing Office, 1965): 526.

'On Water and Waterfronts', in *Beauty for America: Proceedings of the White House Conference on Natural Beauty* (Washington DC: US Government Printing Office, 1965): 141, 154–8.

'Landmarks of Beauty and History', *With Heritage So Rich* (A Report of a Special Committee on Historic Preservation under the auspices of the United States Conference of Mayors with a grant from the Ford Foundation), eds Albert Rains (chairman) and Laurance G. Henderson (director), (New York: Random House, 1966): 28–33; (new edition, National Trust for Historic Preservation: 1999): 131, 133.

'Urban Rehabilitation and Adaptive Use in the United States', *Historic Preservation Today* (Charlottesville: The University Press of Virginia for The National Trust for Historic Preservation and Colonial Williamsburg, 1966).

The Modern American City (Princeton, NJ and London: Van Nostrand Reinhold, 1968).

(with John Pollacco) *Jamaica: Conservation and Development of Sites and Monuments* (final report UNESCO Mission to Jamaica, September 1968 to April 1969), (Paris: UNESCO, 1969).

(with John Pollacco) *Indonesia, Final Report: Cultural Tourism in Central Java* (Paris: UNESCO, 1970).

'Divers Surprises and Little Conceits: A Note on the Renaissance Tradition of Garden Design', *Classical America*, 1/2 (1971): 45–50.

'Highway as Environment' (New Haven, Yale University Department of City Planning Highway Research Project, 1971).

'The Planning Syndrome in Western Culture', in George Fox Mott (ed.): *Urban Change and the Planning Syndrome* (*The Annals of the American Academy of Political and Social Science*, 405) (January 1973): 95–103.

'The United States: Federal Funds for Rescue', *The Conservation of Cities* (Paris: UNESCO, 1975).

Article in *The Man-Made Landscape* (Paris: UNESCO, 1977).

A World with a View: An Inquiry into the Nature of Scenic Values (New Haven, CT: Yale University Press, 1978).

Annex D: Bibliography

L&G: Landscape and Garden
AR: Architectural Review
RIBA: Royal Institute of British Architects

Adams, Thomas, and G.P. Youngman, 'Gardens Will be More Free and Flowing', *Gardens and Gardening* (London: The Studio, 1939): 14–15.

Agar, Madeline, *Garden Design in Theory and Practice* (London: Sidgwick & Jackson, 1911).

Anderson, Dorothy May, *Women, Design and the Cambridge School* (West Lafayette, IN: PDA Publishers, 1980).

Anon., 'Garden Work by Christopher Tunnard', *L&G* (Spring 1937): 39.

Anon., 'House in Surrey', *AR*, 82 (October 1937): 117–22.

Anon., 'Garden by Christopher Tunnard, A.I.L.A.: Printstyle Place, Bidborough', *L&G* (Spring 1938): 42.

Anon., 'Television of Garden Planning', *L&G* (Summer 1938): 118.

Anon., 'House at Hampstead', *AR*, 85 (April 1939), pp. 187–9.

Anon., 'An Exhibition of the "Work of the Landscape Architect" at the Royal Institute of British Architects, 66, Portland Place, W.1, June 1939', *L&G* (Summer 1939): 102.

Anon., 'The All-Europe House: Designed by Elizabeth Denby, Garden Layout and Planning by Christopher Tunnard', *RIBA Journal*, 46, series 3 (26 June 1939): 813–19.

Anon., 'Flats in Palace Gate, Kensington', *AR*, 85 (1939): 173–84.

Anon., 'House at Galby (sic), Leicestershire', *AR*, 90 (November 1941): 132–3.

Anon., 'What Is Happening to Modern Architecture?', *Museum of Modern Art Bulletin*, 15 (Spring 1948): 14.

Anon., 'Project UN HQ, NY, entrance to 47th Str', *AR* 106 (1949): 336.

Baker, Geoffrey, 'Equivalent of a Loudly-Colored Folk Art is Needed', in *Landscape Architecture*, 42 (1942): 65–6.

Bennett, Harvey, 'Balance and Proportion in Landscape Design', *L&G*, 2/4 (1935): 132–3.

Bijhouwer, J.T.P., 'Het Amsterdamsche Boschpark', *De 8 en Opbouw*, 8/2 (1937): 1–10.

Bijhouwer, J.T.P., *Waarnemen en Ontwerpen in Tuin en Landschap* (Amsterdam: Kosmos, 1954).

Birnbaum, Charles A., and Robin Karson (eds), *Pioneers of American Landscape Design* (New York: McGraw-Hill, 2000).

Bramwell, Anna, *Blood and Soil: Walther Darré and Hitler's 'Green Party'* (Bourne End: The Kensal Press, 1985).

Brett, Lionel, 'Doubts on the MARS Plan for London', *Architect's Journal* (9 July 1942): 23–5.

Brown, Jane, *The English Garden in Our Time* (Woodbridge: Antique Collectors' Club, 1986).

Brown, Jane, *The Art and Architecture of English Gardens* (New York: Rizzoli, 1989).

Brown, Jane, *Eminent Gardeners: Some People of Influence and Their Gardens 1880–1980* (New York: Viking, 1990).

Burke, Sir Bernard, *A Genealogical and Heraldic History of the Landed Gentry of Great Britain*, 13th edn, edited by A. Winton Thorpe (London: Burke's Peerage, 1921).

Cane, Percy, *Modern Gardens: British and Foreign* (London: The Studio, 1926–7).

Cane, Percy S., 'Public Parks', *Garden Design* (1930): 174–7.

Cane, Percy S., *Garden Design of Today* (London: Methuen, 1934).

Cane, Percy S., '21, Addison Road, Kensington', *Garden Design*, 18 (1934): 41–5.

Canneel-Claes, M.J., *Association Internationale des Architectes de Jardins Modernistes* (AIAJM), (privately printed, n.d. [1937]); Landscape Institute Library.

Canneel-Claes, M.J., *Association Internationale des Architectes de Jardins Modernistes* (AIAJM) (privately printed, n.d. [1938]); Huib Hoste papers, Katholieke Universiteit Leuven.

Cautley, Marjorie Sewell, *Garden Design: The Principles of Abstract Design as Applied to Landscape Composition* (New York: Dodd and Mead, 1935).

Clark, Frank, 'Lord Burlington's Bijou, or Sharawaggi at Chiswick', *AR*, 95 (May 1944): 125–9.

Clark, H.F., 'Eighteenth Century Elysiums: The Role of "Association" in the Landscape Movement', *Journal of the Warburg and Courtauld Institutes* VI (1943): 165–89.

Clark, H.F., *The English Landscape Garden* (London: Pleiades, 1948).

Clark, H. Frank, 'The Principles of Landscape Design', *Architectural Design*, 23 (March–April 1954): 83, 116, etc.

Colvin, Brenda, 'Some Differences in French and English Garden Design', *L&G* (Autumn 1937): 142–4.

Crowe, Sylvia, *Garden Design* (London: County Life, 1958).

DeAngelis, James P., 'Christopher Tunnard: The Transportation Connection at Yale' (paper to Association of Collegiate Schools of Planning/ Association of European Schools of Planning congress in Oxford (1991)); published in 1999 on the Internet as http://members.bellatlantic.net/~vze29nc2/resume/TUNNARDF.html .

Deming, Elen, 'Christopher Tunnard, Modern Landscape Architecture and the "Empathic" View of Japan', *Journal of the New England Garden History Society*, 4 (Spring 1996): 30–7.

Denby, Elizabeth, *Europe Re-housed* (London: Allen & Unwin, 1938).

Dunington-Grubb, H.B., 'Modernismus Arrives in the Garden – To Stay?', *Landscape Architecture*, 32 (1942): 156–7.

Eckbo, Garrett, Daniel U. Kiley and James C. Rose, 'Landscape Design in the Urban Environment', *Architectural Record*, 85 (May 1939): 69–77.

Eckbo, Garrett, Daniel U. Kiley and James C. Rose, 'The Rural Environment,' *Architectural Record*, 87 (1939): 68–74.

Eckbo, Garrett, Daniel U. Kiley and James C. Rose, 'The Primeval Environment', *Architectural Record*, 88 (1940): 74–9.

Eckbo, Garrett, *Landscape for Living* (New York: Duell, Sloan and Pearce, 1950).

Eden, William Arthur, 'The English Tradition in the Countryside II', *AR*, 77 (1935): 142–52.

Eden, William Arthur, 'The English Tradition in the Countryside III', *AR*, 77 (1935): 193–202.

Eden, William Arthur, 'The New Landscape Architecture' (review of *Gardens in the Modern Landscape*), *RIBA Journal*, 46 (6 March 1939): 464–5.

Elliott, Brent, *Victorian Gardens* (London: Batsford, 1986).

Elrington, C.R., *et al.* (eds), 'Hampstead: Frognal and the Central Demesne', *A History of the County of Middlesex. Volume 9: Hampstead, Paddington* (1989): 33–42.

Faludi, Andreas, *A Reader in Planning Theory* (Oxford: Pergamon Press, 1973).

Floyd, Margaret Henderson, *Architectural Education and Boston: Centennial publication of the Boston Architectural Center 1889–1989* (Boston, MA: Boston Architectural Center, 1989).

Frost, A.C., 'Finella: A House for Mansfield D Forbes, Esq.', *Architectural Review*, 66 (1929): 265–72.

Fry, Maxwell, *Fine Building* (London: Faber & Faber, 1944).

Gabo, Naum, 'Constructive Art', *The Listener*, 16 (408), (4 November 1936): 846–8.

Gaus, John Merriman, 'The Graduate School of Design and the Education of Planners' (internal report) (Cambridge, MA: Yale University Graduate School of Design, 1943).

Giedion, Sigfried, *Space, Time and Architecture: The Growth of a Modern Tradition* (Cambridge, MA: Harvard University Press, 1941).

Giedion, Sigfried, *Walter Gropius: Work and Teamwork* (New York: Reinhold, 1954).

Glazebrook, Mark, *John Tunnard* (exhibition catalogue) (London: Arts Council, 1977).

Goldsmith, Margaret Olthof, *Designs for Outdoor Living* (New York: George W. Stewart, 1941).

Griswold, Mac and Eleanor Weller, *The Golden Age of American Gardens: Proud Owners, Private Estates, 1890–1940* (New York: Harry N. Abrams, 1991).

Gropius, Walter, *Rebuilding Our Communities* (Chicago: Paul Theobald, 1945).

Gropius, Walter and Maxwell Fry, 'Cry Stop to Havoc', *AR*, 77 (1935): 188–92.

Hanson, Brian, 'Rhapsody in Black Glass', *AR*, 162 (July 1977): 58–64.

Harris, C. Britton, 'Plan or Projection: An Examination of the Use of Models in Planning', *Journal of American Institute of Planners*, XXVI/4 (1960).

Harvey, Sheila (ed.), *Reflections on Landscape: The Lives and Works of Six British Landscape Architects* (Aldershot: Gower Technical Press, 1987).

Hastings, Hubert de Cronin, 'Exterior Furnishing or Sharawaggi: The Art of Making Urban Landscape', *AR*, 95 (January 1944): 2–5.

Hudnut, Joseph, 'Space and the Modern Garden', *Bulletin of the Garden Club of America*, 7 (May 1940): 18–22; reprinted in Tunnard, *Gardens in the Modern Landcape* (1948): 175–8.

Hudnut, Joseph, 'The Political Art of Planning', *Architectural Record*, 94/4 (October 1943): 44–8.

Hudnut, Joseph, 'A "Long-haired" Reply to Moses', *New York Times Magazine* (22 July 1944), p. 16, 36–7.

Hudnut, Joseph, *Architecture and the Spirit of Man* (Cambridge, MA: Harvard University Press, 1949).

Humphreys, A. R. *William Shenstone* (Cambridge University Press, 1937).

Hussey, Christopher, 'A Modern Country House: Bentley, near Halland, Sussex designed for himself by Mr Serge Chermayeff, F.R.I.B.A.', *Country Life* 40 (26 October 1940): 368–71, 390–3.

Hussey, Christopher, 'Carrygate, Leicestershire', *Country Life* (7 August 1942): 266–9.

ICOMOS, *The Monument for the Man* (Paris: ICOMOS, 1964).

Imbert, Dorothée, 'Thomas Church: Defining Styles – the Early Years', in Marc Treib (ed.), *Thomas Dolliver Church, Landscape Architect (Studies in the History of Gardens and Designed Landscapes*, 20/2) (Dumbarton Oaks: 2000): 108.

Imbert, Dorothée, 'Landscape Architects of the World, Unite! Professional Organizations, Practice, and Politics, 1935–1948', *Journal of Landscape Architecture*, (Spring 2007): 6–19.

Imbert, Dorothée, 'The AIAJM: A Manifesto for Landscape Modernity', *Landscape Journal*, 26/2 (2007): 219–35.

Jacques, D.L., 'Landscape Appraisal: The Case for a Subjective Theory', *Journal of Environmental Management*, 10 (1980): 107–13.

Jacques, D.L., 'The Rise of Cultural Landscapes', *International Journal of Heritage Studies*, 1/2 (Winter 1994): 91–101.

Jellicoe, Geoffrey, 'The Dynamic Garden' (review of *Gardens in the Modern Landscape*), *AR*, 85 (1939): 151–3.

Jenkins, Gilbert, 'Cotswold Gardens', *L&G* (Summer 1939): 74–8.

Jones, Margaret E. and H.F. Clark, *Indoor Plants and Gardens* (London: Architectural Press, 1952).

Karson, Robin (ed.), *Influences on American Garden Design: 1895 to 1940* (New York: Garden Conservancy Symposium Proceedings, 1995).

Kitson, Ian, 'A Country House near Leicester', *Landscape Design*, (September 1990): 22–6.

Kitson, Ian, 'Christopher Tunnard at Bentley Wood', *Landscape Design* (January 1991): 10–15.

Korn, Arthur, 'A New Plan for Amsterdam', *AR*, 83 (June 1938): 265–76.

Korn, Arthur and Felix J. Samuely, 'A Master Plan for London, based on research carried out by the Town Planning Committee of the M.A.R.S. Group', *AR*, 91 (June 1942): 143.

Lane, Barbara Miller, *Architecture and Politics in Germany 1918–1945* (Cambridge, MA: MIT Press, 1985).

Leitch, George (chairman), *Report of the Advisory Committee on Truck Road Assessment* (London: Her Majesty's Stationery Office, 1977).

Lowenthal, David, 'Finding Valued Landscapes', *Progress in Human Geography*, 2/3 (1978): 373–418.

Maass, Harry, *Wie baue und pflanze ich meinem Garten* (Munich: F.Bruckmann, 1929).

Maass, Harry, 'Glasschutz im Garten', *Gartenschönheit*, 12 (1932): 162–3.

Marquis, Albert Nelson, *Who's Who in America: A Biographical Dictionary of Notable Living Men and Women of the United States*, 29th edn (New Providence, NJ: Marquis, 1957).

Martin, Megan, 'The Richard Clough Collection of Garden Books', *Insites* 40 (Spring 2004).

McGrath, Raymond, *Twentieth-Century Houses* (London: Faber & Faber, 1934).

McGrath, Raymond, '"Glas im Bau" – a prophetic book', in Sharp, *Essays Presented to Arthur Korn* (New York: George Wittenborn, 1967), pp. 131–41.

McGrath, Raymond and A.C. Frost, *Glass in Architecture and Decoration* (London: Architectural Press, 1937).

Mercer, F.A. (ed.), *Gardens and Gardening*, 6 (London: The Studio, 1937).

Mercer, F.A. and C.H. Holme (eds), *Gardens and Gardening*, 8 (London: The Studio, 1939).

Miller, E. Lynn (ed.), *Landscape Architecture Retrospective 1943*, (University Park, PA: American Society of Landscape Architecture, North Central Section, Pennsylvania Chapter, 1975).

Mumford, Lewis, *The Culture of Cities* (New York: Harcourt, Brace and Co., 1938).

Neckar, Lance, 'Strident Modernism/Ambivalent Reconsiderations: Christopher Tunnard's *Gardens in the Modern Landscape*', *Journal of Garden History*, 10/4 (1990): 237–46.

Neckar, Lance, 'Christopher Tunnard: *The Garden in the Modern Landscape*', in Treib, *Modern Landscape Architecture* (Cambridge, MA: MIT Press, 1993), pp. 144–58.

Oldys, Archibald, 'The End of the Garden' (review), *AR* (April 1933): 167.

Page, Russell, 'Gardens' (review of *Gardens in the Modern Landscape*), *Architects' Journal*, 89 (23 March 1939): 499.

Pearlman, Jill, 'Joseph Hudnut and the Unlikely Beginnings of Post-Modern Urbanism at the Harvard Bauhaus', *Planning Perspectives* 15/3 (July 2000): 201–39.

Pearlman, Jill, *Inventing American Modernism: Joseph Hudnut, Walter Gropius, and the Bauhaus Legacy at Harvard* (Charlottesville: University of Virginia Press, 2007).

Pevsner, Nikolaus, *Pioneers of the Modern Movement* (London: Faber & Faber, 1936).

Pevsner, Nikolaus, 'The Genesis of the Picturesque', *AR*, 96 (November 1944): 139–46.

Powers, Alan, *Serge Chermayeff: Designer, Architect, Teacher* (London: RIBA Publications, 2001).

Richards, J.M., 'Modern Architecture and the Public, The M.A.R.S. Exhibition', *AR*, LXXXI/LXXXIII (March 1938): 116 and 203–4.

Richards, J.M., *Memoirs of an Unjust Fella* (autobiography) (London: Weidenfeld & Nicolson, 1980).

Roth, Alfred, *The New Architecture: Examined on 20 Examples* (Zürich: H.Ginsberger, 1940).

Sharp, Dennis (ed.), Planning and Architecture: Essays presented to Arthur Korn by the Architectural Association (New York: George Wittenborn, 1967).

Sharp, Thomas, *English Panorama* (London: Dent, 1936).

Shepheard, Peter, *Modern Gardens* (London: Architectural Press, 1953).

Simo, Melanie, *The Coalescing of Different Forces and Ideas: A History of Landscape Architecture at Harvard, 1900–1999* (Cambridge, MA: Harvard GSD, 2000).

Snow, Marc, *Modern American Gardens – Designed by James Rose* (New York, Reinhold, 1967).

Soby, James Thrall (ed.), *Arp* (New York: Museum of Modern Art, 1958).

Steele, Fletcher, '"The Voice is Jacob's Voice, but the Hands …"' (review), *Landscape Architecture*, 42 (1942): 64–5.

Stein, Clarence, *Towards New Towns for America* (Chicago: Public Administration Service, 1951).

Streatfield, David, 'The Influence of Japan upon Gardens in California and the Pacific Northwest,' in Karson, *Influences on American Garden Design* (New York: Garden Conservancy Symposium Proceedings, 1995).

Strong, William A., 'It is Modern if it Cares Well for Basic Necessities', *Landscape Architecture*, 42 (1942): 66–8.

Sudell, Richard, *Landscape Gardening: Planning Construction Planting* (London and Melbourne: Ward Lock, 1933).

Treib, Marc (ed.), *Modern Landscape Architecture: A Critical Review* (Cambridge, MA: MIT Press, 1993).

Treib, Marc and Dorothée Imbert, *Garrett Eckbo: Modern Landscapes for Living* (Berkeley: University of California Press, 1997).

Van Doesburg, Theo, 'Towards a Plastic Architecture', in Ulrich Conrads, *Programmes and Manifestoes on 20th-Century Architecture* (London: Lund Humphries, 1970).

Voets, A., 'Jean Canneel-Claes: Bezieler van de Functionele Tuin', *Monumenten en Landschappen*, 6/6 (November 1987): 39–48, 63–4.

Walker, Peter and Melanie Simo, *Invisible Gardens: The Search for Modernism in the American Landscape* (Cambridge, MA: MIT Press, 1994).

Warburton, Ralph, 'A Worldly View of Tunnard at his Best', *Landscape Architecture*, 70/3 (May 1980): 311–13.

Warburton, Ralph, 'Planner's Bio-Brief: Christopher Tunnard (July 7, 1910 – February 13, 1979)', *Planning History Present*, 4/2 (Society for American City and Regional Planning History, 1990).

Warburton, Ralph, 'Christopher Tunnard: The Anticipatory Generalist Planner' (paper to Association of Collegiate Schools of Planning/ Association of European Schools of Planning congress in Oxford (1991).

Warburton, Ralph, 'Christopher Tunnard', *Urban Design and Preservation Quarterly*, 15, 2/3 (Summer/Fall 1992): 4.

Webber, Ronald, *Percy Cane – Garden Designer* (Edinburgh: John Bartholemew, 1975).

Welsh, John, 'Tunnard: The Modernist with a Memory', *Landscape Design* (October 1987): 20–3.

Williams, Bradford, '*Gardens in the Modern Landscape*, by Christopher Tunnard' (review), *Landscape Architecture*, XXIX/3 (April 1939): 145.

Wilson, William H., *The City Beautiful Movement* (Baltimore and London: Johns Hopkins University Press, 1989).

Woudstra, Jan, 'Danish Landscape Design in the Modern Era (1920–1970)', *Garden History*, 23/2 (1995): 222–41.

Woudstra, Jan, 'The Corbusian Landscape: Arcadia or No Man's Land?', *Garden History*, 28/1 (2000): 135–51.

Wojtowicz, Robert, 'City As Community: The Life And Vision Of Lewis Mumford', *Old Dominion University's Quest*, 4/1 (January 2001). Available online at: http://www.odu.edu/ao/instadv/quest/cityascomunity.html, accessed 31 July 2008.

Wrigley's British Columbia Directory (Vancouver, BC: Wrigley Directories Limited, 1918–1932).

Index

Entries in **bold** denote references to figures.